10 Traits of Highly Effective Principals

10 Traits of Highly Effective Principals

From Good to Great Performance

Elaine K. McEwan

CORWIN PRESS, INC.
A Sage Publications Company
Thousand Oaks, California

For information:

Corwin Press, Inc.
A Sage Publications Company
2455 Teller Road
Thousand Oaks, California 91320
www.corwinpress.com

Sage Publications Ltd.
6 Bonhill Street
London EC2A 4PU
United Kingdom

Sage Publications India Pvt. Ltd.
B-42, Panchsheel Enclave
Post Box 4109
New Delhi 110 017 India

Printed in the United States of America

Library of Congress Cataloging-in-Publication Data

McEwan, Elaine K., 1941-
Ten traits of highly effective principals : from good to great performance / by Elaine K. McEwan.
        p. cm.
Includes bibliographical references and index.
ISBN 978-0-7619-4618-2 (cloth) — ISBN 978-0-7619-4619-9 (pbk.)
    1. School principals. 2. School management and organization.
3. Educational leadership. I. Title.
LB2831.9.M42 2003
371.2′012—dc21

                                2003004595

This book is printed on acid-free paper.

09   7   6

Acquisitions Editor:	Robert D. Clouse
Editorial Assistant:	Jingle Vea
Production Editor:	Julia Parnell
Copy Editor:	Marilyn Power Scott
Typesetter:	C&M Digitals (P) Ltd.
Indexer:	Jean Casalegno
Cover Designer:	Michael Dubowe
Production Artist:	Lisa Miller

Contents

To my husband, E. Raymond Adkins

Preface

I conducted my first "research" on the role of principals in the fall of 1984. My superintendent was revising the principals' job description and wanted to know what I did all day. I had been on the job for just a year, and there *were* many days that I didn't seem to accomplish much of anything—at least not anything concrete I could cross off a list at the end of the day. I spent most of my time walking and talking—talking with teachers, wandering in and out of classrooms, meeting with parents in my office, and chatting with students on the playground and in the cafeteria, but I wasn't sure these activities sounded impressive enough for a job description.

I needed something more substantive and decided to ask the 364 students in Grades 1 through 6 what *they* thought I did all day. They took on the assignment with unexpected enthusiasm and wrote short "essays" describing my job as the principal of Lincoln School. Some eager beavers even illustrated their compositions.

There were many astute observers. A fifth grade student laid out this comprehensive job description: "She must be able to talk and listen to children. She must be able to make decisions that are good for the school. She has to learn to manage a school. She should participate in all big school events. She has to have patience with children who are sent to the office and she must deal with problems" (McEwan, 1985, p. 17). I forwarded it to the superintendent immediately. I was amused by the many references to me having coffee and "chit-chatting" with teachers. The students obviously did not understand that I was consulting, mentoring, coaching, and facilitating!

What made me feel particularly good about the responses was that the students were aware of me as an individual. They had perceptions of my involvement in the entire building, and they also noted that my job was the fragmented, multifaceted one that more sophisticated observers have noted (Wolcott, 1973). The students were also able to articulate many of the characteristics needed by effective administrators—patience, intelligence, and flexibility. They even had insights into the stress of being a career woman, wife, and mother.

My fascination with what it takes to be an effective principal has not diminished in the nearly twenty years since I did that simple exercise with my students. Now I have a more global perspective, however. During my travels as a consultant, I listen to principals talk about what is working in their schools. They are eager to share the news of rising test scores, empowered teachers, and revitalized learning communities. I also work with principals who are discouraged and frustrated by the demands of the job. As one principal observed, "When I started in this business, my job was to manage the school and keep the parents and teachers happy. Now, to be considered effective, I need to get results." What kind of principal is able to get results with scarce resources, raise achievement and maintain it while building a supportive and caring culture, nurture and mentor novice teachers, energize experienced staff members, and simultaneously leap tall buildings in a single bound? This question motivated me to examine the principalship once again—this time, with the goal of defining the top ten traits of highly effective principals in the age of accountability.

WHO THIS BOOK IS FOR

I have written *Ten Traits of Highly Effective Principals: From Good to Great Performance* for the following audiences:

- Principals at every level who want to notch up their personal effectiveness as well as feel affirmed for what they are already doing well
- Administrative teams who are engaged in study and reflection regarding the role of the principal in improving school performance
- Central office administrators who hire, supervise, mentor, and coach principals
- Teams of teachers who participate in the screening and hiring of principals for their schools
- Educators who aspire to the principalship and are looking for outstanding role models
- College and university educators who train principals

OVERVIEW OF THE CONTENTS

If you are wondering about the origin of the ten traits of highly effective principals, be sure to read the Introduction. It describes in detail the multistep process that I used to identify them. Following the Introduction, you will find ten easy-to-read and highly inspiring chapters—one for each of the following traits:

1. The Communicator

2. The Educator

3. The Envisioner

4. The Facilitator

5. The Change Master

6. The Culture Builder

7. The Activator

8. The Producer

9. The Character Builder

10. The Contributor

Each chapter contains the following features:

- Vignettes describing highly effective principals—true stories from the trenches for each of the ten traits
- A set of behaviors and habits for each of the traits—benchmarks, if you will—to guide and inspire you as you seek to increase your own effectiveness
- Ideas, reflections, and advice regarding each of the traits in the words of more than thirty highly effective principals
- Pearls of wisdom, epigrams, and aphorisms from a wide variety of noted thinkers, theorists, and philosophers regarding the ten traits

Reading the *Ten Traits of Highly Effective Principals* could be compared (if you use your imagination) to attending a week-long seminar with numerous successful principals from every level and kind of school—men and women from across the country who have turned around low-performing schools, helped good schools become great, and raised the standards of excellence in their highly successful schools even higher. At this imaginary seminar, you will have the opportunity to hear keynote addresses as well as participate in numerous small group sessions. You will also be able to ask questions and get honest answers from individuals who have been there and done it with distinction and excellence. There will be occasional drop-in visits from well-known experts and famous people, but the highly effective principals are the stars of this book.

Although each principal whose voice is heard in the following chapters is unique, they do share a number of traits in common—ten, to be precise. Of course, reading about the ten traits as demonstrated in the lives of these inspiring role models won't provide you with a ready-made roadmap to success. In fact, all of the contributing principals would tell you that, as successful as they might seem, they are still works in progress. They see the principalship as an ongoing journey, filled with detours and potholes as well as freeways and straightaways. Although your destination is likely to be similar to theirs, the roadblocks and construction zones that *you* encounter on your journey will be unique to the school in which you work. However, an understanding of the traits, as seen in the lives of these role models, will expand your thinking regarding the variety and quantity of possible itineraries for your trip, enlarge your vision to include a far more expansive horizon, and reveal multiple strategies for finding your way more effectively. My goal is to enable you to pack your briefcase and set out immediately on your own personal journey to becoming a highly effective principal.

When you have finished reading Chapters 1 through 10, you will find two additional features in the Resource section that will make this book useful as a desk reference: (1) a checklist of the nearly 100 benchmarks that define the ten traits and (2) a brand-new Corwin Press feature making its debut in *Ten Traits of Highly Effective Principals*—a facilitator's guide. You can spot the guide very quickly because it is printed on shaded paper for your convenience. The companion to this book, *Ten Traits of Highly Effective Teachers* (McEwan, 2002), has been widely used in graduate classes, study groups, and districtwide staff development courses. I hope that the addition of a facilitator's guide to this book will enhance the ease with which group leaders and teachers can plan their activities and lessons.

ACKNOWLEDGMENTS

This book would not have been possible without the input of nearly 150 individuals—principals, teachers, central office administrators, school board members, university professors, and parents. They took time from more pressing matters to communicate with me via E-mail, snail mail, voice mail, and telephone interviews. I am most appreciative of each of them.

I am especially grateful to the thirty-seven highly effective principals who completed questionnaires, participated in lengthy interviews, or did both. Their names appear here in alphabetical order. You will meet them throughout the book as they share their insights and observations on the ten traits of highly effective principals: Sandra Ahola, Terry Beasley, Sharon Beitel, Regina Birdsell, Kathie Dobberteen, Larry Fieber, Gabe

Flicker, Lorraine Fong, Clayton Fujie, Margaret Garcia-Dugan, Michelle Gayle, John Giles, Patricia Hamilton, Jean Hendrickson, Dawn Hurns, Alan Jones, Mark Kern, Clare Maguire, Lola Malone, Nancy Moga, Tom Paulsen, Douglas Pierson, Larry Pollock, Jim Ratledge, Kathy Schneiter, Carol Schulte-Kottwitz, Byron Schwab, Lois Scrivener, Catherine Segura, Dale Skinner, Mary Ann Stevens, Jeanne Stiglbauer, Marjorie Thompson, Brenda Valentine, Todd White, Tom Williams, and Steve Wilson.

These individuals willingly shared documents, essays, poems, personal writings, news clippings, and videotapes with me and then continued to respond to my requests for additional information with unfailing good cheer and encouragement. They inspired and energized me with their stories. On more than one occasion, I had goose bumps on my arms and tears in my eyes when I concluded an interview.

A round of applause also goes to the following individuals who participated in follow-up interviews regarding specific aspects of the E-mail survey: Charlie Blanton, Dee Cawood, Ken Evans, Bonnie Grossen, Johanna Haver, Don Powers, Marilyn Reed, Katherine Swain, and Linda Thomas. Their insights regarding the traits of highly effective principals were particularly helpful.

My special thanks to Jack Lowe, Jr., the president of TD Industries in Dallas, Texas. Jack is a trustee on the Dallas Independent School District Board and a practitioner of the servant-leadership approach to management, the philosophy which drives his company's success. His keen insights regarding the similarities and differences between business and education, as well as his big-as-all-Texas sense of humor, would make him a wonderful presenter for a principals' conference.

I am indebted to my former superintendent, John E. Hennig, who gave me the opportunity to become an elementary school principal. The principalship enabled me to grow more as a professional and a person than any job before or since. I was compelled to examine what was most important about schooling, my work, and my life. I faced failure, discouragement, and tough moral choices as well as success, achievement, and enormous satisfaction—often on the very same day. That is what I loved most about the principalship—a new challenge every day.

I am profoundly grateful to my husband, E. Raymond Adkins. He is my copy editor, encourager, and biggest cheerleader. Writing a book is a lengthy and often frustrating process—proposal, contract, research, writing, submission, copyediting, page proofs, and finally publication. He has been there for every step of this book—providing a sounding board and a strong shoulder to lean on. His patience is unfailing, his honesty unrelenting, and his common sense invaluable.

Corwin Press gratefully acknowledges the contribution of the following reviewers:

Dr. Paul G. Young
NAESP President
Principal
West Elementary School
Lancaster, OH

Mr. Phil Silsby
Principal
Belleville Township High School, West
Belleville, IL 62226

Mr. Glen Clark
Principal
American Fork High School
American Fork, UT

Ms. Bonnie L. Tryon
Principal
Golding Elementary School
Cobleskill, NY

Ms. Kim Janisch
Principal
Watertown High School
Watertown, SD

Introduction

"Far better it is to dare mighty things, to win glorious triumphs, even though checkered by failure, than to take rank with those poor spirits who neither enjoy much nor suffer much, because they live in the gray twilight that knows not victory nor defeat."

—T. Roosevelt (1899, as
quoted in Safire, 1997, p. 514)

Theodore Roosevelt's stirring words in the above quotation may sound a bit dramatic to describe the mundane job of a school principal, but to those courageous individuals who compete daily against opponents like mediocrity, poverty, low expectations, distrust, and apathy, his sentiments are apt. Jeanne Stiglbauer, principal of Dreher High School in Columbia, South Carolina, describes herself as a "warrior on a steed," but since she played Division I basketball at the College of Charleston, I picture her more as a competitor in high-tops. But whether astride a horse, on the court, or

---

AUTHOR'S NOTE: I am indebted to the many talented and highly effective principals who shared their opinions, reflections, ideas, and experiences regarding their life's work with me. During the months of June through November 2002, they kept my inbox filled with E-mail, my post office box filled with snail mail, and my phone messaging system filled with voice mail. Their voices are heard throughout the book. Every individual with whom I communicated is quoted by name. However, to save the busy reader time, I have omitted dated citations for these quotations unless they have appeared in a published work or an unpublished document authored by the individual, were communicated to me during some other time period than June through October 2002, or appear in a sidebar or context where the citation is needed for clarity. I have included more detailed descriptive information about principals and their schools where appropriate to the context. In all cases, however, I identify the name, level, and geographical location of a principal's school the first time his or her name is mentioned. In subsequent references, only principals' names are provided. An alphabetical list of the highly effective principals with their current positions can be found in Resource A.

in the hallways of her high school, she knows what it takes to win against tough competitors. She began her administrative career at nearby Hand Middle School where she presided over that school's renaissance. It was featured as *Time* magazine's Middle School of the Year for 2001 (Morse, 2001), the same year that Jean was named National Distinguished Principal from South Carolina by the National Association of Elementary School Principals (NAESP 2001a).

Rather than rest on her laurels, however, Jeanne accepted a new challenge. She was recruited by her superintendent and community to go for a "repeat" at nearby Dreher High School. Raising achievement in a high school that had seen five principals come and go in four years was her biggest challenge to date, but Jeanne laced up her high-tops and hit the court running. The high school was in desperate need of what Michael Fullan (2001) calls "reculturing—a contact sport that involves hard, labor-intensive work" (p. 44). Reculturing is not unlike fighting for an offensive rebound under the basket and then going around three defenders to score. Jeanne is taking the ball to the basket at a new level where she is on her way to another successful season.

Not every highly effective principal arrives like a warrior on a steed *or* a hoopster in high-tops. Margaret Garcia-Dugan arrived for her first day as the principal at Glendale High School in Arizona in high heels and a suit, looking every bit the professional that she is. She didn't take long to settle in to her office. She was immediately on the move, and during her decade-long tenure at Glendale, she "managed by walking around" every single day. "I'm not a sit-down principal," she explains. "My job was to be in the building, working harder than anyone else, always available to teachers, parents, and students. I let other people go to conferences and join organizations. I was at school, on the job."

Margaret is what they call in administrative jargon, a "visible presence." Every time a student or a teacher looked up, there was Margaret. She walked softly but carried a big note pad to leave encouraging messages for teachers and write reminders to herself. She was focused on two goals for her students: academic achievement and safety. She tells aspiring principals, "Just because your door has a sign on it that says 'principal' doesn't make you the leader *or* a highly effective principal. It's the trust people have in you based on your actions that allows you to lead."

Margaret and her visible presence have moved to central office in the Glendale Union High School District where she is now in charge of curriculum and instruction, but you can bet she won't be there when you call. She'll be out walking the halls and classrooms of her district's nine high schools. When she stops in at her former campus, she'll find the teachers there are still getting results. Before Margaret arrived in 1992, the staff at

Glendale didn't know how high they could soar. Now they've been featured in a video series showing teachers in other schools how to get results (Association for Supervision and Curriculum Development, 2001).

Larry Fieber (1999) found "a school in disrepair, misbehaving children, lack of community support, and a tired staff in need of rejuvenation" (p. 12) when he arrived at Parkway Elementary School in Ewing, New Jersey, in 1996. In the words of those with whom he works, he has "transformed the school into a community of learners, set high academic and behavioral expectations, and created a culture where children feel special and safe" (Fieber, 1999, p. 7). For Fieber, being a highly effective principal is "not a job, but a way of life." Fieber's way of life was recognized by the New Jersey Department of Education in cooperation with the New Jersey Principals Association when they named him the New Jersey Principal of the Year in 2000 and by NAESP when they named him the National Distinguished Principal from New Jersey in 2001 (NAESP, 2001a).

Management guru Peter Drucker (2001) agrees that the kind of effectiveness demonstrated by Stiglbauer, Garcia-Dugan, and Fieber is a way of life. He writes, "Effectiveness . . . is a habit; that is, a complex of practices. And practices can always be learned. Practices are simple, deceptively so; even a seven-year-old has no difficulty in understanding a practice. But practices are always exceedingly hard to do well. They have to be acquired, as we all learn the multiplication table; that is, repeated ad nauseam until [it] has become an unthinking, conditioned reflex, and firmly ingrained habit" (p. 205).

In spite of the undeniable importance of the principalship to many scholars (Sergiovanni, 1992, 1996, 2000, 2001), school leadership occasionally disappears completely from the radar screen of educational reform. In the 1960s and 1970s, for example, the innovations du jour were teaching strategies and organizational improvement. Thankfully, the research undertaken about what makes schools effective brought the educational community to its senses with the message that principals really do matter (Manasse, 1982, p. vii). But then along came class size reduction, mandated standards, teacher leaders, democratic schools, and more curricular innovations—each one touted as *the* answer to improving student learning.

Recently, however, the principalship has zoomed back into view again. Policymakers have discovered that teachers, tests, and textbooks can't produce results *without* highly effective principals to facilitate, model, *and* lead. A variety of panels and initiatives—all focused on a redefinition of the principal's role—have called for a new kind of principal leadership in the building of caring, learning, and leading communities (Olson, 2000; Richard, 2000):

- Leadership for Student Learning: Reinventing the Principalship (Institute for Educational Leadership, 2000)
- The Principal, Keystone of a High-Achieving School: Attracting and Keeping the Leaders We Need (Educational Research Service, 2000)
- Trying to Stay Ahead of the Game: Superintendents and Principals Talk About School Leadership (Public Agenda, 2001)
- Priorities and Barriers in High School Leadership: A Survey of Principals (National Association of Secondary School Principals, 2001)
- Leading Learning Communities: Standards for What Principals Should Know and Be Able to Do (NAESP, 2001b)

A MATTER OF DEFINITION

Defining highly effective principals like Jeanne Stiglbauer, Larry Fieber, and Margaret Garcia-Dugan in only ten words is a formidable task. I discovered just how difficult very early in my conversations with them and other successful principals. To make the job more manageable, I have taken some literary license with the meaning of the term *trait*. Webster's defines it as "a distinguishing quality or characteristic" (McKechnie, 1983, p. 1936), but the traits that I will describe in the chapters ahead are not as singular, simple, or straightforward as implied by the dictionary definition. Although I have labeled each "trait" with a catchy word or two, the traits I will discuss are definitely more akin to concepts or constellations than single traits. But *Ten Concepts (or Constellations) of Highly Effective Principals* doesn't quite have the same ring to it as *Ten Traits of Highly Effective Principals*. I hope that you will be able to momentarily suspend Webster's definition of *trait* and live with my more comprehensive interpretation, at least until you finish reading the book.

Also, for purposes of our discussion in the chapters ahead, the word *effective* will not be used exclusively. Rather, terms like *successful*, *outstanding*, and *excellent* will be used interchangeably—not only to make for less repetitive and more interesting reading but also to accommodate the variety of ways people describe the principals whom they consider to be the very best. The understood definition of *effective* along with the aforementioned terms will be Webster's: "producing a decided, decisive, or desired effect (result or outcome), producing an intended effort" (McKechnie, 1983, p. 577). The efforts of the principal *must* contribute to and ultimately produce an intended effort in order to qualify for the "highly effective" seal of approval. Sergiovanni (2001) provides a more comprehensive description of effectiveness: "achieving higher levels of pedagogical thoughtfulness, developing relationships characterized by caring and civility, and achieving increases in the quality of student performance on both conventional and alternative assessments" (p. 204).

THE ORIGIN OF THE TEN TRAITS

Developing the final list of ten traits along with the accompanying definitions was a several-step process. First, I read widely in the education literature regarding the traits, characteristics, and behaviors of effective principals. I paid particular attention to the research that illuminates the relationship between what principals do while they are "principaling" and how well their students achieve. I also consulted the leadership and management literature, looking for guidance from psychology and the business world that might inform the practice of school leadership in this age of accountability.

Using that information, I put together a list of thirty-seven items that I loosely called traits. They were in no particular order of preference on my part and can be found in Figure I.1. Some of the "traits" are multifaceted and open-ended in nature (e.g., knowledge of curriculum and instruction), while others are more one-dimensional and specific (e.g., flexibility). Some define a particular state of "being" (e.g., authentic), while others focus on some type of "doing" (e.g., ability to teach students). I then sent this list of traits via E-mail to an eclectic group of 175 individuals (principals, superintendents, central office administrators, staff developers, university professors, teachers, parents, school board members, and education activists) around the country.

I asked the respondents to choose the ten traits from my list that they believed were essential to being a highly effective principal. They were not asked to rank them, although many did. They were not expected to make editorial comments or share personal observations about the traits, but many could not help themselves. Some respondents even added other traits to the list (e.g., flair and courage). Some of the more creative contributors grouped or reorganized the traits in ways that made sense to them. I appreciated their efforts, and their thinking definitely helped to inform mine. Everyone had opinions, it seemed, regarding what principals should "be" and "do" in order to merit the "highly effective" label. Some even gave me nonexamples—"principals I wish I had never worked for."

The 108 individuals who responded are what statisticians would call a sample of convenience: They were conveniently available as part of my E-mail directory and were willing to participate. This convenient sample was both geographically and professionally diverse. For example, it included a twenty-something political science major from Swarthmore

Figure I.1   List of Traits Sent to Respondents via E-mail

Flexibility

A sense of humor

Transparency

Instructional leader

Ability to communicate

Foresight

A servant's heart

Empathy

A sense of calling

Energy and drive

Enthusiasm

Authenticity

A sense of purpose and mission

Slow and steady

Charismatic

Motivational

Knowledgeable about teaching and learning

Caring

Human relations skills

The ability to teach students

The ability to teach adults (teachers and parents)

The ability to listen

A sense of accountability to parents and community

Intelligent

Likes students

Able to deal with change and ambiguity

Ability to convince people to change

High moral character

Honesty

A team player

Trustworthiness

A role model for students and teachers

A take-charge kind of person

A learner

Organized

Loyal

High expectations

Figure I.2   Number of Respondents in Each Category

Category	Number of Respondents
Teachers	36
Principals	25
Central Office Administrators	14
College and University Educators	7
State and County Offices of Education Staff	9
Parent Activists	6
School Board Members	5
State Principals Organization Staff	4
State School Board Association Staff	1
School Secretary	1
Total Number of Respondents	**108**

who is currently teaching kindergarten in the inner city of Philadelphia, a midwestern sixty-year-old retired superintendent with a Ph.D., and a middle-aged aspiring principal with a background in business from the Pacific Northwest. The sample of convenience contained more women than men, however, and that lack of balance can definitely be seen when the total number of respondents (108) is disaggregated by gender: eighty-five women and twenty men. The categories into which the respondents fall and the number of individuals from each category who responded can be found in Figure I.2.

Despite their diversity, the respondents were in *strong* agreement regarding the priority of three major trait areas: communication, instruction, and sense of purpose and mission. Figure I.3 shows the list of traits ranked by the number of votes each received.

The top vote getter of any single trait on the survey was *ability to communicate* (seventy-four votes). The next two highest fall into what I have labeled the Educator traits: (1) *instructional leader* (seventy-one votes) and (2) *knowledgeable about teaching and learning* (sixty votes). It surprised me that many individuals cast votes for both of these learning-related traits. I interpreted this dual voting pattern to mean one of two things: either (1) *instructional leadership* and *being knowledgeable about teaching and learning* meant two different things to the respondents, or

Figure I.3   List of Traits Ranked by Number of Votes Received

Ability to Communicate 74

Instructional Leader 71

Knowledgeable about Teaching and Learning 60

A Sense of Purpose and Mission 51

Human Relations Skills 44

Flexibility 42

High Expectations 42

Sense of Humor 40

Organized 40

Listener 36

Energy and Drive 35

A Learner 34

A Sense of Accountability to Parents and Community 33

Motivational 30

Trustworthiness 29

Enthusiasm 28

Likes Students 27

High Moral Character 25

A Team Player 24

A Role Model for Students and Teachers 23

Able to Deal with Change and Ambiguity 22

Intelligence 23

Ability to Teach Adults (Teachers or Parents) 18

Ability to Convince People to Change 18

Honesty 16

A Servant's Heart 15

Caring 15

Empathetic 14

A Sense of Calling 14

Take-Charge Kind of Person 12

Foresight 11

Authenticity 8

Ability to Teach Students 7

Loyal 4

Charismatic 1

Slow and Steady 0

Transparency 0

(2) a focus on learning by the principal was so important that they wanted to vote for it twice. Following *ability to communicate, instructional leader,* and *knowledgeable about teaching and learning,* the next highest vote getter was *a sense of purpose and mission* (fifty-one votes).

Overall, it can be said that respondents believed that highly effective principals were mission-driven individuals with strong communication skills, a high level of knowledge about teaching and learning, and the ability to provide instructional leadership. At the opposite end of the vote continuum, only about 10 percent of the respondents believed that highly effective principals should be *take-charge* individuals (twelve votes) and only one vote was cast for *charismatic* principals.

Once the votes were counted, I grouped almost all of them into ten broad trait categories and began searching for a precise but memorable word to capture the essence of each category, along with some descriptive phrases to further define the trait. Figure I.4 lists the broad trait categories and displays the related traits from the survey that I placed into each category. In some cases, I chose a unique term that I borrowed from another source to label a trait category or constellation. For example, I first encountered the term *envisioner* in the transcript of a speech by George Fisher (1989) to a group of middle managers at Motorola, Inc. It seemed the ideal word to describe the cluster of traits related to focus, mission, and vision. The term *activator* is used by the Gallup Organization in their Strengths Finder program (Buckingham & Coffman, 2001); it was the perfect word to encompass the qualities of energy and enthusiasm that highly effective principals must have to keep up with the myriad demands of their jobs. I borrowed the term *change master* from the title of Rosabeth Moss Kanter's (1983) classic volume, although my definition of the term differs somewhat from Kanter's.

The next step was finding a diverse group of highly effective principals on which to "test" my ten traits. I located principals from schools of different sizes, demographics (urban, suburban, and rural), kinds (private and public), and levels (K–12) in various locations around the country (New Jersey to Hawaii, Florida to Oregon, Connecticut to Texas, and places in between). I specifically sought out individuals who had faced different kinds of challenges in their principalships. In order to qualify for this list, individuals had to show evidence that they had either helped bring about the renaissance of a failing school, brought a good school to greatness, or been able to take over a highly effective school and maintain or even boost its level of accomplishment. Documentation included test scores or rankings based on a state assessment or rating program. Many, although not all, of the highly effective principals have received national awards—either personally or on behalf of their schools. There are twenty-one women and

Figure I.4   Ranked List of Traits Grouped Into Trait Categories

Trait Number 1: Communicator

Ability to communicate 74[1]

Listener 36

Empathetic 14

Trait Number 2: Educator

Instructional leader 71

Knowledgeable about teaching and learning 60

A learner 34

Intelligent 23

Ability to teach adults (teachers or parents) 18

Ability to teach students 7

Trait Number 3: Envisioner

A sense of purpose and mission 51

A sense of calling 14

Trait Number 4: Facilitator

Human relations skills 44

Likes students 27

A team player 24

Caring 15

Trait Number 5: Change Master

Flexibility 42

Able to deal with change and ambiguity 22

Ability to convince people to change 18

Foresight 11

Trait Number 6: Culture Builder

High expectations 42

Trait Number 7: Activator

Sense of humor 40

Organized 40

Energy and drive 35

Ability to motivate 30

Enthusiasm 28

Take-charge kind of person 12

Trait Number 8: Producer

Accountability to parents and community 33

Trait Number 9: Character Builder

Trustworthiness 29

High moral character 25

Role model for students and teachers 23

Honesty 16

Authenticity 8

Loyal 4

Trait Number 10: Contributor

A servant's heart 15

Low Vote Getters

Slow and steady 0

Charisma 1

Transparency 0

[1]Italicized traits received the highest number of votes in their category.

sixteen men in the group. An alphabetical list of their names and current job assignments, as of publication, can be found in Resource A.

I had multiple goals in mind as I interviewed these highly successful principals: (1) to determine whether the ten traits I had identified were recognized by these individuals and those with whom they worked to be descriptive of them; (2) to ascertain if there were any traits I had omitted from the list or, conversely, if any trait was thought to be repetitious or inappropriate; and (3) to record the stories and experiences of these administrators as they described how the traits affected and motivated their lives. Where applicable, I also reviewed award applications, newspaper articles, personal writings, and videotapes related to the principals and their schools. During the interviews, I continued to fine-tune the list of traits in an effort to capture the essence of effectiveness in the principalship as illustrated in the lives of these individuals.

I have presented the traits in the order indicated by the respondents' voting, although my goal was not to produce a definitive, ranked list of traits but rather to explore and illuminate the critical behaviors, attitudes, and beliefs of highly effective principals from several perspectives: (1) my own personal experiences as a principal, (2) the current literature in the field, and (3) numerous highly effective principals. To that end, I have included one trait in the final list that received very few votes overall but clearly emerged as central in the stories of effective principals as well as in the literature: the concept of servant-leadership as seen in Trait 10, Contributor. Furthermore, it is my belief that highly effective principals, while certainly having some traits that are more dominant than others, *must* possess all of these traits in some measure to be effective. I have tweaked and fine-tuned the list of ten traits right up to my deadline. I do recognize, however, that only when *you* read this book, talk about it with your colleagues, and reflect on its meaning for *your* practice will the book *really* be done.

I second Max DePree (1987), who, in his introduction to *Leadership Is an Art*, wrote, "In some sense, every reader 'finishes' every book according to his or her experiences and needs and beliefs and potential. . . . The ideas here have been in my mind for quite a few years—changing, growing, maturing. I will continue to think about them long after this book is published, and I trust you will too" (p. 3).

THE TEN TRAITS OF HIGHLY EFFECTIVE PRINCIPALS

Here then are the ten traits of highly effective principals that will be described, discussed, and dissected in the chapters ahead. A one-page list of the ten traits suitable for reproduction is included in Resource B.

Chapter 1: The Communicator

The highly effective principal is a communicator—a genuine and open human being with the capacity to listen, empathize, and connect with individual students, parents, and teachers in productive, helping, and healing ways, as well as the ability to teach, present, and motivate people in larger group settings.

Chapter 2: The Educator

The highly effective principal is an educator—a self-directed instructional leader with a strong intellect and personal depth of knowledge regarding research-based curriculum, instruction, and learning who motivates and facilitates the intellectual growth and development of self, students, teachers, and parents.

Chapter 3: The Envisioner

The highly effective principal is an envisioner—an individual who is motivated by a sense of calling and purpose, focused on a vision of what schools can be, and guided by a mission that has the best interests of all students at its core.

Chapter 4: The Facilitator

The highly effective principal is a facilitator—a leader with outstanding human relations skills that include the abilities to build individual relationships with parents, teachers, and students; collaborative teams with staff members and parents; and a schoolwide community of leaders.

Chapter 5: The Change Master

The highly effective principal is a change master—a flexible, futuristic, and realistic individual who is able to both motivate and manage change in an organized, positive, and enduring fashion.

Chapter 6: The Culture Builder

The highly effective principal is a culture builder—an individual who communicates and models a strong and viable vision based on achievement, expectations, character, personal responsibility, and accountability.

Chapter 7: The Activator

The highly effective principal is an activator—an individual with gumption (drive, motivation, enthusiasm, energy, spunk, and humor) enough to spare and share with staff, parents, and students.

Chapter 8: The Producer

The highly effective principal is a producer—a results-oriented individual with a strong sense of accountability to taxpayers, parents, students, and teachers who translates high expectations into intellectual development and academic achievement for all students.

Chapter 9: The Character Builder

The highly effective principal is a character builder—a role model whose values, words, and deeds are marked by trustworthiness, integrity, authenticity, respect, generosity, and humility.

Chapter 10: The Contributor

The highly effective principal is a contributor—a servant-leader, encourager, and enabler whose utmost priority is making contributions to the success of others.

About the Author

Elaine K. McEwan is a partner and educational consultant with The McEwan-Adkins Group, offering workshops in instructional leadership, team building, and raising reading achievement, K–12. A former teacher, librarian, principal, and assistant superintendent for instruction in a suburban Chicago school district, she is the author of more than thirty books for parents and educators. Her titles include *Leading Your Team to Excellence: Making Quality Decisions* (1997), *The Principal's Guide to Attention Deficit Hyperactivity Disorder* (1998), *How to Deal With Parents Who Are Angry, Troubled, Afraid, or Just Plain Crazy* (1998), *The Principal's Guide to Raising Reading Achievement* (1998), *Counseling Tips for Elementary School Principals* (1999) with Jeffrey A. Kottler, *Managing Unmanageable Students: Practical Solutions for Educators* (2000) with Mary Damer, *The Principal's Guide to Raising Math Achievement* (2000), *Raising Reading Achievement in Middle and High Schools: Five Simple-to-Follow Strategies for Principals* (2001), *Ten Traits of Highly Effective Teachers: How to Hire, Mentor, and Coach Successful Teachers* (2001), *Teach Them ALL to Read: Catching the Kids Who Fall Through the Cracks* (2002), *7 Steps to Effective Instructional Leadership, 2nd Edition* (2003), and *Making Sense of Research: What's Good, What's Not, and How to Tell the Difference* (2003) with Patrick J. McEwan.

Elaine is the education columnist for the *Northwest Explorer* newspaper and a contributing author to several online Web sites for parents, and she can be heard on a variety of syndicated radio programs helping parents solve schooling problems. She was honored by the Illinois Principals Association as an outstanding instructional leader, by the Illinois State Board of Education with an Award of Excellence in the Those Who Excel Program, and by the National Association of Elementary School Principals as the National Distinguished Principal from Illinois for 1991. She received her undergraduate degree in education from Wheaton College and advanced degrees in library science (M.A.) and educational administration (Ed.D.) from Northern Illinois University. She lives with her husband and business partner E. Raymond Adkins in Oro Valley, Arizona. Visit her Web site at www.elainemcewan.com where you can learn more about her writing and workshops and enroll in online seminars based on her books, or contact her directly at emcewan@elainemcewan.com.

The Communicator

1

"Seek first to understand, then to be understood."

—Covey (1990, p. 255)

I recently had my annual eye exam and while the doctor was adjusting his high-tech equipment to examine the inner workings of my eyes, he asked me what kind of books I wrote. I was impressed that he had taken the time to read the registration form I'd completed and told him that I wrote for educators—mainly, school principals.

"Do you have children in school?" I asked.

"Oh, yes," he answered, and told me their ages. His children were doing well, he assured me, but he was concerned about the principal. The doctor's diagnosis—inability to communicate.

He explained: "The consensus in my neighborhood is that he doesn't know how to listen. If you have a concern or a problem, you get a fifteen-minute appointment during which the principal talks "at" you. Then he glances at his watch, apologizes for having to end the appointment, and you're ushered out."

I could tell what he was thinking: "Even my bedside manner is better than that." And he was right.

Stephen Covey (1990) calls communication "the most important skill in life" (p. 237), and the 108 individuals who responded to the survey I sent out agreed with him, giving *the ability to communicate* more votes than any of the other thirty-seven traits listed. Successful principals are communicating virtually 100 percent of the time they are on the job—listening, speaking, writing, and reading. Even when they don't think

> "The message is the message received"
>
> —Diekman (1979, p. 21)

they're communicating, they are. How they stand, how they shake people's hands, and even what they wear send messages to the people in their school community. Communication is "the sending and receiving of messages both verbal and nonverbal" (Diekman, 1979, p. 4), but just because a message is sent and even seems to have been received, is no guarantee that the communication is effective.

No matter how clear, direct, and seemingly incontrovertible what we communicate may seem to *us*, we are really only communicating *our* perception of the subject under discussion. And if our goal is to be effective communicators, we must continually seek to understand what the individuals across the table from us are thinking and feeling, particularly if they were the ones who came to see us in the first place.

The average principal conceivably communicates with thousands if not tens of thousands of individuals during a school year. The formats and the forums are varied: writing a newspaper column, presiding over graduation exercises, reporting to the board of education, visiting with parents at open house, addressing the student body during an assembly. Each individual who reads or listens to what the principal has to say forms an opinion and makes a judgment. "He's a straight shooter," says one parent about the principal. "She's nice," says a student. "He's fair," says a teacher. "She'll give you an honest opinion," says a colleague. "OK, but I don't understand a word he says," observes another parent. Many principals are probably unaware of how frequently what they have to say as well as their communication styles are the topics of conversation when teachers, parents, and students "dish" about the principal.

The number one priority of a principal's job description is to communicate in appropriate, productive, meaningful, helpful, and healing ways with teachers, students, parents, colleagues, as well as a vast array of others, whether individually, in small groups, or en masse. The message is unmistakable: If a principal can't communicate—with people of all ages, socioeconomic and educational levels, and every color, race, and creed—going to work every day will be both painful and unproductive.

The principal with the brusque "bedside manner" may well be a caring and committed educator who knows a great deal about curriculum and instruction. Unfortunately, all of his knowledge won't do him much good, if he can't or won't take the time to listen.

Listening attentively and empathetically to the concerns and problems of people is just part of what Communicators do. Highly effective principals also write newsletters, sell bond issues, summarize school improvement plans, tell stories, talk with parents about discipline and achievement concerns, share information at staff meetings, mentor teachers, teach lessons, chair committees, conference with teachers, counsel with students, present workshops, recruit volunteers, bargain new contracts, interview candidates, write grants, and motivate students.

The highly effective principal is a Communicator—a genuine and open human being with the capacity to listen, empathize, interact, and connect with individual students, parents, and teachers in productive, helping, and healing ways, as well as the ability to teach, present, and motivate people in larger group settings.

COMMUNICATOR EXEMPLAR: MICHELLE GAYLE

Michelle Gayle has been the principal of Griffin Middle School (776 students) in Tallahassee, Florida, for two years. Since transferring from an elementary assistant principal's position she held for two years, Michelle hasn't missed a beat. She owes her quick, smooth start to her top-notch communication skills. She is relaxed with adolescents, empathetic with parents, and forthright with teachers.

Michelle's mantra when it comes to communicating is "Open and honest, no matter what." Many administrators love the "honest and open" approach when they are the ones "telling it like it is," but Michelle is always willing to hear the truth from others; "the good, the bad, and the ugly," she calls it. She constantly seeks out reactions, perceptions, opinions, and input from everyone in her school community.

> "Nature has given us one tongue, but two ears, that we may hear from others twice as much as we speak."
>
> —Epictetus

Here are just a few of the ways that she seeks to understand what people are thinking and saying about Griffin Middle School:

- She interviews students and parents who are transferring out of Griffin to private, home, or public schools (both in and out of the district). "I ask them to share something positive about their experience at Griffin as well as the one thing they would tell me, now that they don't have to worry about any consequences."

- She routinely calls parents at random to ask them what's going well at school for their students, what they appreciate most about the school, and what they would change if they could.

- She asks all teachers, parents, and graduating eighth graders to evaluate her performance, using a district-designed instrument plus three open-ended questions she has added to the evaluation: What do I do that you value? What do I do that you don't appreciate? What else would you like to share with me that will help me grow as a professional?

• She makes a point of talking with parents when she meets them outside of school. She always asks how things are going and if they have any suggestions. She immediately feeds back the positive comments to the teachers via E-mail.

Effective communication is a two-way process, and after Michelle listens, she always has something to say that's worth hearing. She characterizes her communication style as "hands-on" but what she really means is "face-to-face." She is one part mother, one part grandmother, and one part preacher. Your mother lays it on the line, your grandmother loves you to death, and your preacher lays down the law. Michelle seems to do all three simultaneously.

She moves effortlessly from counseling with parents to schmoozing with students, to talking instruction with her teachers. With parents, Michelle actively listens and empathizes. "Number one for me is respect," she says. "I want the parents of my students to feel the respect I have for them. If they can sense in what I say and how I say it that they are partners in what we are doing, they will be more willing to trust the way I handle difficult situations. I also want them to know that we support them—that whatever is going on with their children and in their families, we will be there to help."

> "If you don't stand sincere by your words how sincere can the people be?
> Take great care over words, treasure them."
>
> —Lao-Tzu (6th century BCE/1988)

Michelle's communication style with students is impromptu and even a little goofy sometimes. "If I see students I want to chat with, I'll slip up alongside of them in the hallway and make my conversation as unobtrusive as possible. Middle school students can't stand to be in the spotlight so I try to make my communication style fit their needs. I might say softly, 'I heard about your mom. Is there anything I can do to help?' or 'I'm sorry about that math grade. Let us know if you'd like some help raising it.'"

Michelle is one of those people who just exudes energy, especially early in the day. She's out at the student drop-off area on most mornings, talking to kids, chatting with parents, and even waving to perfect strangers on their way to work. She wasn't sure how her sleepy students would react to her bright and early exuberance, but she's discovered they're paying attention even when she thinks they're not. "I'll come up with a crazy word for the day. For example, we have different schedules for different days of the week and I'll think of a good word that starts with "B" for a "B" schedule day. At first, I thought maybe I was going too far with my silliness, but then later in the day when I was in a classroom and the teacher used the word, one of the students said, 'That's Ms. Gayle's word from this morning.'"

Michelle knows that you can't fool middle schoolers. "I'm the real me wherever I am and whomever I'm with." With middle school students, flexibility is the key, and Michelle's motto is "Be ready for anything."

"These kids have so much going on internally. One minute they're on top of the world. Next minute, they don't know what's going on. They don't mean to be that way. This is just where they are." Obviously Michelle adores them, but that doesn't mean she cuts them any slack for their behavior. She is quite comfortable gathering the boys in the gym to talk frankly about the dress code or pulling all of the girls into the auditorium to address issues of sexual harassment.

She is as empathetic and energetic with her teachers as she is with parents and students. She enjoys putting teachers in groups—not "feel-good" groups, as she calls them, but groups in which folks may disagree strongly with one another.

"I think it's important for teachers to learn how to communicate with the people they don't necessarily see eye to eye with. I tell them, 'I want to hear the good, the bad, and the ugly.' If we don't get the truth out, we're just playing feel-good, happy games, and that doesn't help anybody.'"

Griffin Middle School's current academic focus is reading: The entire staff received seventy hours of intensive training associated with the Florida Reading Initiative over the previous summer. Michelle is constantly on the lookout for teachers who are implementing what they learned in their training. "I do a daily E-mail bulletin to the teachers with the usual announcements about meetings, substitutes, and deadlines. But I generally include one or two Hats Off announcements that highlight something positive I saw, related to the reading initiative. Now I have teachers E-mailing me with invitations to their classrooms." Michelle chuckles at her cleverness. "I know they just want to make the Friday Focus."

Michelle has a vision for raising communication to a new level in her school. She explains, "Although Griffin Middle School has always enjoyed a rich tradition of excellence, it really didn't have what I'd call a true middle school mindset. People were divided into departments, and they didn't necessarily speak the same language about students and instruction. My goal is to help people appreciate the value of teamwork and recognize the power of collaboratively wrestling with issues related to teaching and learning. I'm encouraging them to work together in groups and to observe one another's teaching and then talk about what they've seen."

Michelle isn't just *listening* and *talking* to teachers. She's communicating in other ways as well. She wants her teachers to keep on learning, and to that end she has been putting articles and information in their mailboxes.

She says, "I read a lot . . . a real lot. One of the things I pride myself on is reading and sharing. I'll ask teachers, 'Can we get together and talk about this for five minutes?'"

One of Michelle's teachers observed, "I haven't read this much since graduate school." Effective communication is two-way, however, so it wasn't until a teacher shared an article with Michelle that she knew her message about reading and sharing had been received and understood. "I was almost in tears," she said. "It was a wonderful moment." Communicators are like that. They love the excitement and energy that is generated through what Harriet Lerner (1991) calls "the dance of connection."

COMMUNICATOR BENCHMARKS

The connections that Communicator principals make with the students, parents, teachers, and other individuals who pass through their lives each year may number in the tens of thousands. Many of these interactions are heartwarming and memorable, others are filled with tension and uncertainty, but Communicator principals survive and thrive on this whirlwind of words by keeping it simple. They know that above all else, they must attend, listen, seek to understand, empathize, tell the truth in love, and make connections, for "communication seems to work best when it is so direct and so simple that it has a sort of elegance" (Kotter, 1996, p. 89). The following Communicator Benchmarks are guaranteed to result in "elegant" communication.

1.1 Communicators Attend

Attending is not going to football games, concerts, and fun fairs, but rather the first and most basic task of being a helpful, healing, and productive communicator. Monitor yourself or others during most interactions, and you will notice how rare it is that people are being fully attentive to one another. While addressing you and purportedly listening, a friend may also be engaged in a number of simultaneous activities—looking over your shoulder, waving to someone walking by, or rustling through papers. Such divided behavior hardly inspires your confidence, nor do you get the feeling that you are all that important to your friend during that moment in time.

We are all tempted to multitask, but effective principals have learned, sometimes the hard way, to give those with whom they meet their complete and undivided interest. They use their bodies, faces, and eyes to say, "Nothing exists right now for me except you. Every ounce of my energy and being is focused on you." Successful principals structure their one-on-one meetings with individuals in an atmosphere that is free from interruptions. They hold their conversations at round tables where they can sit side by side (or face to face). They never sit behind their desks. They clear away clutter and remove distracting items from their desks and tables. The same electronic devices that interfere with the operation of an aircraft during flight also interfere with effective communication in the principal's office. Communicators turn off their telephones, computers, cellular phones, palm pilots, pagers, CD players, and any other electronic communication devices. They know how to focus on a real person for a face-to-face conversation for as long as it takes to make a connection. They recognize the healing and helping power of attending to people, particularly those who are troubled or distraught.

> "Listen a lot, speak a little.
> One word is enough to make a lot of trouble.
> A fool speaks a lot, a wise man thinks instead.
> One word is as good as nine."
>
> —Finnish proverb
> (Sawyer, 2001, p. 59)

1.2 Communicators Listen

Activator Exemplar Todd White was only twenty-eight when he was named the principal of San Souci Elementary School in Greenville, South Carolina. He says, "I learned how to listen from the teachers there. They taught me to sit down, look people in the eye, and listen to them." Sometimes, his teachers had to tie Todd down to get his attention, but once they did, he was a quick learner. After one year at this small school, Todd was transferred to Mitchell Road Elementary, a low-performing school of 660 students.

During his first day on the job, a veteran staff member asked him if he listened to teachers. Todd looked her straight in the eye and informed her as only a true Southern gentlemen who has learned to listen can, "Yes ma'am, I do. You don't get to be in charge of a school this size at the age of twenty-nine and *not* listen to teachers."

A major difference between highly effective principals and their less effective colleagues is that successful administrators learn early in their careers that the ability to listen isn't just a nice thing to do: It is an essential skill to surviving and thriving in the principalship.

Brenda Valentine, principal of Kanawha City Elementary School in Charleston, West Virginia, admits that one of the things she had to work on at the beginning of her career was listening. She says, "I was young when I became a principal, and one of my first challenges was dealing with parents who had what I call 'tunnel vision.' I discovered that caring parents tend to be more focused on their children's individual needs and less concerned about general school policy and procedures. Sometimes, their expectations seemed unrealistic. At first I was defensive, but I've learned that no matter how far off on a tangent parents may go, if I listen, clarify, and make a genuine effort to solve their problems, they will leave my office feeling that it wasn't a waste of their time to see me." Brenda knows that being a Communicator doesn't mean giving people exactly what they want. "I can't make everybody happy. I do try to make sure that they have been heard, and if warranted, I implement a change."

As a beginning principal, Mark Kern of New Palestine Elementary School, in Indiana, often heard the words that a teacher or parent was saying to him but sent a completely different message with his body language. He has learned that listening is the key skill that is needed for "centering on people."

"When I am with someone, I need to give that individual my complete attention. If I am not able to give that kind of attention at that particular time, I'm honest with the person. 'I'm sorry, but right now I can't give you the attention you deserve. Can we set up another time to talk?' I try to be sensitive to the other person's needs. For example, if it's an emergency or an extremely urgent matter for them, I do drop what I am doing and give my full attention to them. I try to use good listening techniques, making sure I'm giving them eye contact and not using distracting body language, and making sure I summarize or ask questions to fully understand what they are saying. It's difficult for any of the people in your school— students, teachers, or parents, or other staff members—to trust you completely if they feel you don't listen to them."

> "The best kind of listening comes not from technique but from being genuinely interested in what really matters to the other person. Listening is much more than patiently hearing people out."
>
> —Farson (1996, p. 62)

1.3 Communicators Empathize

Communicators know how to lay aside their own personal needs to be heard and understood and are able to focus instead on hearing and understanding what parents or teachers or students have to say. Even if they have never had identical experiences, they can suspend belief for a moment and imagine themselves in someone else's shoes.

How would they feel? How would they act? Where would they go for help? They use their imaginations. Suppose their child was being evaluated for mental retardation. Would they be calm, trusting, and totally relaxed? Probably not. Suppose their child was being bullied on the playground and they thought no one cared. Would they take it lying down? Walking in someone else's moccasins enables Communicators to understand and respond with caring hearts. Communicators know how to engage their imaginations and allow their empathy to flow.

1.4 Communicators Disclose Themselves to Others

Self-disclosure is a technique by which Communicator principals demonstrate authenticity, genuineness, and humanness to others. The purpose of self-disclosure is to share a personal experience in order to show others that they are not alone, thus creating a stronger communication connection. However, too much talking about oneself can interfere with the ability to listen and to focus on the other person's problems.

Terry Beasley, principal of Fairhope Elementary School in Alabama encourages students and teachers to persevere through tough learning challenges by sharing his personal childhood difficulties with learning to read. Contributor Exemplar Lola Malone, principal of Tyson Elementary School in Arkansas, inspires her students to try harder in the face of discouragement and to be patient with those who need more time to learn by sharing the story of her failing grade in college Spanish.

> "Managers think the people with whom they work want them to exhibit consistency, assertiveness, and self-control—and they do, of course. But occasionally, they also want just the opposite. They want a moment with us when we are genuinely ourselves without façade or pretense or defensiveness, when we are revealed as human beings, when we are vulnerable."
>
> —Farson (1996, p. 39)

1.5 Communicators Get the Whole Story

Communicators are sensitive to the kinds of responses and attitudes that principals can display that can distress and anger parents, like automatically backing teachers against parents and students without really hearing the issue from the parents' or students' perspectives. Dawn Hurns, principal of Palm Springs North Elementary School in Hialeah, Florida, realized that sometimes she was making decisions without complete information and then would have to change her mind after "filling in the blanks." Now she uses the phrase "Let me think about it" more often and asks "Why?" and "Can you give me more details on that?" She says, "I have become more discriminating about the information that is brought to me. I don't readily accept everything at face value and do more research."

1.6 Communicators Ask the Right Questions

Certainly the most obvious and direct way to gather information or encourage individuals to explore a particular issue in depth is to ask them a series of questions. The problem with questions, as natural as they may seem in the course of a conversation, is that they often put another individual in a subordinate position in which the principal is the interrogator and expert problem solver: "Tell me what the situation is and I will fix it." For that reason, Communicators only use questions in extended conversations when they are unable get individuals to reveal information in other ways. One notable exception to the rule of avoiding questions unless they are open-ended in nature, is when it is important to gather very specific information in a potentially threatening or dangerous situation. Another exception would be the kind of informal and sometimes almost rhetorical questions that one asks in brief encounters and interactions in more public places.

1.7 Communicators Say What They Mean and Mean What They Say

Margaret Garcia-Dugan is straightforward, direct, and uncomplicated. She is definitely a Horton Award winner, named after one of my favorite Dr. Seuss characters, Horton the elephant. Horton repeats over and over, "I meant what I said, and I said what I meant" (Seuss, 1940, p. 16). Margaret says what she means and she means what she says. Furthermore, she is consistent and doesn't keep changing the rules—another "no-no" for those who aspire to be effective communicators.

"When I communicated my expectations to teachers and students," she explains, "I tried to be as clear and simple as I could be. I repeated my expectations every chance I got. The more frequently they heard what my expectations were and the more they saw how closely my actions aligned to what I said, the clearer they became as to what their actions and attitudes needed to be."

1.8 Communicators Can Accept Criticism

What is your first reaction when someone winds up and throws you a highly critical curve ball? If you are honest, you must admit that criticism is tough to take. When we've worked hard, done our best (or so we thought), and have had good intentions, we want full credit for an assignment well done. We are generally not eager to be critiqued by someone with less experience or fewer degrees.

Highly effective principals, on the other hand, are able to handle criticism (from both staff members and parents) with aplomb. They never engage in arguments, raise their voices, respond in kind with inflammatory remarks, or take a defensive posture. In fact, they often look back on a difficult situation with satisfaction as they reflect on how their ability to listen and learn, as difficult as it seemed at the time, changed their lives.

Activator Exemplar Todd White remembers the first time he encouraged his faculty to tell him what he needed to do to be more effective. He says, "I had to hold my assistant principal down because she kept wanting to argue with the teachers and defend me. But I knew it was important for me to hear what they had to say and learn from it."

Communicators know when to agree with the critic, when to make a conciliatory statement, when to share their own personal feelings in a moment of self-disclosure, *and* when to acknowledge the criticism and move ahead to the next item on the agenda (Parkhurst, 1988, p. 103).

1.9 Communicators Can Give Correction

In her book of essays titled *High Tide in Tucson,* Barbara Kingsolver (1995) tells of her Kentucky grandfather, who dispensed words of wisdom from his front-porch rocking chair. My favorite quote, and one I often share with principals during workshops on how to deal with angry parents, is: "If you never stepped on anybody's toes, you never been for a walk" (p. 45). It's impossible to be a highly effective principal without stepping on a few toes every now and then. You can't make everybody happy and say positive things all of the time. However, successful principals know that there's a big difference between stomping and stepping.

Zig Ziglar (1986), the popular motivational speaker, uses the term "goodfinding" to describe a mindset of giving compliments and positive feedback to others. He says, "I'm convinced that with commitment and persistence you can find *something* good about any person, performance, or situation" (p. 53). Even this superpositive motivator does concede, however, that there are moments that call for correction and instruction.

In her book, *Fierce Conversations,* Susan Scott (2002) suggests a simple but effective six-step process to use when confronting someone about inappropriate behavior or unacceptable performance: (1) Name the issue, (2) select a specific example that illustrates the behavior or situation you want to change, (3) describe your emotions about this issue, (4) clarify what is at stake, (5) identify your contribution to this problem, (6) indicate your wish to resolve the issue, and (7) invite the other person to respond to what you have said (pp. 149–153). Once you have written a simple statement for each of the six steps, verbalizing the six statements should take no more than sixty seconds.

Here's what one Communicator said in her sixty-second opening statement to a teacher with whom she had a problem:

Issue:	Sue, I want to talk with you about the effect your rudeness to parents is having on your overall credibility as a teacher.
Example:	Yesterday, outside your classroom, you confronted Mrs. Teller in a very hostile tone of voice about the fact that John forgot his homework again. You were overheard by several students and parents.
Emotions:	I am very distressed and embarrassed about this issue and how it reflects on our school.
Clarification:	You have a great reputation as a teacher here, and if the gossip mill gets going, I'm afraid you'll damage it.
Contribution:	I should have talked to you the minute I realized that you were having a problem, but I ignored the situation hoping it would go away. I'm sorry. I didn't help you the way I should have.
Desire to Resolve:	I want to resolve this issue today. I'd like to know when we leave my office today that we won't ever have to discuss this kind of problem again.
Response:	Sue, I want to understand what is happening from your perspective. Talk to me about what's going on here.

At this point, the highly effective principal sits back and stops talking. The rest is up to the teacher (or student or parent). Scott's six-step process is practical proof of Kotter's (1996) description of good communication: "[It] seems to work best when it is so direct and so simple that it has a sort of elegance" (p. 89).

1.10 Communicators Communicate Creatively

Don't wait for parents to call you—reach out and make a connection today. Michelle Gayle periodically opens the school directory and randomly selects several parents to call. "Hello, this is Michelle Gayle," she begins. "I am so proud to serve as the principal of your child's school. I'd like to take two minutes of your time if I could."

Michelle laughs as she reports the usual response to her opening comments: "You're who?" She explains once more who she is and then asks, "What are we doing at Griffin Middle School that you'd like to see continued? What would you like to see us do that we're not doing?"

Michelle takes careful notes and follows up the phone calls with notes or postcards. "Thanks for the time you took with me," she writes. "I will pass on your feedback to the faculty and staff."

Now it's time to communicate the good news to her faculty. "Let me tell you what the parents are saying about you," she says at the next faculty meeting. Then she tells them ten things that parents love about Griffin Middle School. "They love the way you communicate with them. They appreciate knowing when their child is having a problem in class. They think it's fabulous when you work with a student during your planning period to catch them up when they've been in the hospital. They love the assignment notebooks you're using."

> **IT'S BEEN TOLD AND TOLD**
>
> **Terry Beasley, Elementary, Fairhope, Alabama**
>
> Gossip is
> The art of passing
> Information on,
> That does not need
> To be repeated
> And needs be left
> Alone.
> Yes, it's been told
> And told and told
> And now my turn
>   has come,
> To choose abortion
> For this tale
> Or pass it on and on.

1.11 Communicators Disagree Agreeably

Highly effective principals know that only in their dreams will everyone agree with all of their decisions. But they have learned how to disagree in agreeable ways. Mark Kern believes that his most valuable communication tool is his ability to do just that.

"After I've carefully listened to an individual, if the idea that is proposed is one with which I cannot agree for very sound reasons, I tell the individual that I cannot agree with their position or grant their request and give them my reasons. I'm always courteous and respectful of their needs and viewpoint. While everyone's first choice is to gain my total support or agreement for what they are proposing, most individuals are satisfied that I gave them a fair hearing and made my decision taking into account what they had to say."

1.12 Communicators Pay Attention to Parents

Communicators aren't pushovers, and they never permit themselves to be backed into corners, steamrolled, or threatened by overly aggressive and hostile parents. They follow some simple rules to protect themselves as well as their staff members. They take careful notes, keep superiors informed, and consult with mental health and law enforcement professionals. They are well informed about school board policies, the legal rights of parents and students, as well as their own rights and responsibilities. They frequently invite others to attend meetings with hostile parents to help defuse explosive situations, and they know the law with regard to their obligations to report possible child abuse.

Communicators also know, however, that there are some very real and legitimate reasons for parents to be angry, and they are able to listen, apologize, and take action if it is needed. Communicators recognize the importance of paying attention to parental concerns in a timely way. Circling the wagons to protect incompetent staff members or stonewalling in the hope that a problem will disappear usually only makes an unfortunate situation more explosive. Kosmoski and Pollock (2000) suggest the following guidelines:

- "Consider all complaints or accusations as serious and valid until proven otherwise" (p. 30). (Most parents find lodging a complaint against an individual teacher or against a school policy to be a stressful and difficult situation. They do not do it lightly and need to be treated with respect.)
- "Promptly rectify any valid misunderstanding or complaint of which you have accurate and direct knowledge" (p. 30). (Unfortunately, ignoring a problem won't make it disappear.)
- "Do not equate staff support with blind blanket protection" (p. 30).
- "Do not feel threatened when an individual lodges a complaint or voices an accusation. By coming to you, it implies that the person respects and trusts you" (p. 30).

1.13 Communicators Connect Emotionally and Professionally With Staff

Communicators know that it is essential to have interactions and conversations with staff members that are both personal *and* professional. Steve Wilson, principal of Centura Elementary School in Cairo, Nebraska, says, "I touch base with each of my faculty and staff members as often as I can. I want to know what is happening with these people both at school and at home so that I can help them be the best they can be every day. It is important to me that teachers understand that I care about them personally, their classroom performance or their performance in another staff

"I am known for keeping my word. I have been told numerous times that people feel comfortable confiding in me because they know that I will keep their confidences."

—Principal Dawn Hurns

function, and where they need to improve. This collegiality helps build trust and professional respect, and helps me to raise the bar for high expectations of personal performance in a nonthreatening way. This also helps build the foundation for a learning-centered environment."

1.14 Communicators Communicate With Students

Communicator Principals know how to communicate with their students. Elementary principals know that it's important to be concrete when they want their students to remember an important concept or idea. When Facilitator Exemplar Doug Pierson talks to his students at Hamilton Elementary School in Rhode Island about the importance of apologizing to someone they've wronged, he gives them more than just words to help them remember his four-step process for apologizing.

"I teach them one step for each of the four fingers on their right hand. The pointer finger stands for addressing the person by name. The middle finger stands for looking the person in the eye. The ring finger stands for telling the person exactly what it is that you're sorry about. And the pinky stands for being sincere."

Doug knows that his system is working when he sees a student standing in front of a wronged classmate with his hand behind his back holding up one finger at a time.

Larry Pollock, principal of Juanita Elementary School, in Kirkland, Washington, uses a thumbs-up signal to communicate the work ethic that prevails at Juanita School. One thumb up means "Try your best." A second thumb up stands for "Don't give up."

"What amazes me, " says Pollock, "is the profound impact that a little object lesson like this can have on young minds. A parent recently told me that she and her first-grade son were working a challenging puzzle together. When she suggested putting it away because it was too difficult, her child responded with my "thumbs-up" lesson. 'Oh no,' the child said, 'Mr. Pollock says "Try your best and don't give up.'"

Lest you think that object lessons and acronyms are only for little kids, think again. Character Builder Exemplar Tom Paulsen, of Naperville Central High School in Illinois, uses

> "There are three principles in man's [and woman's] being and life, the principle of thought, the principle of speech and the principle of action. The origin of all conflict between me and my fellow-men is that I do not say what I mean, and that I do not do what I say. For this confuses and poisons, again and again and in increasing measure, the situation between myself and the other man, and I, in my internal disintegration, am no longer able to master it but contrary to all my illusions, have become its slave."
>
> —Buber (1948/1958, p. 158)

the acronym RESPECT as the basis for his annual graduation speech. It is a character-building program at the high school and stands for responsibility, equality, sincerity, pride, empathy, communication, and trust. Communicators never miss an opportunity to communicate in positive and productive ways with their students.

1.15 Communicators Can Talk to the Boss

One of my former principal colleagues and I often discussed her seeming inability to communicate with our boss, the superintendent. "You always get what you want," she complained. I couldn't argue with her. She was right. "Even if I ask for the very same thing that you do, he says 'no' to me and 'yes' to you. He must like you better than he likes me."

I disagreed with her. "I think your problem is the way you're communicating with him," I said.

"Oh, so I've got to polish up my tongue so it's silver like yours?"

Actually, there was nothing wrong with her tongue at all. It's just that our boss was a Reader, not a Listener (Drucker, 1999), and she was a Talker, not a Writer. She presented her proposals and requests verbally, completely unaware that our boss didn't learn well by listening. I, on the other hand, being a Reader myself, just naturally put anything I wanted to discuss with him in writing, always giving him a copy beforehand.

He needed to see and digest the printed word before he could render a positive decision. Confronted with a barrage of words, he often just said no, feeling confused and frustrated.

Peter Drucker (1999) points out, "Very few people even know that there are Readers and there are Listeners, and that very few people are both. Even fewer know which of the two they themselves are" (p. 169). Communicators quickly figure out the most effective ways to communicate with their superintendents or supervisors. My colleague tried the "printed word" approach and left the superintendent's office with exactly what she came for.

1.16 Communicators Connect in Productive, Helping, and Healing Ways

Highly effective principals know how to help staff, students, and parents explore problems, confront difficult issues, and consider possible solutions. They use three communication strategy tool kits as needed (Kottler & McEwan, 1999; McEwan, 1998).

Successful principals always open their *responsive strategy tool kit* first when talking with parents, students, and teachers about problems: (1) decelerate, (2) attend, (3) listen, (4) open the mind, and (5) empathize. Once they have listened and fully understand the issues, they turn to the tools in their *exploratory tool kit*. This set of tools is useful for gaining more information from an individual than has been initially shared and includes (1) questioning, (2) reflecting content, (3) reflecting feelings, (4) self-disclosure, and (5) summarizing.

The final *tool kit of action strategies* is opened only after the responsive and exploratory tools have been well used: (1) problem solving, (2) goal setting, and (3) reality therapy. *Problem solving* and *goal setting* are familiar terms, but *reality therapy* as I define the term may be new to you—helping students, parents, and teachers to confront their problems realistically and objectively by means of telling the truth in love. This process is rarely accomplished in one meeting or encounter and takes patience and discretion. It is an ongoing process, sometimes taking place over several years but often resulting in changed teachers, parents, and students.

1.17 Communicators Care Enough to Send the Very Best

In this age of E-mail communication and instant messaging, the art of sending cards and notes is vanishing. There is something quite uplifting, however, about receiving a handwritten thank-you note or word of encouragement. Nancy Moga, principal of the Callaghan Elementary School in Covington, Virginia, often recognizes and encourages members of her school community in writing. In fact, during one school year, she sent 144 notes and messages to a teacher who needed extra support. Most Communicators can't measure up to Nancy's record, but they do know the importance of personal, handwritten communiqués.

Facilitator Exemplar Doug Pierson was overspending his budget on "store-bought" cards and is now buying attractive computer paper to make his own. "I send cards to parents and teachers all the time: thank-you notes, tough-times cards, and birthday greetings." As if that weren't enough, twice a year (summertime and Christmastime), Doug also writes to all of his teachers from home.

> "If we genuinely respect our colleagues and our employees, those feelings will be communicated without the need for artifice or technique. And they will be reciprocated."
>
> —Farson (1996, p. 37)

1.18 Communicators Know How to Schmooze

One of my fellow Corwin authors, Robert Ramsey (2002), has written a very helpful book on communication: *How to Say the Right Thing Every Time: Communicating Well With Students, Staff, Parents, and the Public.*

I particularly enjoyed the section he titled, Smooth Schmoozing: How to Make Small Talk. He says that "schmoozing is a dance and if possible, you want to lead" (p. 127). He recommends sticking to such safe conversational topics as traffic, weather, arts, sports, news, and the family.

I've always been a fairly effective schmoozer, but I have only recently learned the power of schmoozing about sports. Having been a sports illiterate for most of life, only my marriage to a die-hard sports fan has motivated me to read *Sports Illustrated* and keep up with various sports teams around the country. Now I can schmooze with the coaches and former coaches who attend my workshops. After a few minutes of discussing the latest ups and downs of their local teams, we have "bonded," so to speak. They are far more inclined to listen to what I have to say when the workshop begins, if I can make a communication connection over football or basketball.

Good principals never underestimate the importance of small talk. As Ramsey (2002) notes, "Obviously making small talk at social events, at the market, or on the street corner is not the most important thing you do as a school administrator. But it isn't chopped liver either" (p. 130).

> **WHERE DREAMS LIVE . . . AND DIE**
>
> **Terry Beasley, Elementary, Fairhope, Alabama**
>
> Words are important after all—
> Beginning and ending conflict,
> Inspiring and discouraging thought.
> Creating the magnificent
> And the unwanted—
> And should not be spoken lightly;
> And are not easily taken back.
> As the bit guides the way of the horse,
> And the rudder the path of the ship,
> Words rule the affairs of men
> Bringing to each generation
> A taste of heaven and a taste of hell.

1.19 Communicators Write, Speak, and Teach

Communicators are adept at writing, speaking, and teaching. No one does it with more enthusiasm and expertise than Terry Beasley. He writes poetry (notice his poems in the sidebars) which has been published by both the Alabama and American Poetry Societies; presents at meetings and conventions like the National Council of Teachers of Mathematics; teaches graduate classes and serves as a senior thesis advisor at the University of Mobile; writes and reviews curriculum in reading and mathematics; and somehow also manages to teach Sunday School, serve as a worship moderator, and narrate religious dramas.

SUMMING IT UP

Communicator principals engage in a nonstop merry-go-round of conversations, interactions, communications, connections, exchanges, and contacts with people. Some may last only a few moments and be quickly forgotten; others are ongoing and life changing. Effective principals handle them all with skill, courtesy, and savoir faire. They are able to connect with sullen seventh graders as smoothly as with suave bankers. They can communicate with senior citizens as readily as they can with the senior class. They can sit down with distraught parents and put them at ease as comfortably as they can take the podium in front of an auditorium full of

Figure 1.1   Communicator Benchmarks

Trait Number 1: The highly effective principal is a Communicator—a genuine and open human being with the capacity to listen, empathize, interact, and connect with individual students, parents, and teachers in productive, helping, and healing ways, as well as the ability to teach, present, and motivate people in larger group settings.

- 1.1 Communicators attend.
- 1.2 Communicators listen.
- 1.3 Communicators empathize.
- 1.4 Communicators disclose themselves to others.
- 1.5 Communicators get the whole story.
- 1.6 Communicators ask the right questions.
- 1.7 Communicators say what they mean and mean what they say.
- 1.8 Communicators can accept criticism.
- 1.9 Communicators can give correction.
- 1.10 Communicators communicate creatively.
- 1.11 Communicators can disagree agreeably.
- 1.12 Communicators always pay attention to parents.
- 1.13 Communicators connect emotionally and professionally with staff.
- 1.14 Communicators communicate with students.
- 1.15 Communicators can talk to the boss.
- 1.16 Communicators connect in productive, helping, and healing ways.
- 1.17 Communicators care enough to send the very best.
- 1.18 Communicators know how to schmooze.
- 1.19 Communicators write, speak, and teach.

hormonally charged middle school students and keep them mesmerized. Communicators know the power of words as well as the value of silence. They understand this timeless truth: "Communication is a people-process. And effective communication is simply good 'people relations.' It's not a matter of technique or gimmicks; it is a matter of sensitivity and understanding and responsiveness" (Diekman, 1979, p. 13).

The Educator

"*To be an Educator, one must eat and sleep teaching and learning. Educators are constantly thinking about how to organize a school and instruction so that all students can learn.*"

—Educator Exemplar, Alan Jones

In the spring of 2001, a brief article appeared in *Education Week* describing a program under way in the Los Angeles Unified School District (LAUSD)—an effort by the eleven local district superintendents to "rethink" how principals should do their jobs (Stricherz, 2001). The program, funded by the Broad Foundation at a cost of more than $200,000 over two years, was designed and conducted by Lauren Resnick of the University of Pittsburgh. LAUSD's spokesperson said one goal for principals included spending time in classrooms, school halls, and teacher's lounges acting as instructional leaders. The foundation's director of program development, Dan Katzir, is quoted as saying that "the foundation is agnostic on whether instructional leadership raises student achievement," but they wanted to help out the new LAUSD superintendent, former Colorado governor Roy Romer (p. 5).

Although the 108 respondents to the trait survey were not asked to give their personal definitions of instructional leadership or share what they believed about the relationship of instructional leadership to student achievement, they were most definitely *not* doubtful about its importance to being a highly effective principal. You may recall from our earlier discussion that the survey trait *instructional leader* received the second highest number of votes overall (71), while a related trait, *knowledgeable about teaching and learning,* received the third highest number of votes (60). Furthermore, when the vote totals for the traits that were eventually grouped in the Educator category were combined, the grand total was 213: instructional leader (71), knowledgeable about teaching and learning (60), a learner (34), intelligent (23), ability to teach adults (18), and ability to teach students (7).

If Mr. Katzir, program director for the Broad Foundation, or any others are interested in deepening their understandings about the relationship between instructional leadership behaviors and student achievement, I could recommend some excellent books to them (Blase & Blase, 1994, 1998a, 1998b; Blase & Kirby, 2002; McEwan, 2002), as well as research studies (Heck, Larsen, & Marcoulides, 1990) and reviews (Hallinger & Heck, 1996a, 1996b).

Those interested in pursuing the topic of instructional leadership could begin with a very early study from Andrews and Soder (1987). Rather than merely describing instructional leadership behavior, they sought to show how this behavior affected the performance of students, particularly low-achieving students. They administered questionnaires to teachers in the sixty-seven elementary schools and twenty secondary schools of the Seattle, Washington, school district. Eighteen different interactions that occur between principals and teachers were measured in four key areas: the principal as resource provider, the principal as instructional resource, the principal as communicator, and the principal as visible presence. Their findings showed that the normal equivalent gain scores of students in schools led by strong instructional leaders (as perceived by the teachers in those schools) were significantly greater in both total reading and total mathematics than those of students in schools rated as having average or weak leaders (as perceived by the teachers in those schools).

More recently, Hallinger and Heck (1996a), in a synthesis of fifteen years of research on how principals impact their schools, concluded that principals exercise a *measurable,* though indirect, effect on school effectiveness and student achievement. About the *indirect* aspect, they write, "The fact that leadership effects on school achievement appear to be indirect is neither cause for alarm or dismay. . . . Achieving results through others is the essence of leadership" (p. 39). Regarding the current state of knowledge about the effects of instructional leadership, Blase and Kirby (2002) conclude, "In sum, although the study of instructional aspects of leadership and student achievement has been shown to be complex and empirically challenging (Hallinger & Heck, 1996a, 1996b), and although a number of scholars have acknowledged the dearth of studies of the relationships among leadership, teaching, and student achievement (Leithwood, Begley, & Cousins, 1990), some direct and indirect links to student achievement have been found" (Blase & Kirby, 2000, p. 3).

If there are those who are still unconvinced regarding instructional leadership after reading the aforementioned books and studies, they might benefit from spending a day with the thirty-seven highly effective principals who participated in this study. They would discover, as they listened to their inspiring stories, that principals *do* matter—a great deal. That we have not yet fully determined the precise "how" of this impact is cause for continued speculation and investigation by theorists and researchers. However, those of us who deal with the realities of failing schools on a daily basis know that we must pay close attention to what *is* working in the lives of these highly effective administrators. We must carefully examine their priorities; conversations; behaviors; activities; and interactions with teachers, parents, students, and the public, and then seriously consider how they have gone about creating learning-centered schools, particularly in those instances where a school was failing abysmally when they were hired.

I have chosen to use the term *Educator* (rather than *instructional leader*) in this book for three reasons: first, *Educator* implies a more mediated or indirect relationship between the behaviors of effective principals and student learning, a position that is in keeping with current thinking and research; second, the term *Educator* is more amenable to the role of parents, teachers, and principals as learners; and third, it is a more inclusive term that encompasses the behaviors and activities of the principal that may seem only tangentially related to learning but upon closer examination are at the heart of creating a learning community.

Heck et al. (1990) write, "Our results indicate that many of the important instructional leadership variables influencing school achievement are not related to the regular clinical supervision of teachers. . . . While regularly observing teachers and conferencing with them regarding instructional improvement is admittedly an important aspect, our results show that principals' time and attention are focused on a variety of additional activities" (p. 120).

These observations of Heck and his colleagues (1990) confirm what you will discover as you make your way through this book: To be an Educator also means being a Facilitator who is a Change Master, Culture Builder, Envisioner, and Producer. While the list of Educator benchmarks may at first glance seem all too short for the central purpose of schooling, don't forget there are nine chapters of supporting benchmarks.

The highly effective principal is an Educator—a self-directed instructional leader with a strong intellect and personal depth of knowledge regarding research-based curriculum, instruction, and learning who motivates and facilitates the intellectual growth and development of self, students, teachers, and parents.

EDUCATOR EXEMPLAR:
JEAN HENDRICKSON, ELEMENTARY

Jean Hendrickson is the principal of Mark Twain Elementary School in Oklahoma City, Oklahoma. When she said good-bye to her affluent suburban school principalship in 1999 and took on the challenge of revitalizing a seemingly irreparable inner-city school using the Core Knowledge (CK) curriculum as her cornerstone, there were those who wondered if her vision wasn't a bit unrealistic. However, if people tell Jean that something won't work, that's her signal to prove them wrong.

Larry Lezotte (1992) observes, "One of the best kept secrets in education is that students *do* tend to learn those things they are taught" (p. 62), and no one knows that secret better than Jean. As a CK national trainer, Jean understood the power and deeply appreciated the value of a content-rich curriculum that includes Language Arts (reading, writing, grammar and usage, fiction, nonfiction, drama, poetry, speeches, sayings and phrases), World History, American History, Geography, Science, Mathematics, Visual Art, and Music. She also knew the history and genesis of CK. Its founder, E. D. Hirsch, Jr., did not develop the curriculum for affluent students in privileged schools but for students just like those at Mark Twain: 48 percent Hispanic, 15 percent African American, 15 percent Native American, and 22 percent Caucasian. The big questions: Would the teachers at Mark Twain buy into Jean's recommendation, *and* would they be able to pull it off?

Jean was determined to narrow the "learning gap" described by Hirsch, but she had some groundwork to lay before she could begin making her vision a reality. The former principal had lasted only one year, and in his wake he left a divided staff, disenfranchised parents, and discouraged students. Why did the Oklahoma City superintendent of schools tap Jean for the job? She says, "I believed in the community's capability to mobilize their resources for children, and I am committed to the fact that all children can learn. My mission is to create the most effective, comprehensive learning environment for children that we possibly can."

What does an Educator principal do first? Listen. Jean recognized the opportune moment and seized it when a staff member at Mark Twain with whom Jean had once worked called her early in the summer. She asked if Jean would be interested in meeting with the staff, and Jean immediately said yes. They reserved a restaurant meeting room where Jean listened to the teachers talk for more than two and a half hours. They were hurt, angry, and disillusioned.

Then it was Jean's turn to talk. She told them that she didn't do mediocrity well and believed with all her heart that there was no excuse for not providing the same kind of challenging and meaningful learning environment for the students at Mark Twain that the students in her former school had enjoyed. She agreed to listen to their heartaches and empathize with their devastating experiences for a while but told them to be prepared at some point to lay their anger aside, pick up their plan books, and move forward.

Jean laid out the basics of the CK curriculum to the teachers. They were highly skeptical of her proposal but had no other alternatives to offer. They were at the end of their proverbial ropes and virtually certain that *their* students could never handle the rigor of the CK curriculum with its emphasis on history, art, and literature. The teachers were also insecure about their own abilities to teach CK—Ancient Egypt in first grade, Ancient Greece in second grade, Ancient Rome in third grade, Europe in the Middle Ages in fourth grade, and the cultures of the Aztecs, Incas, and Mayans in fifth grade.

Jean challenged the teachers while at the same time pledging her unqualified support to them: "If you will commit to creating a new understanding of what school is about for our students," she said, "I will provide all of the training and resources you need to be successful. I will be there for you every step of the way. At the end of five years, if we haven't made huge strides, if we haven't been able to do this together, then I will admit that you were right and I was wrong. I will take full responsibility for the failure." Jean understood the trepidation her teachers were feeling, but she was

---

GET OUT OF YOUR OFFICE AND INTO CLASSROOMS

Communicator Exemplar Michelle Gayle, Middle School, Tallahassee, Florida

I'm in classrooms every day. I might participate with the class in the lesson, work with individual students if they're doing an assignment, or give the teacher a word of encouragement if it's appropriate. I also regularly substitute in classrooms. It started off as a budget decision because my school was in the red on the substitute line item, but I've discovered that getting hands-on in the classroom affords me incredible opportunities to interact with students in a totally different context. I can observe their class work and make note of problems to discuss later with the teacher. Another way I keep track of kids is to constantly look at data—classroom tests, report cards, and grade books. I ask teachers all the time—"let me see your grade book." Teachers know I'm checking to see how certain students are doing.

TEACH TO THE OUTCOMES

Nancy Moga, Elementary, Covington, Virginia

Four years ago, we weren't at all pleased with our school's test results on the Virginia Standards of Learning. Doing things the same old way was not getting the results we needed. I knew we had excellent teachers, but we were focused on the wrong content. I led the teachers through a process to determine how much time to spend teaching each objective and where to put our emphasis. The process had to be broken into small bits so we could see progress and make sure that what we were doing would lead to results we wanted to see. It worked, and we became the first school in our district and the only school within fifty miles to be fully accredited by the state. Soon another school in the district joined our ranks, and now all but one has achieved the highest status. The central office administrators soon realized that if a school like ours, where there was a high percentage of free and reduced lunch students and only a handful of families with college degrees, could obtain the top results, so could the others.

confident—in her teachers, in the program, in the students and parents of Mark Twain, *and* in her own ability to help make it happen.

Jean gave the teachers time to think about her offer individually, call her with questions, and then get together again privately to talk with each other. The summer stretched on, but before the school year began, she had received a 100 percent signed commitment from the staff indicating their willingness to undergo thirty hours of intensive CK training, one night a month, for three to four hours, over the course of the year. The next step involved integrating the CK content with the Oklahoma state standards and then determining what resources and materials were needed for classrooms and libraries. Jean continued to support and encourage her teachers' growing abilities to master the intricacies of a totally new curriculum while they planned for a full-scale implementation the following year. She wanted the change to be meaningful and lasting. She took her time.

While teachers were experimenting with new ways of looking at curriculum and instruction, Jean was thinking about ways to create a learning environment for parents and their preschool children. She enlisted community partners and opened up the school to a variety of outside agencies. Jean asked parents what they needed and then put together programs and services that met those needs—a Parent Resource Room, a full day Head Start program, GED and ESL classes, a full-time parent advocate, and a Success by Six program. Monthly coffees, parenting classes, and a parent-edited newsletter drew even more parents into the Mark Twain learning community. The school soon became a beehive of learning—for teachers, students, *and* parents. Jean obtained resources to improve reading instruction at school and family literacy at home, always balancing the priorities of teachers and parents but ever mindful that raising achievement depends on a strong parent-school partnership.

Improvement at Mark Twain has been solid and steady. The teachers have acquired a tool kit of strategies and an appreciation for how much their students *can* learn. Parents have been welcomed into the school and have become a part of the learning community in a variety of important ways. As E. D. Hirsch, Jr., says, "The more you know, the more you can learn." The students, parents, and teachers at Mark Twain are a testimony to the power of that statement.

EDUCATOR EXEMPLAR: ALAN JONES, HIGH SCHOOL

Alan Jones retired in June of 2002 after seventeen years as the principal of Community High School in West Chicago, Illinois, with a host of achievements to his credit. Currently an assistant professor of education at St. Xavier College in Chicago, Alan left a legacy of educational excellence in this small, working-class community. A highly trained and knowledgeable faculty, award-winning programs, and myriad extracurricular opportunities for students in drama and music are commonplace features in prestigious private schools, but they are seldom found in public institutions where one-third of the students are Hispanic. The recruitment of top-notch faculty has always been a priority for Alan, and the staff members he has hired, coached, and mentored during his tenure would be welcome at any college or university. Sixty percent of the faculty have earned master's degrees and some also have Ph.D.s. They have written textbooks, presented regularly at national conferences in their disciplines, and been honored with state and national teaching awards. Alan has provided the encouragement *and* procured the resources to make it happen.

In 1993, Community High School received a Blue Ribbon of Excellence Award. "It was a big deal for the school," Alan concedes. "I didn't want to do it originally because I felt it would take me away from other more important priorities, but the superintendent thought the community needed that designation to make it aware of what a great school it had, and he insisted we do it."

In the end, the affirmation and encouragement that Alan personally received from the experience enabled him to continue the sometimes discouraging work of an Educator—pushing the boundaries of what his faculty thought was reasonable for a high school to do and be. One of the Blue Ribbon site visitors told Alan during the visit, "You have a very special high school. You are doing all the right things."

The right things that Alan was doing were centered on learning for all students, not just the college-bound and highly motivated ones but also those who often slip below a high school principal's radar screen—bilingual students, potential dropouts, and special education students. Alan says, "I was concerned about the harshness of our high school and the lockstep mentality of many teachers; I wanted to build a kinder and gentler culture where all of our students could be successful."

Alan calls the opportunities to make learning more meaningful for these students "my chances to churn and burn." He says, "These opportunities to make a significant difference happen to every principal, but you have to know what you're doing so that you end up with meaningful change. So frequently, administrators just send teachers chasing their tails, and they end up doing the same things they were doing ten years ago."

Alan's opportunity to "churn and burn" with the special education delivery model grew out of his teachers' frustrations: They were attempting to implement an inclusive model with a self-contained mentality.

"The first inclination of many principals, when confronted by a problem like this, is to buy a photocopy machine and hire two more aides," Alan says, somewhat tongue in cheek. "But I saw this as a pivotal opportunity to change the entire focus of special education in our school—to bring it out of a closet and make it an integral part of the high school learning community."

"Since high schools are departmentally driven," Alan explained, "it made sense to decentralize special education and send the teachers out as 'entrepreneurs' to create their own schedules and develop their own ways of doing business with each individual department."

Alan had done a great deal of thinking and reading about inclusion and the problems inherent in high school implementation long before his teachers came to him. He was prepared to ask the probing questions that would eventually generate systemically sound solutions, but rather than giving *his*

LINK INSTRUCTION TO STANDARDS

Kathie Dobberteen, Elementary, La Mesa, California

When I came to my school, it was a typical elementary school staffed by caring teachers who believed that the low socioeconomic status of their students automatically dictated low achievement. Because we knew that change was needed, we grasped at everything new. We focused on multicultural education for a time, to build acceptance for our culturally diverse population. Then we emphasized conflict resolution to minimize disciplinary issues in the hope that students would become more self-reliant and take ownership of their learning. None of these programs had any impact on student achievement. Then through several district-level initiatives we began to look at data and its disaggregation as a means to improve every area of curriculum and instruction. Our program used to be defined by a teacher's favorite theme or area of instructional expertise. Now, we are focused on standards combined with effective instruction to ensure that students meet those standards.

solutions to the teachers, he guided them through a critical inquiry of the problem.

Although frustrated with their old ways of doing business, the teachers were understandably nervous about implementing the new model. "What's our role?" they asked Alan.

"You're not teachers anymore," he said. "You're facilitators. Your bottom line is to meet the needs of the special education students who are enrolled in the department to which you are assigned. You'll work in partnership with the department chairpersons."

The plan sounded wonderful on paper, but bringing it to fruition required an infusion of money, several additional staff members to give each department its own facilitator, the approval of the board of education, and most challenging of all, the cooperation of the department chair-persons. Alan made it all happen within a matter of weeks. Educators can "churn and burn" when the lives and learning of their students are at stake.

> "Carpe diem."
> Seize the day.
>
> —Horace (65–8 B.C.)

Another one of Alan's "churn and burn" experiences concerned truants—the students who continually fall through the cracks and eventually just disappear. Alan tells this story with all the drama of a soap opera. First he sets the scene: "We were all in my office (the truant officer, the guidance counselor, and the assistant principal in charge of discipline) talking about the number of kids who had been absent for more than thirty school days and were naturally failing every subject. The guidance counselor and the assistant principal had plans for getting tougher. They included calling the students' homes more often and leaning harder on their parents—all of the stuff we'd been doing forever, with no success."

"Finally, the truant officer turned to the group and announced, 'Unless you're willing to change the way you do school with these kids, forget it.'"

That got everybody's attention. "These kids don't do gym," the truant officer asserted. "They won't come to school at 7:00 a.m. They want to take the courses *they* want to take."

Alan listened carefully, as he always does when staff members express frustration. He asked the truant officer what *she* would do differently, and she told him. "I've been given a truancy grant from the county, and if the district will put some money with it, I'd like to take a bunch of these kids and do school another way. Give me a classroom somewhere and some options. I want to start school at 10:00 a.m. I want to eliminate the gym requirement, and I'd like to offer correspondence classes to give the kids more options." Alan was on board with everything but dropping the gym requirement. He could see trouble ahead on that issue.

He told the truant officer, "They can't graduate unless you figure out some way for them to do gym."

The truant office fired back, "They don't want to take showers or wear gym uniforms. These kids are different. They have dyed hair, nose rings, and wear leather. They can't stand those coach types yelling at them to win one for the Gipper at 7 o'clock in the morning."

Alan did see her point but knew that few others on his staff would be so understanding. He faced another pivotal decision-making point.

As he reflected on this experience, he said, "Here I am, thinking to myself, 'This is a wonderful teacher with a fabulous idea that really makes sense. On the other hand, the institutional restraints are enormous. If I go too far beyond the boundaries of the faculty's understanding, the whole thing could backfire on me." In the end, Alan "churned and burned" on this decision too. He got approval from the Board of Education that included the funds he needed to support the program.

"We put eighteen of the most truant students in one classroom, and it was a giant success story. Kids who had missed thirty days of school were suddenly there every day, working on correspondence classes from the University of Nebraska. But boy, did I take a lot of flak over that class. 'Who are these kids? You're compromising our standards.' I had to fight continually for that program. Pretty soon, the graduation rate began to move up. The program tripled in size to three classrooms, two teachers, and several aides."

Solving the gym problem took a little more creativity. Alan and the teacher worked out an arrangement so that her students could take their credits in the summertime, in a class designed just for them. Alan says with a chuckle, "It's really something to see this group of kids in their leather jackets and chains running around the track. We discovered that they will do physical exercise for somebody they like, *if* they get to wear their own clothes while they're doing it."

Of course, there were those who continued to question Alan's judgment. He laughs out loud. "I had somebody complain that the kids weren't taking showers after they ran. I told the complainer that if I had to choose between the competing priorities of graduation and hygiene, I'd pick graduation any day!"

EDUCATOR BENCHMARKS

Educators will go to any lengths to ensure that every student has the opportunity to learn. The following benchmarks offer some specifics about how they are doing it.

2.1 Educators Believe
That All Students Can Learn, and They
Develop Programs to Help Them Succeed

The almost time-worn statement of belief, *All can learn,* is all too easy to say. Making it happen on a daily basis is never easy. Educator principals know that one size rarely fits all. Sometimes programs must be tailored to meet the needs of small groups of students. Highly effective principals have the courage it often takes to step out and meet those needs. Whether establishing a program for truant students, redesigning the special education delivery model, or changing the way his school "did" bilingual education (see Chapter 7), Alan Jones never lost sight of his vision to create a more humane and caring high school environment where *all* students could learn. Jean Hendrickson pursued the goal of learning for all by giving every student a content-rich curriculum. Kathie Dobberteen knows that students learn as individuals, not as groups, and has targeted specific groups of at-risk students for skill-based booster sessions along with enrichment and acceleration opportunities for high achievers.

2.2 Educators Provide
Training and Support For Teachers

Highly effective principals do not expect teachers to "go it alone." They understand the critical importance of providing training and coaching to their teachers. They also never underestimate the importance of "being there." Alan Jones advises that supporting teachers instructionally, particularly during the implementation of a new program, is the heart of leadership. He says,

Too often, school leaders adopt a program and then immediately go back to the buses, budgets, and boilers. But rarely is a program completely understood by staff members at the outset. That is not to say they aren't on board or eager to participate, but frequently they simply do not have a complete conceptual understanding to sustain what they are doing. The role of the leader, then, is to be in the right place at the right time, ready to engage staff members in various aspects of the inquiry process that will lead them to a deeper understanding of the beliefs, goals, and practices of a specific program. Sometimes it can take years to get staff members beyond a kind of rote implementation where they are merely connecting the dots with no sense of the big picture. Oh, things may seem OK, but usually following a period of initial optimism, there is what Fullan calls "an innovation dip." Real leaders stick around and are available to patiently respond to this confusion and to help staff members through these dips. They understand the time and energy required to bring about meaningful and lasting change.

Patricia Hamilton, principal of Arbuckle Elementary School in California, regularly helps her teachers to reflectively examine their teaching.

Three times a year, the reading specialist and I meet with each teacher to review student assessments and to discuss the instructional goals they have set based on their students' identified weaknesses. During these reflective conferences, teachers often identify areas they would like to pursue educationally. Sometimes we schedule staff development to address a need. But frequently, a grade level will take on an action research project to investigate some aspect of instruction in their classrooms.

My challenge is to help teachers break down their goals into small enough chunks so they can determine how well they are doing at shorter intervals along the way. I use a cognitive coaching dialogue at these conferences to encourage the teachers to think reflectively about their goals and the results they have achieved.

RAISE ACHIEVEMENT CHILD BY CHILD

Kathie Dobberteen, Elementary, La Mesa, California

I know the reading levels of every child in my school and I talk regularly with every teacher about how their students are doing. I feel personally responsible for every child who can't read at grade level and for accelerating and enriching the curriculum of students who are gifted. I am always looking for additional interventions or strategies. If there's a specific student I'm concerned about, I constantly ask the teachers, "How's Carina doing?" or "What else can we do to make a difference for Jason?" I share the responsibility with teachers for the achievement of their students. I will move heaven and earth to make sure that our students can read.

2.3 Educators Create Cognitive Dissonance

Carl Glickman (1993) defines successful schools as "those that have set educational goals and priorities and accomplished them over time" (p. 16). He goes on to describe several lesser known characteristics that he believes are fundamental to these schools, the first being that "faculty in successful schools are less satisfied with regard to their teaching than are faculty in the less successful schools" (p. 16). Glickman suggests that this sense of cognitive dissonance regarding current practices and organizational structures is a strength. Who stirs up this dissatisfaction? Educators.

Highly effective principals ask probing questions, foster serious discussions about programs and policies, and frequently question teachers' long-held beliefs about schooling. Alan Jones sees this as one of the major roles of an Educator, but it is often an arduous and even lonely one. Lest the reader think that Alan is a superprincipal who disappears into a phone booth to emerge with a "Super Program" in his briefcase, he makes it clear that the eventual success of any program is years in the conception (thinking, talking, and reading) and many years in the implementation (again, thinking, talking, and reading). Alan's superintendent would have been happy to see him stop doing all that reading, thinking, and talking and head off instead to a Rotary meeting once in a while, but Educators have a different agenda—meeting the intellectual and achievement needs of all students.

2.4 Educators Establish, Implement, and Achieve Academic Standards

Larry Pollock and his staff have raised student achievement substantially on the Washington state assessment in just two years. In a school that had previously never performed *at*, let alone *above* the district's average, their results are impressive. They used many of the suggestions found in *High-Velocity Culture Change* (Pritchett & Pound, 1993) to get results in a hurry. Larry explains how he and his staff tackled the challenge:

- *Don't do it all.* We needed to focus, focus, focus and give up on lesser priorities. I became the gatekeeper who protected the school from the constant pressure to add programs and features, most of which were of limited benefit to learners or diluted our efforts.
- *Keep it simple.* We discovered that highly detailed school improvement plans were an obstacle. Instead, we wrote brief outlines of strategies to get our students performing, modifying them as needed. If you can't say it in a compelling, simple way, it probably will be forgotten.
- *Work together.* We quickly achieved whole-school agreement on the strategies we would use.
- *Make student performance the only thing.* Get kids reading, solving problems, computing, and writing all the time, and continually collect evidence of their growth and success.

2.5 Educators Focus on Instruction

High school principal Jeanne Stiglbauer organizes biweekly Learning Walks™ for her teachers. Developed by the Institute for Learning at the University of Pittsburgh (Providence Schools, 2002), the activity is designed to focus a small group of individuals visiting a classroom on how teachers teach, how students learn, what gets taught to whom, and how the school is organized to enable students to meet the standards (Learning Research and Development Center, 2002, p. 2). Although in some districts Learning Walks™ include only central office administrators and principals (e.g., Los Angeles Unified School District, Providence Schools), Jeanne has trained her teachers in the methodology and believes that the walks are far more meaningful and nonthreatening if she isn't a part of the group.

The purpose of the walks is not evaluative, and teachers are given guidelines regarding what is appropriate and acceptable to include in their discussion of what they see happening in classrooms. The teachers who are going on the walk choose a topic on which to focus, such as the student work product or the teacher's use of the inquiry method. They then spend fifteen to twenty minutes in each of several classrooms observing, taking notes, and talking with students about what they are learning and why they need to know it. Jeanne has rearranged lunch schedules to give departments shared planning time in which to have follow-up conversations about their Learning Walks™.

2.6 Educators Model Continuous Learning

Facilitator Exemplar Doug Pierson loves to learn so much that he has been taking beginning music lessons with his fifth graders for the past three years. So far, he has studied the cello, violin, and clarinet. He explains that he would be less inclined to change instruments so frequently if second-year lessons were offered, but since his students move on to middle school for their second year of lessons, Doug moves on to learning another instrument with each new crop of fifth graders. Doug suggests that middle and high school principals could learn alongside their students if they signed up for a foreign language they did not know or took a challenging new science or math class. Doug says, "There's nothing quite as exhilarating as becoming a learner on the same level as one's students. The perspective one gains from an experience like this is totally different than just sitting in a classroom and observing a lesson."

TALK ABOUT INSTRUCTION

**Kathie Dobberteen,
Elementary,
La Mesa, California**

Before we made the commitment as a staff to leaving no child behind, our weekly staff meetings were devoted to disseminating information and addressing general schoolwide issues. Now, teachers meet in grade-level teams at least twice per month. They work on long- and short-term plans, analyze their students' work, and discuss ways they can help more students to reach the standards. Over time, our focus has become the constant refinement and improvement of our instructional delivery system.

2.7 Educators Develop Teacher Leaders

Sandra Ahola, principal of K–8 Pomfret Community School, in Connecticut, believes that empowering teachers to become leaders in her school is her number one priority:

> My philosophy is to play to people's strengths. I do not believe in spending 90 percent of my time trying to fix, change, or improve 10 percent of the staff. Instead I spend 90 percent of my time with 90 percent of my teachers, and I "feed the leaders." I encourage, enable, empower, find funds, give release time, and provide praise.
>
> Finding each person's area of strength and building on that strength is the key to success. I put items in the bulletin to affirm teachers school-wide, send teachers to school board meetings to talk about the wonderful things they are doing, and also send them personal notes they can put on their bulletin boards. I let them and everyone else know what a good job they are doing. I have found that these leaders are then able to bring everyone else along behind them.

> "The role of the leader is to ensure that the organization develops relationships that help produce desirable results."
>
> —Fullan (2001, p. 68)

2.8 Educators Pay Attention to What Matters Most

"What should I do?" asks the new principal, "to ensure that all of my students are learning?" "Pay very close attention to the teaching in your school," highly effective principals advise. "Be there—everywhere, every-day—asking questions, offering assistance, talking to students, and observing teachers." Educators are able to distinguish activity from achievement and are able to continually refocus their teachers on what matters most. See The Educator's To-Do List (Figure 2.1) for some ideas on how effective principals do it every day.

2.9 Educators Create Learning Communities

What differentiates the average school from a true learning community? DuFour and Eaker (1998) suggest six characteristics of such a community: (1) shared mission, vision, and values; (2) collective inquiry; (3) collaborative teams; (4) action orientation and experimentation; (5) continuous improvement; and (6) a results orientation (pp. 25–29).

Figure 2.1

THE EDUCATOR'S TO-DO LIST

Bonnie Grossen and her staff at the University of Oregon's Center for Applied Research in Education work with teachers in low-performing schools at both the elementary and secondary levels to improve reading achievement. They quickly realized, however, that without the commitment and hands-on involvement from building principals to back up their teaching and coaching efforts, they could well be spinning their wheels. They went to three of their most effective project principals and asked them to list the things they did daily so they could begin to coach less effective principals to include more of these behaviors in their daily routines.

I have adapted and expanded their suggestions into a To-Do List for Today. Reproduce the list on some brightly colored paper. I recommend Pulsar Pink for maximum visibility on your desktop or clipboard. Put today's date at the top of the page, and then check off the items as you complete them. When you do them all, give yourself a silent cheer or a pat on the back.

- *Visit every classroom in your school every day. Develop a checklist with all of the teachers' names and check off those you visit. If you can't get there during class time, pop in before or after school. If you don't make it through the entire list in one day, begin where you left off the next.*

- *Focus on each teacher's instructional delivery. Write a comment directly related to some aspect of instruction for at least five teachers. Make all of your comments positive and descriptive (Faber & Mazlish, 1990). Work your way through everyone on your staff. Be sure to personalize your comments, as your staff members will no doubt be comparing notes over lunch.*

- *Celebrate the academic success of at least five students each day. Make all of your comments positive, personalized, and descriptive. You can deliver them orally, put them in writing, or call their parents to deliver the good news. Of course, to do this, you will need to visit more classrooms, talk to teachers, look at student work samples, and talk to students.*

- *Learn the names of all of your students, and call them by name when you meet them in the hallways, at athletic events, at concerts, or in the cafeteria. If you're not there yet, learn five new names per day. Pick a family with several children and learn their names as a family group. Learn their parents' names as well. You cannot track the academic progress of students without knowing who they are, what they look like, in whose classroom they sit, and what their specific needs are.*

- *Help staff members and students resolve conflicts in an efficient and timely way. Emphasize the need to work together for the overall goal of learning for all students. The place to begin is with your own relationships. If there is someone on the faculty with whom you have had a disagreement or unpleasant conversation lately, tell that person that you miss talking to them and want to repair the rift for the sake of the students. Call a parent with whom you have had a difficult time communicating and share something positive (related to the academic success of one of their children). "What if their children have not experienced any academic success?" you may ask. Set about finding how you and the teachers can make this happen—even in the smallest of ways.*

- *Support teachers in their disciplinary actions with students. Affirm teachers who have particularly challenging classes this year. Praise their classroom management skills (be descriptive and specific) and ask if there's anything you can do to help them. Look upon this responsibility as the most basic foundation to academic success for all.*

- *Ensure that teachers have the training, materials, and protected time to do their jobs. Minimize interruptions from the intercom. Ask the teachers with whom you talk each day if there's anything you can do to help them be more effective on the job. Follow through in a timely way on these requests.*

- *Plan a coaching session with every teacher. Teach a lesson while a teacher observes you and then schedule a time for you and the teacher to talk about how you could improve your lesson. It's amazing how much you can accomplish in a coaching session if you take the focus off the teacher and put it on yourself.*

Kathie Dobberteen and her staff at La Mesa Dale School in California built their learning community with these six characteristics in mind. They vowed that the demographics of their school would not be an excuse for low achievement and in 1996 committed to a goal of grade level or above reading for every child. Kathie's expectations for student achievement are extraordinarily high as are her expectations for teachers. She has not, however, expected them to do "more with less." She has worked tirelessly to facilitate teamwork, find funding for additional staff members, and provide staff development:

We have moved from a few team-teaching situations with the majority of classrooms still operating independently to the current status where it is truly a whole-school approach to instruction. Grade levels align curriculum to the standards, plan instruction, and provide for individual student needs. As a school, we have moved from merely making lesson plans to analyzing instruction, setting goals and objectives for student learning, and then collecting data to ensure that the desired learning occurs. Individual teachers no longer enter their classrooms and close the door to the outside world. As teams, they meet and plan together; they no longer are responsible for just their particular students. Instead, as a grade level, they are responsible for the entire student body at that grade level.

Our program used to be defined by a teacher's favorite theme and instructional expertise. The program is now defined by the standards and appropriate instruction to ensure that students meet those standards. Our staff now believes that every student can be taught our new rigorous California State Standards but that we have to provide additional time and interventions to make sure this happens. Some examples of the practices that have changed include the structure of both our reading and math programs. We have organized our reading program so that it is much more balanced and each year have looked for ways to make improvements. We started by hiring additional reading specialists for first and second grade. The next year, we hired college student aides so that we could complete guided reading in thirty-minute sessions for all students in each classroom. This meant that more time was available for other language arts activities, especially shared reading and writing. The following year we began conducting guided process reading Monday through Friday (instead of Monday through Thursday) to provide 20 percent more guided process reading instruction. We targeted vocabulary, higher-order thinking skills, and a writing connection to be included in this thirty-minute period. (Dobberteen, 2001, p. 3)

La Mesa Dale was named a California Title I Distinguished School and a National Title I Distinguished School, and Kathie and her staff received a School Change Award from the Chase Manhattan Bank and Fordham University recognizing their accomplishments. In the spring of 2002, the goal they had set in 1996 was nearly reached: 92 percent of their students were reading above grade level.

Figure 2.2   Educator Benchmarks

Trait Number 2: The Educator is a self-directed instructional leader with a strong intellect and personal depth of knowledge regarding research-based curriculum, instruction, and learning that motivates and facilitates the intellectual growth and development of self, students, teachers, and parents.

2.1   Educators believe that all students can learn, and they develop programs to help them succeed.
2.2   Educators provide training and support for teachers.
2.3   Educators create cognitive dissonance.
2.4   Educators establish, implement, and achieve academic standards.
2.5   Educators focus on instruction.
2.6   Educators model continuous learning.
2.7   Educators develop teacher leaders.
2.8   Educators pay attention to what matters most.
2.9   Educators create learning communities.

If you asked Kathie how she and her teachers have achieved this kind of success for students who typically fall through the cracks, she would tell you that they had a compelling vision and a mission that was measurable. Once they zeroed in on exactly what they wanted to do, they never lost their focus. Teachers were constantly engaged in solving instructional problems using the inquiry method. They worked collaboratively to design lessons and notch up their teaching performance. Their student achievement moved steadily upward, but they never stopped setting small incremental goals focused on results.

SUMMING IT UP

To be the kind of principal that Alan Jones so eloquently described at the beginning of the chapter is an all-consuming endeavor. Educators are constantly thinking, planning, and developing—seeking collectively with their teachers for ways to improve instruction and engage more students. Their work is never done, but then, learning is the passion of highly effective principals. They can say with Yeats (as quoted in Fitzhenry, 1986), "Education is not the filling of a pail, but the lighting of a fire" (p. 89). Educators are like Olympic torchbearers—moving through their schools day after day, keeping the flame of learning burning.

The Envisioner

"There is no more powerful engine driving an organization toward excellence and long-range success than an attractive, worthwhile, and achievable vision of the future, widely shared."

—Nanus (1992, p. 3)

What is the secret weapon of school leaders who achieve great things? What sets them apart from their colleagues who talk about what they're going to do but never manage to get it done? According to Collins (2001), highly effective individuals have mastered the hedgehog concept—the ability to focus on one big idea and follow it through to completion. Collins's idea for the hedgehog concept came from a slim volume titled *The Hedgehog and the Fox: An Essay on Tolstoy's View of History* (Berlin, 1970). Berlin's inspiration for his book's title came from a single line in an obscure Greek poem by Archilochus: "The fox knows many things, but the hedgehog knows one big thing" (p. 1).

I have never personally witnessed a fox trying to catch a hedgehog, but apparently, in spite of the fox's multiple and creative approaches to solving the problem of what to have for dinner every night, he never succeeds in nailing his needle-covered prey. The single-minded hedgehog consistently reverts to the one big thing he does best: roll up into a very prickly and impenetrable ball. Berlin likens individuals who can focus on a big idea and accomplish it, to the hedgehog. He compares folks whose fertile minds are overflowing with so many fabulous ideas that they seldom finish anything they start, to the fox.

For there exists a great chasm between those, on one side, who relate everything to a single central vision, one system less or more coherent or articulate, in terms of which they understand, think and feel—a single, universal organizing principle in terms of which alone all that they are and say has significance, and, on the other side, those who pursue many ends, often unrelated in some *de facto* way, for some psychological or physiological cause, related by no moral or aesthetic principle: these last lead lives, perform acts, and entertain ideas that are centrifugal rather than centripetal, their thought is scattered or diffused, moving on many levels. . . . The first kind of intellectual and artistic personality belongs to the hedgehog, the second to the fox. (Berlin, 1970, pp. 1–2)

There is a second quality that sets apart highly effective principals from their "so-so" colleagues: a vision. Highly effective principals are able to look at low-performing or even failing schools and envision what they will look like after the mission has been achieved. Less-effective educators prefer excuses to envisioning.

The state of Arizona plans to impose a new accountability system in 2003, similar to those already in place in many states. In a newspaper article describing the expected fallout from the new system, a Phoenix-area superintendent bemoaned the unfairness of it all: His four schools would be labeled *underperforming*. He was looking for sympathy from the public for all of the inconvenience this would create for him (Kossan, 2002). He had the audacity to whine about the "devastated teachers, frightened parents, and angry students" with whom he would have to deal. "It takes a lot of nurturing and motivation. Once they get through the hurt, you work to get them centered and focused again" (p. B1). This beleaguered administrator seemed oblivious to the question that was on most people's minds as they read the article: What had he and his principals been focused on prior to this? Highly effective principals (and superintendents) don't make excuses. They envision a high-performing district (or school) and then enable and empower parents, teachers, and students to make it happen. Envisioners are compelling individuals. If they were selling life insurance, you'd buy more than you needed. But thankfully for the education profession, these highly persuasive and visionary individuals are focused on students. They remind me of high-spirited racehorses whose vision is narrowed during the big race by blinders. Highly effective principals are not distracted by what some think should be done or by what others believe can't be done. Their eyes are fixed on the finish line.

> "It is only with the heart that one can see rightly; what is essential is invisible to the eye."
>
> —Antoine de Saint-Exupéry

The highly effective principal is an Envisioner—an individual who is motivated by a sense of calling and purpose, focused on a vision of what schools can be, and guided by a mission that has the best interests of all students at its core.

ENVISIONER EXEMPLAR: LARRY FIEBER

Larry Fieber is the principal of Parkway Elementary School in Ewing, New Jersey. He never aspired to be an elementary school principal. In fact, he spent twenty-one years as a high school social studies teacher and assistant principal for discipline before he was called to work at the elementary level. The invitation came from a neighboring school district that was looking for a disciplinarian who could restore order and dignity to a school that had hit rock bottom. In addition to a student body that was out of control, Larry found low academic expectations, a crumbling school plant, dissatisfied parents, and demoralized teachers. Many principals pale at the thought of a challenge like this. Envisioners get visions.

Producer Exemplar Dale Skinner, principal of Eduardo Villarreal Elementary School in San Antonio, Texas, believes, "Only those that can see the invisible accomplish the impossible." He and Larry wear the same kind of magic glasses that enable them to envision a future that others cannot see. The superintendent thought he was hiring a disciplinarian. Little did he know: He was getting a hedgehog. Larry had one big idea that he clung to tenaciously: creating a school where everybody would be somebody—a learning community where parents, teachers, and students would actually choose to be. His mission was thought to be impossible by many.

> "A leader needs to be able to envision success instead of failure."
>
> —Principal Lois Scrivener

Larry started by ordering bumper stickers to hand out to everyone: *Parkway School: Where Everyone Is Someone.* Then he systematically began to make his vision a reality by challenging teachers, parents, and children to believe that achieving a strong school identity, educational excellence, and a safe and orderly environment were within their grasp. He was able to set high academic and behavioral expectations while still remaining open, positive, and accessible. He invited parents to partner with the school and assured them that their voices would be heard and valued. He pledged his full support for professional inservice training and classroom

> "When I reflected on my own experience, it struck me that when I was most effective, it was because I knew what I wanted. When I was ineffective, it was because I was unclear about it."
>
> —Bennis (1989, p. 20)

instructional materials to his teachers. He further promised them his unequivocal backing for their all-out implementation of the district's behavioral expectations.

Larry's superintendent just wanted someone to control student behavior at Parkway. How was he to know that he had hired an envisioner who would bring about a renaissance at the school? In just six years, what many believed to be a "mission impossible" has become a vision realized. Here are just a few of the ways that Larry empowered, enabled, and energized his teachers, parents, and students to partner with him in this accomplishment:

- The PTA sponsors over fifteen committees. They have undertaken special projects, such as the construction of playground equipment, the design of an outdoor courtyard classroom, and the funding of enrichment programs.
- The College of New Jersey recognizes Parkway School as a laboratory school. College students learn from Parkway teachers while providing instructional support to students.
- Teachers extend themselves well beyond the school day assisting students with academics. Exemplary enrichment programs, field trips, and schoolwide activities rival those in the most affluent districts.
- Students' special deeds of service and kindness are recognized during morning announcements.

"The practice of leadership requires, perhaps first and foremost, a sense of purpose—the capacity to find the values that make risk-taking meaningful."

—Heifetz (1994, p. 274)

The superintendent who hired Larry had this to say about his Envisioner principal: "Of all the important things Mr. Fieber has done for the Parkway School, his ability to instill pride in the school and in each student for their accomplishments is the most important" (Fieber, 2000). Larry knew long before his students did that they had innumerable reasons to be proud of their school and their personal accomplishments. He can see the invisible. It's part of what Envisioners do.

ENVISIONER BENCHMARKS

Much of what Envisioners do is unseen. It takes place in their thought lives, during quiet times of reflection and meditation. After all, one does not pick up a meaningful mission or vision at a convention or by leafing through the latest issue of *Educational Leadership.* Meaningful missions and visions emerge from wrestling with difficult issues. Becoming an

Envisioner is not for the faint of heart. It requires the kind of commitment that is often in competition with life's other priorities. Envisioners don't go home when the bell rings. They wake up in the middle of the night thinking about the students who aren't learning. They drive their families and friends a little crazy with their fixation on school. They are hedgehogs and as we discovered earlier in the chapter, hedgehogs do get a little prickly sometimes.

As one of the several superintendents with whom Educator Exemplar Alan Jones worked during his tenure as a high school principal said to him, "You know, Al, you're probably one of the most outstanding principals I've ever met, but you're quite a load." Al wasn't sure if this statement was a compliment or not. He looked quizzically at his boss, who elaborated: "You won't give anything a rest. That keeps an edge on things. It's a creative place around here, with high standards, but it's certainly not a place for the complacent or the comfortable."

> "Leaders spend considerable effort gazing across the horizon of time, imagining what it will be like when they have arrived at their final destinations. Some call it vision; others describe it as a purpose, mission, goal, or even a personal agenda. Regardless of what we call it, there is a desire to make something happen, to change the way things are, to create something that no one else has ever created before."
>
> —Kouzes and Posner (1987, p. 9)

3.1 Envisioners Are Hedgehogs

Focus is the force that enables Envisioners to intuitively know whether or not a particular action or decision will move their school forward or take it off course. They are patient when they need to be but, more often than not, demonstrate an urgency and relentlessness when it comes to moving their schools forward. They persevere in the face of setbacks, are courageous when their values are questioned, and know how to close their eyes and ears to the "birdwalks" that distract their less focused colleagues. They have what the Japanese call *hoshin* (ho-sheen), a sense of direction that points their internal compass toward "true north." They realize that they cannot do it all but know with certainty exactly what to eliminate to be most effective. They have the ability to block out the irrelevant, ignore the inconsequential, and disregard the unimportant. They have the discipline that is required to focus their limited resources on the task at hand.

3.2 Envisioners Feel Called

There are more than a few administrators who have been "called" to their jobs, not by a desire to make a difference in the world but by the sirens

<table>
<tr><td>

THE GREATEST CAREER EVER INVENTED

Activator Exemplar Clare Maguire, Elementary, Grover, Missouri, has two framed quotations hanging in her office. One is a quote from Arnold Palmer: "Golf is deceptively simple and endlessly complicated. It satisfies the soul and frustrates the intellect. It is at the same time rewarding and maddening—it is without doubt the greatest game mankind has ever invented." The other framed quotation is Clare's version of Palmer's words: "Running an elementary school is deceptively simple and endlessly complicated. It satisfies the soul and frustrates the intellect. It is at the same time rewarding and maddening—it is without doubt the greatest career mankind has invented."

</td></tr>
</table>

of power and paychecks. To them, becoming a principal is the next rung to climb on the career ladder, and they are ready to step up. Highly effective principals, however, feel called not to a job per se but to the opportunity to make a difference, change the educational landscape, heal an ailing school, or work for the concepts of equity and excellence.

The term *calling* evokes a religious image, and indeed when one feels God's calling to a vocation, it is much harder to ignore the message. Lois Scrivener, principal of Holy Name of Jesus School in Indialantic, Florida, could be a principal anywhere, but she has chosen to be a Catholic school principal because she believes she has been called to be God's hands and heart in the world and in so doing make a difference in the lives of children. Lois explains, "It is when I make a difference that my job becomes joyous—joy because of a smile, a glint in an eye, a hug, a note, or a picture from a child to say thank you."

Like Lois Scrivener, Educator Exemplar Alan Jones could have been a principal anywhere, but he felt called to West Chicago, Illinois, a blue-collar community with a high percentage of minorities, not exactly where one might expect to find a philosopher who quotes John Dewey. Alan's friends gently ribbed him from time to time about his career options. "You could be working in Wilmette or Glenview (affluent northern suburbs of Chicago). What are you doing in West Chicago?"

But Alan felt called there to make a difference for the students who arrived at his school without a built-in support system or the advantages of a learning-centered home environment. He believes that "the only kids who are succeeding in many schools today are the ones whose parents have provided them with the prior knowledge and skills to navigate the system. Too many of the other kids just get chewed up and spit out. What a tremendous waste of talent." Alan felt called to help those students make it through the system. It is his proudest achievement—giving disenfranchised students the opportunity to be successful, both academically and in life.

3.3 Envisioners Have Resolve, Goals, and Lifevision

Envisioners demonstrate three different kinds of *purpose* in their lives. The first kind can be seen in the *resolve* they exhibit when committed to a specific cause, ideal, value, or principle. Purpose in this context is related to an individual's strength of character—the ability to stand up for a strong belief, even in the face of extreme pressure and opposition.

Standing up to central office is never easy, but Activator Exemplar Todd White has always been clear on his bottom line—creating a safe and secure environment in which his students and teachers can learn. "The mission of Mitchell Road Elementary School is to offer students a quality education in a safe, inviting environment and to help them learn responsibility, self-discipline, and respect for others" (White, 1999). The incident that precipitated Todd's stand concerned the placement of a highly troubled student who had put the lives of more than thirty Mitchell Road students at risk earlier in the year. Now the word came down from central office that he had to re-enroll the student in his school.

> **PURSUING A DREAM**
>
> **Steve Wilson, Elementary, Cairo, Nebraska**
>
> "I believe that a principal must lead by example. My childhood dream was to become a pilot. Unfortunately, my career choice has not given me the economic freedom to pursue this dream. However, I have found another way of realizing it. I belong to the Experimental Aircraft Association and over the past twelve years have been building my own aircraft from a set of plans. Most people in the community know this about me and frequently ask how the project is progressing. I see a relationship between pursuing this dream and realizing the dreams my teachers and I have for our school. They are big and they are difficult and they may take some time, but we never give up."

"It was the most outrageous thing I've ever done," Todd said, "but I told my boss, 'You can either have me as a principal in the building, or you can have that student in the building. But you can't have both.'" That kind of resolve is uncommon in education.

"I suppose some people would call it insubordination," Todd says, "but I was willing to give up my job because I believed that this student did not belong in my school after the things he had done there. I believed that the safety of my teachers and students was at stake. I didn't think or plan what I did ahead of time, but I quickly made up my mind that I'd rather work at Wal-Mart then have to live with myself in that situation." The mission of Todd's school meant more to him than his job.

Margaret Garcia-Dugan became an activist for English language instruction for bilingual students because of what she saw happening repeatedly to her students. "It was close to educational malpractice, in my opinion, to keep a child in bilingual education for five or six years, with only limited opportunities to learn English vocabulary. Our students would get to high school and be absolutely lost." Margaret worked actively for the passage of Proposition 203, an English-only initiative in Arizona, but it wasn't easy. "People called me a racist and the poster girl for Prop. 203," she says with a wry smile. "But my board of education backed me completely."

Purpose can also be thought of as "that which a person sets before himself as an object to be reached or accomplished" (McKechnie, 1983, p. 1465)—*a specific goal to be attained.* Kathie Dobberteen's goal was to prove to one and all that the demographics of her school didn't have to determine the students' achievement. Her commitment to that goal could be seen in everything that happened in her school. A La Mesa Dale student once commented to a group of visitors, "Our teachers won't let us fail" (Dobberteen, 2001, p. 12). The visitors, part of a California Distinguished School visitation team, later wrote, "There is a pervasive focus on the improvement of academic achievement. The 30 Day/30 Minute Goal Setting System . . . and the principal's monitoring of the reading progress of every classroom are prime examples of this focus. [La Mesa Dale] feels and sounds and looks like a school that has made significant progress in the last four years" (Dobberteen, 2001, p. 12).

> "Human beings cannot live wholly and fully without giving themselves without reservation to something beyond themselves."
>
> —Bennis (1989, p. 11)

The third kind of purpose refers to the overall meaning and life goals of Envisioners—their raison d'être, if you will. Cox and Liesse (1996) call this kind of purpose *lifevision* (p. 8). Highly effective principals are deeply committed to worthy ideals and values (e.g., equity or excellence); they derive meaning in their lives from this commitment, and they are constantly reflecting and reexamining their personal and professional goals based on this commitment. A lifevision serves multiple functions in the lives of Envisioners:

- *It sustains them through difficult times.* "I focus on how important this job is, so that even if I'm really stressed or tired, I feel as though my day has been worthwhile" (Kathie Dobberteen).
- *It puts joy into their lives.* "I'm so excited. The night before school starts, I won't sleep. I love school. I feel so very blessed to be able to do something I love. I have such a passion for what I do. It's not just a job or a career for me: It's a heart-felt mission" (Michelle Gayle).
- *It energizes and renews them.* "The daily quest to achieve lofty goals constantly energizes me. I always have tremendous enthusiasm and energy at work" (Dale Skinner).

3.4 Envisioners Can See the Invisible

Vision is a driving force that reflects the highly effective principal's image of the future, based on personal values, beliefs, and experiences. Descriptors such as *universal, immeasurable, an object of the imagination,* and *unusual discernment* or *foresight* come to mind. Vision is not what you will do tomorrow but where you are going in the next five or ten years.

Alan Jones explains, "As a leader you have to be able to see what your school can become, and the picture has to be a detailed one, in my opinion. The thing that disappoints me about so many of my colleagues is that when you ask them to describe their vision for schools, they describe 'what is,' not 'what could be.' They aren't able to see beyond today."

Constructing a personal vision requires background knowledge. It requires having a philosophy of education. It demands a vocabulary that can communicate that vision in meaningful ways to those who may not see the invisible. Envisioners have a set of fundamental core beliefs about schooling to guide them, ballast, if will you, to keep them from living what Alan describes as "a life of nothing more than buses, budgets, and boilers."

> "The heart of leadership has to do with what a person believes, values, dreams about, and is committed to—the person's personal vision."
>
> —Sergiovanni (1992, p. 57)

3.5 Envisioners Know Where They Are Headed

Mission is the direction that emerges from the vision and guides the day-to-day behavior of the school. A mission is developed collectively with staff, parents, and community but reflects the vision that highly effective principals have communicated to others. Descriptors such as *measurable, obtainable,* and *directional* come to mind when reflecting on the concept of mission. Beware of missions that are self-centered: *We will be the best school in the county;* missions that are meaningless: *All of our students will be able to handle the "real world";* or missions that say nothing about the purposes of schooling: *All of our students will value diversity, appreciate harmony, and facilitate cooperation.*

Larry Pollock says, "It's all too easy to say that we expect every child to learn, but the key to achieving this goal lies in a 'take no prisoners,' relentless approach to address the needs of nonproficient learners and to assist all students to realize their potential." Not only did Larry have a vision (expecting every child to learn), but he and his staff developed a mission to get there (address the needs of nonproficient learners). Their mission statement reads, "We envision every learner becoming a powerful mathematician, effective writer, responsible citizen, and confident reader" (Juanita School, 2002). Just to make sure no one forgets the mission, they've created an acronym. PERC stands for powerful, effective, responsible, and confident—just the kind of learners Larry envisioned his school would have. Envisioners facilitate the development of missions that speak to the needs, desires, and dreams of their school communities while focusing on a worthy vision of schooling.

Communicator Exemplar Michelle Gayle put revisiting Griffin Middle School's mission statement at the top of her agenda when she came aboard as principal. "When I was hired, the first thing I did was review the mission statement that was currently in place. I told the staff, 'This is not just a piece of paper you put up on the wall and forget about. It has to be a living, breathing document that articulates the focus of the school.'"

> "The main thing is to keep the main thing, the main thing!"
>
> —Barksdale (as quoted in Labovitz & Rosansky, 1997, p. 4)

In some schools the mission statement is developed with much discussion and deliberation. It drives instruction and improvement. In other schools, no one remembers who wrote it, much less when it was written. Michelle says, "When my teachers saw how serious I was about the mission, they suggested a number of revisions. I made sure they understood that all of the decisions we made from that day forward would be tied to that mission."

3.6 Envisioners Have Compelling Visions

To a person, highly effective principals are passionate people with compelling visions that have captured the hearts and minds of their staff members. Compelling visions are simple but elegant. They speak to unmet needs and unrealized potential in school communities. One word sums up Educator Exemplar Jean Hendrickson's vision: equity. She knew that the teachers at Mark Twain School did not enjoy seeing their students fail. She sensed their deep frustration and lack of efficacy and was able to convince them that both they and their students deserved the same kind of opportunities and success as her former teachers and students had enjoyed in their more affluent school. She offered to help them meet their needs for personal fulfillment while at the same time bringing equity to the students of Mark Twain. It was an offer they couldn't refuse.

Producer Exemplar Dale Skinner is driven by a vision that is equally compelling: instructional excellence. If we teach students what they need to know in a highly effective way, they will learn. Kathie Dobberteen and the staff at La Mesa Dale Elementary School in California were awarded one of six School Change Awards given yearly by the Chase Manhattan Bank and Fordham University, in 2001, for bringing about meaningful and sustained change in their school. This vision drove their change process: "We refuse to let demographics determine the destiny of our students."

Visions don't have to focus on student achievement per se, although student learning is *always* the bottom line. Many principals use other metaphors or paradigms to motivate students, empower faculty, and engage parents. Contributor Exemplar Lola Malone and Character-Builder Exemplar Tom Paulsen embrace visions that are grounded in character development. They believe that when students work hard, persevere, have determination, are honest, and share what they have with others, they will soar to unheard-of achievement levels.

Kotter (1999) says, "Without a sensible vision, a transformation effort can easily dissolve into a list of confusing and incompatible projects that can take the organization in the wrong direction or nowhere at all. . . . In failed transformations, you often find plenty of plans and directives and programs, but no vision" (p. 81). The ancient author of Proverbs was more succinct: "Where there is no vision, the people perish (Proverbs 29:18). Whether you prefer the Proverbs' version or the Harvard professor's pontifications, the message is the same: You need a compelling vision to make things happen!

> "It is so easy to become pulled from the school's focus with a myriad of 'things-to-be-done.' Focusing on what is best for children is key."
>
> —Principal Patricia Hamilton

3.7 Envisioners Can Articulate Their Visions and Then Make Them Happen

There is an expression in religious circles that aptly summarizes a trap that one can fall into while envisioning: "He's so heavenly, he's no earthly good." Failing to connect with the real world is as worthless as not having a meaningful vision. Envisioner principals are able to articulate their dreams and visions to ordinary teachers and parents in the real world. They are practical, action oriented, and down-to-earth individuals. A vision without an action plan is useless. A vision without the people to implement it is worthless. A vision without training and money and time is just "pie in the sky." Envisioners are able to make their visions and dreams happen.

Figure 3.1   Envisioner Benchmarks

Trait Number 3: The highly effective principal is an Envisioner—an individual who is motivated by a sense of calling and purpose, focused on a vision of what schools can be, and guided by a mission that has the best interests of all students at its core.

3.1   Envisioners are hedgehogs.
3.2   Envisioners feel called.
3.3   Envisioners have resolve, goals, and lifevision.
3.4   Envisioners can see the invisible.
3.5   Envisioners know where they are headed.
3.6   Envisioners have compelling visions.
3.7   Envisioners can articulate their visions and then make them happen.

SUMMING IT UP

We began this chapter with the story of the hedgehog and the fox, and that is the way we will end it. "The fox knows many things, but the hedgehog knows one big thing" (Berlin, 1970, p. 1). To become an Envisioner, you must first figure out what your "big thing" is. You *must* have a vision. Without one, you cannot become a highly effective principal. *Average* principals keep the buses, budgets, and boilers humming. *Good* principals are warm and caring people. *Great* principals do and are all of the aforementioned *plus* they have focus, purpose, vision, and mission.

The Facilitator

"The first order of business [is to begin] on a course toward people-building with leadership that has a firmly established context of people first. With that, the right actions fall naturally into place."

—Greenleaf (1982, p. 17)

Every administrative team has at least one business official who signs the checks and balances the budget. Bill, a very likeable former high school math teacher, was our accountant in residence. I enjoyed his organized style and no-nonsense reports but couldn't understand his intense dislike for any activities designed to increase teamwork or strengthen working relationships.

"I can't stand that 'touchy-feely' stuff," he would say with disdain; "Let's just cut to the chase." He considered any conversation that wasn't related to the bottom line to be a waste of time. If he were reading *Ten Traits of Highly Effective Principals*, he would no doubt skip this chapter and go straight to Chapter 9 that features Producer principals. "Who has time for building relationships when there's work to be done?" he would ask. As for Greenleaf's epigraph at the top of the page, he would raise a skeptical eyebrow and say, "People first? I don't think so."

I can understand Bill's abhorrence of time wasting; most administrators share this view. However, his distaste for the "touchy-feely" stuff belies an ignorance of the impact, either positive or negative, that relationships can have on both student achievement and employee productivity. Carl Rogers (1957), the eminent psychotherapist, was fascinated with the correlation between what he called the facilitative conditions (e.g., understanding, caring, and genuineness) and learning in the classroom. He hypothesized that students would learn more and behave better if taught by high-facilitative teachers (i.e., individuals with high levels of understanding, caring, and genuineness) as compared with students taught by low-facilitative teachers. Aspy and Roebuck (1977) tested Rogers's hypothesis in a variety of classroom and school studies.

They reported their findings in a book, the title of which should be emblazoned on the walls of all of the teachers' lounges in America: *Kids Don't Learn From People They Don't Like* (Aspey & Roebuck, 1977). The studies described the students of high-facilitative teachers, those individuals who are empathetic, genuine, and have respect for students. These

> "In all things, we learn only from those we love."
>
> —Goethe (as quoted in Flesch, 1957, p. 199)

students were found to make greater gains on academic achievement measures, including both math and reading scores, and present fewer disciplinary problems (p. 46). The same powerful dynamic that drives student achievement to higher levels when teachers and students have thriving relationships also holds true for the principal-teacher connection. Anderson (1998) observes, "People don't change for leaders they don't like" (p. 12). Relationships drive school improvement.

During the past twenty-five years, the Gallup organization has conducted several major research studies among managers and employees regarding the characteristics of effective managers as well as the specific working conditions that improve employee productivity (Buckingham & Coffman, 1999, 2001). Many of these characteristics and conditions have to do with the quality of relationships in the workplace. I have reworded some of the Gallup survey questions to make them more germane to school settings. When staff members can answer *yes* to these questions, their productivity, motivation, and loyalty will be high, according to Gallup's research (Buckingham & Coffman, 1999):

- In the past seven days, have teachers and other staff members received recognition or praise from the principal for effective instruction, their caring attitudes toward students, or special attention and service to parents?
- Does the principal give evidence of caring personally about staff members as people?
- Does the principal encourage and facilitate the personal and professional development of staff members?

- Do the opinions of all staff members count when important decisions are made?
- Does the mission of the school make staff members feel as though their work is important?
- Does every staff member have a best friend at school?
- Do staff members have opportunities to learn and grow through the work they do? (p. 28)

If Bill, the business manager, were reading this chapter, I hope that by now he would have concluded that productivity in a school *does* depend to a large extent on how well people get along with each other *and* how they are treated by their administrators. Highly effective principals know how to bring out the best in their staff members. They mentor, coach, enable, facilitate, praise, develop, energize, counsel, and empower people of all ages and abilities.

The highly effective principal is a Facilitator—a leader with outstanding human relations skills that include the abilities to build individual relationships with parents, teachers, and students; collaborative teams with staff members and parents; and a schoolwide community of leaders.

FACILITATOR EXEMPLAR: DOUG PIERSON

Doug Pierson has been a principal for twenty years, the past four years in North Kingston, Rhode Island, but he still considers himself a teacher. Hence the title by which he prefers to be addressed: "principal teacher." It's an apt designation for him since Doug doesn't act like the typical manager or supervisor. He doesn't even resemble the average instructional leader but is more like a lead teacher among many equal teachers. He explains his philosophy: "I know that I don't know it all. No one knows it all, but all of us together can figure anything out." Doug goes to school every day with the goal of empowering, energizing, and enjoying teachers, students, and parents. This man genuinely loves people, and they respond to his warmth and caring with enthusiasm *and* productivity.

If you were to arrive unannounced at Hamilton School, a K–5 school of 475 students, it's hard to predict where you might find Doug. Try the music room, but you probably won't notice him right away. Actually, he's the big kid in the woodwind section trying to keep his clarinet from squeaking. The other students are paying no attention to him. He is one of them—a struggling beginner. In 2002, Doug took violin lessons, and the year before that it was the cello. "We only teach first-year lessons at Hamilton and then the kids move on to middle school," Doug laments. "That's why I have to begin a new instrument every year."

When he took up the cello, he couldn't read a note of music. Some principals might contemplate doing what Doug has done, but there are few who would have the perseverance to attend the weekly lessons, the discipline to practice regularly, and the chutzpah to perform in all of the concerts. Doug's presence in the beginners' orchestra and band has created quite a stir among parents, but this isn't a public relations stunt. He simply enjoys being a student among students.

If you were to arrive at Hamilton on another day, you might find Doug in a classroom playing his ukulele. "I can't sing and play at the same time," he confesses, "so I write the words on chart paper and tack them up around the classroom so the kids can sing along with me." Although the tunes he plays are always the same—"My Bonnie Lies Over the Ocean," "Clementine," and "Down in the Valley"—Doug writes new words by request.[1] "Can you believe they pay me for this stuff?" he asks with a twinkle in his eye. Don't let him fool you, however. There's a method to his musical madness.

Doug is building relationships with students that come in handy during disciplinary situations. "If my students get into trouble on the playground—for example, a fight or a scuffle—I'll keep them for an hour to talk about it. I never give tongue-lashings. I teach. We talk about what they did wrong and how to make it right. We talk about things like hurt feelings and apologies. I never *make* students apologize to one another because if I *insist* on it, it's not genuine. Instead, I teach them my four-step apology process, practice it with them a few times, and then just assume they *will* apologize." And they do it for Dr. Pierson—wouldn't you?

If you drop in at Doug's school on another day, you might find him taking some of his paperwork to a quiet classroom so he can meet a pressing deadline. "I have an open-door policy," he explains, "and if I'm in my office, someone is always dropping in to see me." On location, Doug can do two things at once—finish his paperwork *and* be with students. "I might work in a classroom for an hour," he explains, "and I enjoy it so much more than I would shut up in my office." The students know exactly what Doug is doing in that quiet corner of the classroom—his homework. They know when he leads them in singing the homework song that he's "giving homework its due."

> "Communities are collections of individuals who are bonded together by natural will and who are together bound to a set of shared ideas and ideals."
>
> —Sergiovanni (1996, p. 48)

If you interviewed Doug's students, they would tell you that he loves them best. After all, how many principals do you know who will don a cape, tights, and a mask to become Zero the Hero for the first grade's 100th-day celebration? Quite a few, you say? Well, would they mount a horse and ride onto the playground with their cape flying behind them? Well, maybe one or two might. Would they drive up on a motorcycle the next year? Can't think of anybody who would do that for an encore, except maybe Activator Exemplar Clare Maguire whom you will meet in Chapter 7.

Doug's relationships with teachers are as unique as those he has with students. Each grade level team receives three release days per year in order to plan and articulate their programs. Doug doesn't attend these meetings; they provide him with an agenda beforehand and a summary of what was accomplished. "I suggest they go off campus once in a while," he said. "It's far more pleasant to spend a day on someone's deck developing curriculum than in some stuffy room at school."

Doug reports that he makes very few decisions anymore. "We recently had to develop a new open house format, and I turned it over to the teachers completely. They also do all of the supply ordering. Each grade level has a per pupil allocation, and they can spend it any way they like. The former principal ordered supplies, and the teachers had to put in frequent requests for what they needed. This way, if the teachers want to economize with certain supplies, they can afford other things they'd like to have—for example, composition books for every child."

Doug's monthly staff meetings are warm and humane. He begins each one with an inspirational story or poem. One Christmas, Doug bought supersized boxes of Kleenex for his teachers because his "readings" made them cry so frequently. He admits to crying right along with them. "I don't mind showing my emotions to teachers," he said. "We console each other, talk each other through hard times, and offer support for one another." He goes on to say, "Don't think we cry all the time, though. We're big on celebrations and parties, too. When I get the test scores and we've improved (which is hard to do when you're already so close to the top), I really pull out all the stops. Music, refreshments, the works."

Doug's teachers would tell you that they are his favorites. He covers for them in their classrooms when they have dentists' appointments, house closings, or funerals. And he stays out of their way and lets them teach. Of course, he's always in their classrooms, but he's there to help—to assist students who are having a difficult time, to teach a poetry unit, sing one of the songs he's written, or even to do his homework. Whenever he observes a lesson, he notices all the good things the teachers do, and even when he has suggestions for improvements, they are always positive. He has trained parents to go to teachers first with problems, and if they should by chance come to him first, he gently sends them right back to the teachers. Doug is always available to his staff—ready to talk about anything, professional or personal. He's the kind of principal that makes everybody want to work harder, do more, come earlier, and stay later.

Of course, the parents of Hamilton School think that Doug really loves them best of all. On Tuesday mornings he serves tea and Danish for an hour and a half and invites parents in to chat about anything they'd like. He says it's more like a cocktail party (without the alcohol, of course) than a parent-principal conference. Parents know they can talk to him about school problems *or* about the new book they're reading. Whenever they volunteer, they get a handwritten thank-you note from Doug. He often calls parents with good news about their children, and they are regularly invited to serve on a variety of schoolwide committees.

After spending time with Doug, I am convinced that he loves them all—parents, teachers, and students—with the same degree of intensity and commitment. He magically manages to sprinkle praise, attention, celebration, good humor, music, and an occasional word of suggestion or gentle correction equally throughout his school community. The people with whom he works reward him in kind.

FACILITATOR BENCHMARKS

Facilitators have different priorities than their more task-oriented colleagues. They recognize that the secret to being highly effective *and* achieving the mission of the school does not lie in "doing," but rather in "being"—being with people.

4.1 Facilitator Principals Bond People Together Into a Community of Leaders

Community is the new educational buzzword of the twenty-first century, but talking about a community is far easier than creating one. Most educators, if asked to define the term as exemplified in a school setting, would no doubt include the concepts of caring and learning as discussed in Chapter 2 (Educator), Chapter 6 (Culture Builder), and Chapter 9 (Character Builder). However, when it comes to defining, much less creating, a *community of leaders*, principals have a more paradoxical goal. Their training and on-the-job experiences do not generally support and nurture the concept of shared leadership, and there are few models to follow for creating and sustaining a community where *everyone* is a leader. Questions and doubts abound. How can *everyone* be in charge? Where *does* the buck stop? What *is* my job?

Sergiovanni (2001) calls this new approach, "leadership by building, bonding, and binding." (p. 145). When staff members (as well as parents and students) are part of a community of leaders, everyone accepts responsibility for learning, knows the reasons behind what they are doing, and is committed to the mission of the school. When teachers (or students and parents) are "told" what to do or manipulated and coerced into compliance, they simply play the game by the rules and punch out when the day is over. They act as subordinates (or hangers-on) rather than committed followers. "[When] followership is established, bureaucratic and psychological authority are transcended by moral authority" (Sergiovanni, 2001, p. 150).

Highly effective principals recognize the power inherent in building a community of leaders. When a newspaper reporter asked Doug what he had done at Hamilton to help students achieve a 100 percent on the state assessment (the first school in Rhode Island ever to do so), he said, "I just stay out of the teachers' way." The reporter was incredulous. She, of course, just assumed that *he* had directed, or told, or at the very least motivated the teachers or students in some extrinsic way. "No," she insisted, "what did *you* do?"

As a principal teacher, Doug understands how to facilitate a community of leaders: empower teachers, students, and parents on behalf of the school's mission; provide the support and resources they need to function autonomously; and remove the bureaucratic obstacles from their way (Sergiovanni, 2001, p. 151). Once Doug does that, he simply gets out of the way.

> "Empowerment is the natural complement to accountability."
>
> —Sergiovanni (2001, p. 151)

4.2 Facilitators Tap the Potential of People

Creating a community of leaders is a synergistic effort involving all of the people in a school, not just the individuals with degrees and certificates. When teachers experience the empowerment and sense of efficacy that result from assuming leadership roles, they pass them along in their interactions with students and parents. When parents share leadership responsibilities, they become a part of the school community in new and remarkable ways. Highly effective principals are simultaneously able to hold people (including students) responsible for their own learning and growth, relinquish control and responsibility for decision making, develop independent thinkers, and actively engage people in reaching mutual goals.

In a community of leaders, everyone's potential is appreciated, tapped, and developed. Tom Williams, principal of Walton-Verona Elementary School in Verona, Kentucky, suggests, "In order to create an

> "Anybody could lead perfect people—if there were any. But there aren't any perfect people. . . . It is part of the enigma of human nature that the 'typical' person—immature, stumbling, inept, lazy— is capable of great dedication and heroism if wisely led. Many otherwise able people are disqualified to lead because they cannot work with and through the half-people who are all there are. The secret of institution building is to be able to weld a team of such people by lifting them up to grow taller than they would otherwise be."
>
> —Greenleaf (1977, p. 21)

atmosphere where all students can learn, you have to generate a sense of teamwork with the parents and community. Having a strong volunteer program has resulted in a two-fold benefit for us: (1) parents and community members are actively involved in the life of the school, thereby removing the barriers that once existed, and (2) the presence of volunteers increases our ability to meet the needs of students by giving teachers more flexibility in planning instruction and offering tutorial and enrichment classes."

4.3 Facilitators Say "We" Instead of "I"

Brenda Valentine is up-front about who gets the credit at her school: "The success of our school is not about me; it's about the parents, the teachers, and the students working collaboratively together." John Giles, principal of Hinckley Elementary School in Ohio, reports that *all* the members of his staff put 100 percent of their effort into helping kids be the best they can be. "We are an Ohio Hall of Fame school, and this is a direct reflection of everyone's efforts."

Facilitator Exemplar Doug Pierson adds, "I'm proud to say that our school is a high-achieving school. This has been true for several years. As a consequence we have attracted the attention of the state media, the state department of education, and a visit from the state commissioner of education." He goes on to say, "Our entire school faculty and staff must take credit for these accomplishments."

4.4 Facilitators Favor People Over Paperwork

Highly effective principals find ways to get their paperwork done when people aren't around. They can't bear to shut their office doors when teachers, parents, and students are in the building. Communicator Exemplar Michelle Gayle is often in her office before sunrise on Saturday mornings to catch up on paperwork. Doug Pierson rises at 3:30 a.m. to write, read, and reflect so he can spend his school day with people, not paper. Highly effective principals have discovered that the concept of "quality time" is a misnomer in schools. It's always the *quantity* of time spent with people that counts.

"Open-door" policies are routine. "I only close my door when I'm in a confidential conference," was the usual response. Highly effective principals know they are responsible for the "paper" part of their job descriptions, but they find ways to solve the administrivia problem. Producer Exemplar Dale Skinner hired a high-level administrative clerk (in addition to his secretary) to ease some of the paper burden. What is he doing with the time he has gained? Coaching teachers, of course.

4.5 Facilitators Build Up Emotional Bank Accounts

In his training program, *Principle-Centered Leadership*, Stephen Covey (1993) describes a practice that is the hallmark of highly effective principals: making regular and sizable deposits to the emotional bank accounts they hold with parents, teachers, and students. Here's a personal example of how the process works: I recently made a huge withdrawal from the account I have with my daughter. Nearing the completion of her dissertation, she had become almost paralyzed by the pressures of finishing, applying for jobs, starting a family, and dealing with a temperamental professor. I had been living with pressures of my own: book deadlines, workshops, and the preparation of my first online seminar. Emily had called to talk with me at an inconvenient (for me) time. I offered unwanted advice in a critical and impatient tone. I failed to listen carefully for what was really needed and instead gave her my ill-considered opinion. I'm afraid I overdrew my account with one hasty comment. After reflecting on the conversation, I quickly realized that I needed to make a big deposit and fast. I drafted an E-mail to her: "In doing the research for my book, I've been thinking a lot about the characteristics of people that make them successful. Here are some of the things I believe have made you successful in the past and will contribute to your being a highly effective person in the future." I went on to specifically describe the ways in which she is thoughtful, sensitive, creative, loyal, family centered, intelligent, and honest.

> "I take time to meet with every staff member each day to let them know I care. I take whatever time is needed to make sure that each staff member feels needed and appreciated. This kind of attention to staff members reflects in their efforts and their willingness to go the extra mile for students."
>
> —Principal John Giles

Seeking to understand, appreciate, and affirm another individual, whether a teacher, student, parent, or someone in your own family, is the equivalent of an emotional deposit. On the other hand, demanding to be heard and understood first is an emotional withdrawal. Keeping a promise is a deposit; breaking a promise is a withdrawal. Apologizing to someone is a deposit; being arrogant or defensive is a withdrawal. Highly effective principals regularly put "money" away in their accounts, not for a rainy day but for the relationships they are building with parents, teachers, and students.

4.6 Facilitators Cultivate Their Own Well-Being

To interact in positive and healing ways with large numbers of diverse individuals takes overwhelming amounts of emotional, psychological, and physical energy. Make no mistake, the acts of motivating, mentoring, empowering, coaching, counseling, facilitating, and praising are joyful and rewarding. But they can also be intense and draining. To avoid burnout, Facilitator principals pay attention to their own well-being. They deal with the inevitable "pain" of leading and have developed coping mechanisms to manage their own anxieties. They define who they are from within, based on their values, principles, and beliefs, not on what others think of them. They know that "they are not their jobs."

> "Skillful leaders rely less on authority and dictums and more on collaboration and negotiation."
>
> —Stowell and Starcevich (1998, p. 11)

When I quizzed the highly effective principals regarding how they keep emotionally, physically, and spiritually healthy, most of their responses fell into four categories: family, fun, faith, and fitness (both mental and physical). They are extraordinarily well-adjusted and healthy individuals—excellent role models for their staff members, students, and parents.

- I cook without a recipe, take a nap on a Sunday afternoon, and pull weeds in my garden (Nancy Moga).
- I read, swim, and eat out. I love to be pampered by someone else on the weekends (Lois Scrivener).
- I always have tremendous enthusiasm and energy at work. Unfortunately, by the time I get home, I am often drained. I try to work out consistently and play golf on the weekends (Dale Skinner).
- I pray a lot. My faith has carried me through the hardest of times. Also, I've learned from my husband to leave my worries at work (Catherine Segura).

Some highly effective principals restore their energies through networking and mentoring relationships:

- I have engaged a coach to help improve my performance (see Building Champions, 2002). We have twice-monthly phone conferences on various aspects of leadership and personal growth (Gabe Flicker).

- I am part of a collegial group of six elementary principals—three men and three women. We are from different districts and meet once a month for lunch and conversation. This group supports, reinforces, and nurtures me (Byron Schwab).

Facilitators recognize that caring for themselves is not selfish but essential. John Giles says, "I have to put my needs first because if I'm not at 100 percent, I can't help others."

> **NURTURE RELATIONSHIPS**
>
> **Larry Pollock,
> Elementary School,
> Kirkland, Washington**
>
> I always make this statement in a faculty meeting at the beginning of the school year and reiterate its sentiment periodically:
> The problems that we have will pass, but the hurtful comments we make about or to one another will never be forgotten. A relationship is too important to lose over a problem. In tough situations, preserve the relationship, no matter what.

4.7 Facilitators Value Diversity

One cannot be a Facilitator without valuing the variety and diversity of the individuals in a school community. There are many different templates for approaching the task: multiple intelligences (Gardner, 1983, 1999), thinking styles (DeBono, 1999), or individual strengths as identified by the StrengthBuilders program (Buckingham & Coffman, 2001).

My favorite model for helping team members value, understand, and work well with one another comes from Edward DeBono's (1999) *Six Thinking Hats.* I have used this approach with parents, administrators, as well as teacher teams, and I'm certain it could be adapted for use with student leader teams as well. DeBono uses hats of different colors as metaphors for six unique thinking or problem-solving styles. For example, he describes White Hat thinking as a straightforward approach, based on facts and figures. In contrast, Red Hat thinkers rely on gut-level feelings, intuition, and prior experiences. DeBono discusses both the value and the necessity of having all of the perspectives included in decision-making and problem-solving processes.

I purchased six different hats in colors to correspond with DeBono's (1999): a red beret, a white hard hat, a green cowboy hat—well, you get the picture. I use the hats in a humorous but

> "Meaningful 'team' is always a result of pursuing a demanding performance challenge."
>
> —Katzenbach and Smith (1993, p. 9)

concrete way to demonstrate that although everyone has a *preferred* way of approaching problems and making decisions, an individual can always put on another hat and use a different thinking style. I also emphasize how using a combination of all of the approaches can improve the quality of any decision or implementation. Rather than taking the "too many cooks spoil the broth" approach, People-Centered principals believe that "two [or even more] heads are better than one."

4.8 Facilitators Share the "Power Pie"

Power in the principalship reminds me of one of my favorite Old Testament stories (I Kings 17:8–15, *The Living Bible*). I call it the "Elijah Effect." Starving from days of wandering in the desert, the prophet Elijah encounters a widow who is about to use her last measures of oil and flour to make dinner. He asks if she will share her meal with him, but not unlike many ineffective principals, she believes that sharing what she has will leave her impoverished. Elijah promises that if she will break bread with him, there will be more than enough ingredients to make another loaf, not only for the next day, but for all the days thereafter.

> "Mindful that true words seem paradoxical when the mind is cluttered with untruth, the wise leader embraces paradox.
> By not forcing, he leads.
> By not dominating, he leads.
> By not leading, he leads."
>
> —Autry and Mitchell (1998, p. 214)

Highly effective principals know from personal experience that sharing the "power pie" with staff members, parents, and students will produce the same happy ending for them as it did for the Biblical widow—they will have a far greater and more positive impact on their school community than they ever thought possible. The ways in which the highly effective principals in this book have shared power and accomplished great things in their schools provide ample evidence of the power of the "Elijah Effect". When you share power, responsibility, *and* accountability, your return will exceed 100 percent and continue for as long as you keep sharing.

4.9 Facilitators Accentuate the Positives

Have you ever fallen into the dreaded Criticism Trap (McEwan & Damer, 2000, p. 88)? Parents do it, spouses do it, and even teachers and principals do it. When principals become ensnared in this insidious trap, the only way to get out is to begin keeping track of the ratio of positive, reinforcing comments to the negative comments that are made. In the classroom, effective teachers aim for at least four positive comments to every negative or corrective one. Highly effective principals recommend a nine-to-one ratio to their colleagues who are prone to overcorrect and critique. Highly effective principals major in positives, focus on what's working, and build on strengths rather than highlighting weaknesses.

When I am writing a book, I often send portions of the manuscript to people I know for review. While working on this chapter, I sent it to a principal who had just taken on a challenging new assignment—low achievement, low expectations, and low morale. Having just experienced a "mountaintop" experience in her former school, she was a bit impatient with some of the "naysayers" and "yes-butters" on her faculty and was tempted to resort to corrective measures. Human nature being what it is, we all have a difficult time praising a negative *and* ineffective faulty member. This principal's short note to me attests to the power of praise, however:

"I tried the idea that was suggested in Chapter 4 relative to giving very specific and descriptive praise, especially to a teacher who isn't doing a very effective job. I did it yesterday . . . and lo and behold, the teacher came up to me today and said she wanted to attend an upcoming training session. This is an amazing development from someone who appeared to be 'stuck-in-the-mud.'"

4.10 Facilitators Promote Parental Involvement

> ### IT'S ALL ABOUT RELATIONSHIPS
>
> **Kathy Schneiter, Middle School, Roselle, Illinois**
>
> When I was hired for my first principalship, I had several strikes against me. First, I was the youngest person on my staff. Then, I had been an elementary music teacher, and I'd been hired to be a middle school principal. I was the brainchild of a brand-new superintendent, and to top it all off, I was the first woman principal at the middle school since the early 1980s, and she had been there only two years. With that many strikes against me, I had to listen to what was important to other people. I had to negotiate them on board. Relationships are basic to being a highly effective principal, and I've made the teachers a part of everything that happens in the building.
>
> First, I established a building leadership team. The teachers were used to the "tell me what to do and I'll do it" approach, and being brought into decision making was a new and somewhat fearful experience for them. But they've learned quickly and are now a part of curriculum and hiring decisions.

The multiplicity of ways in which highly effective principals promote parental involvement is a topic for another book (McEwan, 1998, pp. 79–89). Suffice it to say that successful principals never wait for parents to make the first move. They recruit, enlist, invite, cajole, motivate, and when all

> "The collective knowledge of the group is a super-power source. If leaders will open their doors, express their vulnerabilities, and say to their group, 'Let's solve this difficult problem together' then they will receive greater respect and warmth from their employees."
>
> —Kuczmarski and Kuczmarski
> (1995, p. 229)

else fails, offer incentives and rewards to help parents take the first step toward involvement and eventual commitment to the mission of the school. Many parents need to be bathed in love and empathy before they feel safe and welcome at school. They need to be understood and appreciated *before* they are willing to become a part of the school community. Their own personal schooling experiences or previous encounters with less effective schools or principals may have left them feeling prickly and defensive. Highly effective principals are able to help parents like these realize how important they are to the life of the school and to defuse their anger and frustration.

Activator Exemplar Todd White knew that promoting parent involvement would be a challenge when he took his first principalship. His school was in what he called a "working-poor" community, and the former principal had discouraged parents from becoming involved. Todd targeted his first potential parent volunteer on the opening day of school.

"I noticed this truck dropping off a student, and it looked like it belonged to a painter. So the next morning I waylaid the man and asked him if he would be willing to paint the front doors of the school if I furnished the paint." San Souci School had barely survived a tropical storm, and its physical appearance was as grim as the school's culture. Todd picked the brightest color he could find for the front doors: "safety hazard yellow."

"I wanted something bright, cheerful, and inviting for those doors." When the volunteer painter had completed his job, Todd made sure he was publicly recognized for his efforts, and the next thing Todd knew, his painter had recruited additional parents to brighten up dingy classrooms and hallways. Involving parents can be as simple as identifying a job that desperately needs doing and then matching it to a person who has the talent.

Brenda Valentine's school community is a diverse one. Children come from highly affluent neighborhoods as well as from low-income housing. At the outset of her principalship, one group was very involved at school; the other wasn't. Brenda and her staff brainstormed ways to include every parent in PTA and make the meetings more family focused and less like "business meetings." Together they came up with the slogan, "Parents Make a Difference," and had T-shirts made for every parent. They planned a picnic, the sole purpose of which was to get acquainted and have fun. No business allowed. The school's business partner (a bank) furnished a popcorn machine, and the president came and popped corn for everyone. Seven hundred parents and children attended. This event was the beginning of a year of togetherness and fun that included a pumpkin-carving party, a holiday caroling event, and a silent craft auction.

4.11 Facilitators Celebrate

Steve Wilson and the faculty at Centura Elementary School in Cairo, Nebraska, know that there's more to celebrate in Nebraska than the Cornhuskers's latest football victory.

"We celebrate what we have accomplished, and we do it frequently! Our staff members have informal gatherings in homes or at school on a monthly basis. We celebrate the short-term goals we have accomplished, the improvements we've seen in individual student performance, or sometimes we just get together and celebrate making it to that point in the school year. Not everyone attends every time, but everyone makes it to at least one or two "parties" a year.

"We also encourage students to celebrate their personal accomplishments, such as meeting their monthly reading goals, by treating them to an ice cream social, popcorn party, or some other type of break from their daily routines. This builds a positive school climate for everyone; learning is a challenge and very hard work at times. We have to re-energize in order to keep the momentum we need to be successful."

4.12 Facilitators Spend Time With Students

The students at Kanawha City Elementary School look forward to a trip to the principal's office. Brenda Valentine greets all of her students by name and is ready to give them the principal's stamp of approval. This inexpensive but unique way of affirming outstanding work is highly coveted by students and motivates even the most reluctant workers to do their best. The rubber stamp, which Brenda has retooled every few years to keep it current, contains a line drawing of Brenda along with this congratulatory message: The Principal's Stamp of Approval!

> "Leading [a school] from good to great does not mean coming up with the answers and then motivating everyone to follow your messianic vision. It means having the humility to grasp the fact that you do not yet understand enough to have the answers and then to ask the questions that will lead to the best possible insights."
>
> —Collins (2001, p. 75)

> "When the Master governs, the people are hardly aware that he exists. . . .
> The Master doesn't talk, he acts.
> When his work is done, the people say,
>   'Amazing.
> We did it all by ourselves!'"
>
> —Lao-Tzu (6th century BCE/1992, p. 17)

Brenda says, "For primary students I put the stamp right on their work; older students enjoy having the stamp on a business-sized card they can put in their wallets." Brenda's goal is to motivate by affirmation and congratulation.

Her door is also open for students who need a listening ear. One very perceptive young visitor to her office shared this problem with Brenda: "I know I'm going to get into trouble today. I feel really antsy." After a brief chat with Brenda, who assumes the role of counselor on the two days per week when the counselor is at another school, the student returned to class. Brenda didn't have to say much at all. She just listened and gave some of that priceless "wordless advice" she often dispenses—not only to students, but to teachers and parents alike.

SUMMING IT UP

Doug Pierson believes strongly in the importance of relationships. Here's how he describes what it means to him to be a Facilitator:

> I strongly believe that the work of the "principal teacher" is about relationships.
>
> Being a principal teacher is a people-centered job. There is no way that an individual who is not skilled at establishing and maintaining meaningful relationships can be successful. The technical skills needed to manage a school are important, but those are things that most folks can learn and apply. Without the ability to build relationships, however, the amount of knowledge one has relative to pedagogy, curriculum, or school management is meaningless.
>
> All of the skills and talents necessary to create a highly effective school are already present in the staff members of every school building. However, the principal teacher can only access those skills and talents by developing meaningful relationships. There isn't anything that I do that is more important. That doesn't mean other aspects of my work aren't important. They are. My staff and I take very seriously the charge to teach our children to read, compose, and compute. We are very intentional about increasing student achievement, and we are also keenly aware of the importance of

Figure 4.1   Facilitator Benchmarks

Trait Number 4: The highly effective principal is a Facilitator—a leader with outstanding human relations skills that include the abilities to build individual relationships with parents, teachers, and students; collaborative teams with staff members and parents; and a schoolwide community of leaders.

4.1   Facilitators bond people into a community of leaders.
4.2   Facilitators tap the potential of people.
4.3   Facilitators say "we" instead of "I."
4.4   Facilitators favor people over paperwork.
4.5   Facilitators build up emotional bank accounts.
4.6   Facilitators cultivate their own well-being.
4.7   Facilitators value diversity.
4.8   Facilitators share the "power-pie."
4.9   Facilitators accentuate the positives.
4.10   Facilitators promote parental involvement.
4.11   Facilitators cheerlead and celebrate.
4.12   Facilitators spend time with students.

the physical, musical, and artistic aspects of learning. However, all of our efforts are made easier when our top priority is building positive, meaningful, and successful relationships.

NOTE

1. This homework song is sung to the tune of *My Bonnie Lies Over the Ocean.*

Your homework is very important,
Your homework's important to do,
Your homework is very important,
Make sure you give homework its due.

Homework,
Homework,
Make sure you do your homework, for sure,
Homework,
Homework,
Your grades will improve if you do.

You shouldn't do homework for others,
You shouldn't do homework for them,
You should do your homework for yourself,
You surely will benefit then.

Chorus

If homework is done with much effort,
If homework is done with much care,
If homework is done as it should be,
Your teacher will see that you care.

The Change Master

"Change is one thing, progress is another."

—B. Russell (as quoted in
Seldes, 1999, p. 605)

In his book *Overcoming Inertia in School Reform*, one of my fellow Corwin Press authors, R. Murray Thomas (2002), examines five aspects of educational change: (1) why things in education don't change at all, (2) why they don't change enough, (3) why they often change in the wrong direction, (4) why they sometimes change simultaneously in both good and bad ways, and (5) why, even when things do change, sooner or later they go back to the way they were (p. 3). If you have been in school administration for any length of time, you have no doubt experienced all five of these phenomena. In a word, "the more things change, the more they stay the same." Many teachers have their own perspective on change: "This too shall pass." The French teacher might well put it this way: *Plus ça change, plus c'est la même chose* (Karr as quoted in Knowles, 1834/1997, p. 64).

All things considered, it's a pretty depressing state of affairs, not altogether different than the ongoing battle that many of us have with excess weight. We go on a guaranteed-to-lose-weight diet and don't lose a pound. Sometimes we lose weight but hardly enough to make all the effort worthwhile. Occasionally we go on a diet and actually *gain* weight. Then there's the good news/bad news scenario wherein we actually succeed in losing weight but then don't have any clothes that fit our new bodies. But we shouldn't buy a new wardrobe prematurely, because sooner or later, we'll be back to what we weighed before we started the diet.

We have all experienced the vagaries of change—both in our personal and professional lives. Undoubtedly, you can enumerate the innovations, strategic plans, and reorganizations you have lived through or even personally initiated that either just faded away or were run out of town altogether. Most of us would welcome a measure of stability, permanence, and incremental improvement, for a change, no pun unintended—a chance to catch our breath and actually do something long enough to get good at it and see results. That is, unless we're politicians.

Politicos thrive on chaos, and when a school system is wed to politics, as many urban districts are, educators are the beneficiaries of a double dose of change. For example, Michael Bloomberg, mayoral successor to Rudy Giuliani in New York City, succeeded in gaining legislative control of the New York Public School System and appointed former federal prosecutor Joel Klein as Chancellor. Mr. Klein readily admits he knows nothing about education, so he appointed Diana Lam, a change agent par excellence, as the deputy chancellor for teaching and learning (Goodnough, 2002). As the superintendent of four different districts in the preceding twelve years, Lam earned both accolades and enemies (Lewin, 2002). In San Antonio, her policies turned around dozens of low-performing schools while at the same time alienating her school board. In Providence, Rhode Island, she increased student achievement remarkably but did so at the expense of teacher morale. Ms. Lam knows how to raise expectations and make heads roll.

"Charismatic leaders inadvertently often do more harm than good because, at best, they provide episodic improvement followed by frustrated or despondent dependency. Superhuman leaders also do us another disservice: they are role models who can never be emulated by large numbers. Deep and sustained reform depends on many of us, not just on the very few who are destined to be extraordinary."

—Fullan (2001, p. 2)

The question is, can Diana Lam *manage* change? Does she know how to *motivate* change? Is she a *Change Master*? I will let you be the judge of that as you read about how highly effective principals motivate and manage change.

The highly effective principal is a Change Master—a flexible, futuristic, and realistic leader, able to motivate as well as manage change in an organized, positive, and enduring fashion.

CHANGE MASTER
EXEMPLAR: MARJORIE THOMPSON

Now retired, Marjorie Thompson was the principal of Kelso Elementary School in Inglewood, California, for a quarter century. Located across the street from the Los Angeles Forum and a race track turned casino, Kelso existed in a constant state of flux, some would say chaos, throughout Marjorie's career. When she was named principal in 1974, Kelso was a modest-sized K–3 building of 375 children operating under court-ordered integration. In retrospect, 1974 was one of the calmer years of the twenty-five that Marjorie spent in what some would call a tough neighborhood. When the court order was rescinded in 1975, the school was reconfigured as a K–6 building with a 50 percent staff turnover. To give the year some added spice and suspense, a shipment of reading books for the newly arrived upper grade students was somehow "misplaced." Marjorie's sister, also an educator, was so disturbed by the situation that the following summer, she drove a pickup truck load of discarded books from her New Mexico school district to California to ensure that adequate materials would be in place for the next school year.

By the early 1980s, Kelso's enrollment had nearly tripled, and the student body was over 90 percent African American. Children and teachers were crowded into hallways, the cafeteria, and portable units in the parking lot and playground. In a desperate search for more classroom space, Marjorie cut an archway between the teachers' lounge and a storage room and used the space for a classroom. The library and her office were also commandeered for classrooms. She shared office space with the nurse. In spite of the distractions, Marjorie and her teachers were teaching them all to read.

> "Leaders must be able to operate under complex, uncertain circumstances."
>
> —Fullan (2001, p. xiii)

Each new wave of students was lower achieving than the previous group, and Kelso adapted the highly structured reading program used in the primary grades for the upper grades. Marjorie was largely responsible for recruiting and training her own teachers, and it was a full-time job as younger staff members turned over almost as frequently as the students did. A few faithful and highly skilled teachers kept the achievement ship afloat. In 1984, the enrollment hit 1,000, and a year-round schedule was adopted to manage the overcrowding. Marjorie and her faculty were left on their own to design and implement the new calendar. Once again, central office handed them lemons, and they made lemonade.

Marjorie discovered a suitable reading curriculum that would meet the needs of primary students for direct instruction in phonics and also provide challenging literature at the upper grades to increase comprehension skills and vocabulary. Short on funds, she was delighted when Open Court Publishing Company offered to give a set of materials for each grade level to the school in exchange for piloting the materials. After the piloting year, Kelso adopted the program for schoolwide use.

In the mid-1980s, Marjorie and her staff hit another roadblock. The whole-language philosophy hit the California reading scene, and the structured phonics approach of Open Court came under fire from state officials in Sacramento. Marjorie and her administrative colleague at Bennet-Kew School, Nancy Ichinaga, mounted a parent-teacher letter-writing campaign to state officials, and convinced them to readopt Open Court as one of California's approved textbooks. With reading scores that defied demographics, the last thing Kelso students needed was an untested instructional approach in reading.

> "When it is not necessary to change, it is necessary not to change."
>
> —L. Cary, 1641
> (as quoted in Knowles, 1997, p. 64)

In the late 1980s, the Kelso neighborhood underwent yet another transition. Spanish-speaking families began moving in, and a state-mandated bilingual program became the focal point of a second heated battle between the Kelso community and the bureaucracy in Sacramento. Marjorie speaks softly, but once she makes up her mind, her resolve is like steel. She and her staff followed their instincts regarding this newest educational wrinkle and determined to teach all children in English. They were accused of violating the civil rights of Hispanic students and were threatened with the loss of funds. Marjorie says, "It was a tough experience. Both the district and the state harassed us. On one occasion, I was grilled for nearly three hours by state department of education officials. But we stood our ground." Marjorie is far too modest about her role in the bilingual battle. "Actually, I can't take any credit for anything that happened. There were some very articulate parents who were adamant about wanting English-only instruction for their children, and what they were asking for made sense to me," she explains. Once again, Marjorie resisted change that she believed would undermine the academic achievement of her students.

If Marjorie dreamed of a few stable and relatively peaceful years at Kelso before her retirement, it was not to be. The supposedly good news of the California class size initiative was bad news for Kelso. There were few certified teachers available to teach at Kelso and no classrooms in which to house them. Marjorie went to work training the novice hires, observing in their classrooms, and suggesting ways to improve their instruction, while more portable classrooms were moved onto the campus. Intersession classes were once again crammed into the stage, cafeteria, and storage rooms.

Marjorie miraculously managed these myriad environmental changes with a calm approach to problem solving. She maintained her quiet focus on what mattered most for the students and parents in her neighborhood—achievement, most especially learning to read in a safe and caring atmosphere. Marjorie says in her forthright and blunt style, "If you can't read, your life is ruined—you're absolutely crippled." She has dedicated her life to making sure that the kids at Kelso weren't crippled by illiteracy. When she encountered barriers, she systematically set about dismantling them. She is a counselor to parents, teachers, and students alike. She does her best work one-on-one—helping troubled children, advising frustrated parents, and motivating tired teachers. "I'm not really a PR person," she says. "That's just not my style. I don't like talking in front of large groups."

> "The principal must acquire an appreciation for what constitutes genuine change, compared to what was traditionally considered to constitute change."
>
> —Sharon, Shachar, and Levine (1999, p. 65)

The demographics at Kelso are the kind that some teachers and principals use as excuses for low achievement (90 percent free and reduced-price lunch and 100 percent minority), but Marjorie kept the faculty and student body focused on her vision. The students at Kelso have achievement test scores that come close to those of their affluent suburban counterparts in communities like Malibu, Irvine, and Beverly Hills. In 2001-2002, Kelso scored a 9 on California's Academic Performance Index. The top API score in the state is 10 (Brice, 2002). Kelso has been a training ground for dozens of master reading teachers, and the "reading coach" model now being used in many of California's urban areas was developed and polished at Kelso and Bennett-Kew. Marjorie Thompson never sees obstacles—only opportunities, and she has left a legacy of learning to thousands of students and teachers.

CHANGE MASTER BENCHMARKS

Although I chose Marjorie Thompson to exemplify the Change Master trait, all of the highly effective principals I interviewed are skilled in the following aspects of the change process and use them situationally as appropriate: (1) instigating change where and when it is needed (e.g., motivating individuals or groups to change certain aspects of their behavior or attitudes), (2) facilitating a variety of processes to identify problems and possible solutions, (3) procuring the resources to fund the change process, (4) providing the stability and continuity that are needed to sustain meaningful change, and (5) facilitating the response of a school community to ongoing changes in the district or community without losing sight of the mission (i.e., managing and handling environmental change).

5.1 Change Masters Can Handle Uncertainty and Ambiguity

Kelso School is a long way from the rural countryside outside St. Louis County, Missouri, that surrounds Pond School, a two-campus K–6 complex of 640 students. However, its principal, Clare Maguire, has a great deal in common with Marjorie Thompson. They both entered the principalship when women were the exception rather than the rule. Together they could write a book about the changes they have seen in their combined five decades of service to public education. In a day when many school administrators switch jobs faster than professional sports figures are traded to new teams, Marjorie and Clare have been steady and predictable presences in their schools and districts.

As the principal of the only Missouri school to receive *two* National Blue Ribbon of Excellence awards, Clare Maguire has witnessed change at a breakneck pace in her twenty-three years in the Rockwood School District: the suburbanization and gentrification of her rural community, court-ordered desegregation and busing, increased accountability, special education, inclusion, and technology. Of course, there are also the five superintendents and countless central office administrators who have come and gone during Clare's tenure. "Just when you think you have the rules at central office figured out," Clare says, "they change." Even as we spoke, Clare reported that her superintendent had just resigned

---

GET READY TO CHANGE

Catherine Segura, Elementary, Avery Island, Louisiana

I have been a principal for eighteen years. Each year brings new challenges and higher expectations. For me, becoming a "highly effective principal" is an illusive bar that keeps going up every year. Our school has been recognized locally, at the state level, and nationally. Even though each recognition was a milestone of accomplishment and highly celebrated, soon new students arrive, state and federal regulations change, and I have to work harder to keep up. I'm on track, but I haven't arrived yet. I'm still learning.

to take a new job, leaving the district leaderless. Then she added with a chuckle, "Could be my best year yet." The only thing that hasn't changed at Pond over the years is their on-site septic system. Clare still has to supervise its cleaning every summer. After twenty-three years in the Rockwood School District managing, initiating, and motivating change *and* inspecting the septic system at Pond School, Clare can still say, "I'm enthused about the opening of school every year." She is indeed a Change Master.

Clare and Marjorie are the kind of principals that parents, teachers, and students love. They are there. They know everybody and everything, and you can count on them. They are committed to their neighborhoods and constant in their attention to what matters most: success for all students. They are true Change Masters.

5.2 Change Masters Respect Resisters

It takes great skill to listen to and even embrace the "yes-butters" and the "naysayers" who seem to appear out of nowhere whenever change is imminent. Mary Ann Stevens, principal of East Jones Elementary School in Laurel, Mississippi, is an expert Change Master who managed and mastered three communities of resisters. When her school board decided to build a new elementary school to consolidate three old and crowded buildings into one, it selected Mary Ann to be the chief Change Master. She was principal of the largest and most remote of the three schools to be merged, and her timeworn building had been a crucial part of life in its community for more than seventy years. The townspeople were angry and suspicious. Even though their principal had been selected to lead the new, consolidated school, it fell to Mary Ann to bring them, as well as the doubters from the other two schools, on board.

First, she gathered parents and community leaders together and asked them to trust her. She had a reputation for fairness and consistency in the community, and she pledged that she would do all she could to make the transition a smooth one for families and their students, including listening to their concerns. She selected some of the most outspoken critics to serve on a steering committee made up of individuals from all of the closing schools. "I inundated this group with information and asked for their ideas regarding the best way to unite the three communities," said

> "Often those who resist have something important to tell us. We can be influenced by them. People resist for what they view as good reasons. They may see alternatives we never dreamed of. They may understand problems about the minutiae of implementation that we never see from our lofty perch atop Mount Olympus."
>
> —Maurer (1996, p. 49)

DON'T GET TOO COMFORTABLE

Nancy Moga, Elementary, Covington, Virginia

Whenever I think that I've arrived, in the sense of mastering change, something else comes along: a key person resigns, a policy is changed, or a new curriculum guide arrives in the mail. It's a constant cycle of ups and downs. It would be nice if there were more ups than downs, but as quickly as the world is changing and the needs of children are increasing, it's a challenge to climb up the side of the mountain from the valleys to get back to the peaks. Right now I feel as though I've arrived.

I have wonderful new staff members who are quickly learning what to do. I have PTO members who are putting in a new playground. They are keeping me informed and consulting me about controversial decisions but feel empowered with their volunteer work. I have very few new students this year other than the normal move-ins, and since our newcomers are generally families who are choosing or asking permission to come to our school, this makes for a win-win situation. But I can't get too comfortable because I know something is bound to happen soon!

Mary Ann. "Then I put the most vocal opponents to work on plans for the grand opening celebration," she added. "I gave them so much to do, they didn't have time to stir up trouble. Plus, they knew exactly what was going on day by day and were able to share what they knew with their friends in the community. Being included and in the know helped everyone to make a smooth transition."

When did Mary Ann feel as though she had mastered this change? "I got an inkling on the day of the ribbon cutting," she confessed. "Every important person in Mississippi was there. My committee had played a central role in planning the activities and inviting guests. I could tell from the smiling faces I saw as we toured the new building with its state-of-the-art computer center, fully stocked library, and spacious new classrooms, that their feelings of pride and ownership regarding what we had accomplished had overcome their resistance." Mary Ann knew for certain that she had accomplished her goal when she heard people talking about "*our* new school," instead of "*that* new school."

Change Masters know how to help resisters overcome the fears, uncertainties, and even anger that are a natural part of any change process.

5.3 Change Masters Are Futuristic

Change Masters have the ability to see what's coming in the distance and get ready for it. Clare Maguire believes that successful principals must continually remain alert to potential problems or opportunities that lie in the future. Thinking ahead allows breathing room, time to consider the alternatives, and the luxury of developing an action plan to minimize the impact on day-to-day operations. In her case, the future held growth. As word of Pond School's success spread, many younger families began moving into the area, and with new construction popping up in former farm fields, the trend showed no signs of abating. Clare says, "We didn't have space for an addition to the building, and the physical layout of the building was not conducive to the use of trailers. I went to the superintendent and shared my idea for a Kindergarten Center that would ease the overcrowding at the school. The school has been on two campuses for seven years. Yes, there are times when it is inconvenient. However, for seven years we have had the space for optimal class sizes and subsequent maximum learning."

> "God, give us the serenity to accept what cannot be changed;
>   Give us the courage to change what should be changed;
>   Give us the wisdom to distinguish one from the other."
>
> —Niebuhr (1951, p. 7)

5.4 Change Masters Use a Situational Approach

Every school community requires a somewhat different approach to change, but using the wrong one can frustrate or derail needed improvements. Regina Birdsell has been a highly effective principal at Academy Elementary School in Madison, Connecticut, for five of her twenty-one years in administration. Her experiences in a variety of schools and settings have made her a perfect mentor for brand-new administrators. One of the first things she does with novice principals is to help them take stock of their schools. Here's her advice:

If you are hired to lead a school where things haven't been ideal—for example, either the former principal was an authoritarian or the school had no mission—you have a real advantage in that anything you do will be better. If you do a lot of listening and develop a mission jointly with the faculty, you're likely to be successful. However, if the staff in your new setting really seem to like things the way they are but you've seen some things that need to be changed, it's often helpful to meet individually with faculty members to find out where everyone is coming from. What do people feel is worth celebrating about their school? What would they like to see changed? Although your superintendent may have given you marching orders to change things, there's nothing worse than forging ahead without first listening to people.

I also remind new principals how important it is to stay connected to the rest of the district while they are making changes in their own schools. They should avoid alienating their staff members from teachers in other buildings, even as a possible motivator to change. While developing the culture of their own schools is a top priority, they have a responsibility to their fellow administrators to share what they are doing to help improve the system as a whole.

5.5 Change Masters Know That the Power Is Within

We often go looking for answers from experts when change is desperately needed. We may be looking in the wrong places. When I arrived at Lincoln Elementary School as a brand-new principal, I was faced with overall reading achievement in the twentieth percentile. I had never taught a child to read, much less raised reading achievement in a low-achieving school, and I immediately thought in terms of hiring an expert to solve the problem. I contacted an eminent reading professor only to discover that he had never worked with a school as low-achieving as ours and had no idea what to do.

I assumed, quite erroneously, that the faculty was the biggest problem. Although there *were* some serious personnel issues to resolve, the majority of teachers were eager to be a part of the solution. As I listened to them air their frustrations, I discovered the many leadership, cultural, and organizational issues that had tied their hands and sent them scurrying to their classrooms to teach in isolation. The climate had not supported collaboration, the frank discussion of issues had been suppressed, and problems had been swept under the rug. We tapped into our collective wisdom, drew on each other's courage, and in the process discovered that together we were mighty. Just as the compatriots in the Wizard of Oz found that they already possessed the courage and wisdom they were seeking elsewhere, we discovered at Lincoln that the wizard was truly within us.

> "Any attempt to create a better environment for education will have to decrease isolation, increase cooperative planning, and sharply lengthen the amount of time in meetings."
>
> —Joyce, Hersh, and McKibbin (1983, p. 69)

5.6 Change Masters Value the Process

One of the most effective ways to harness the power and talents of your teaching staff is to use process activities that, when done collectively, produce a change in thinking or behavior for the participants. Change Masters use them for a variety of purposes: (1) building and sharing values, (2) strengthening leadership teams, (3) generating ideas, (4) sharing critical information, (5) problem solving, (6) reaching consensus, (7) resolving conflict, and (8) goal setting and planning (McEwan, 1997). Change Masters don't have all the answers by any means, but they are process experts. They are able to help their staff members ask the right questions, debate ideas openly and freely, make quality decisions, and implement with commitment.

My building leadership team and I used the Force Field Analysis process to tease out the specific variables that were keeping us from reaching our goals. Developed by Kurt Lewin in the 1940s, Force Field Analysis helps participants identify an issue and then describe the driving forces that will.push toward or facilitate a solution of the problem as well as the restraining forces that will work against solving the problem. The process encourages group members to verbalize both positive and negative feelings about the situation or the proposed solution. Identification of positive forces enables group members to capitalize and strengthen these forces, and verbalization of the negatives illuminates erroneous information and issues that may be hindering the accomplishment of goals. Once the restraining forces are on the table, they can be managed. Unspoken issues are usually unresolved issues that can pop up to slow down or even sabotage an implementation. The Force Field Analysis always works best when it involves the group members who are most resistant to change and enlists them in solving the problems (McEwan, 1997, pp. 100–101; 2002, p. 166).[1]

DON'T GET SIDETRACKED

Lorraine Fong, Elementary, Inglewood, California

My biggest challenge as a new principal is following in the footsteps of a very high-profile and successful principal. Even though I was the assistant principal and very involved in all of the decisions and activities of the school, now I'm the one who has to keep the mission alive. I have to keep telling myself that we can't maintain the high achievement we've had over a sustained period of time and still implement every single new idea that central office sends our way or that the teachers would like to try. My predecessor was able to say "no" very easily, but I am still learning how.

"If consensus is to be used effectively, all group members must contribute their views on the issue and their reactions to proposed alternatives for group action; no one should be allowed to remain silent."

—Johnson and Johnson (1982, p. 107)

5.7 Change Masters Plan for Short-Term Victories

Kathie Dobberteen and her staff use a 30 Day/30 Minute Goal Setting Plan as recommended by Schmoker (1999).[2] Using this format, grade levels determine their goals based on assessment results and student work samples, decide on improvement strategies, devise a pretest and posttest, set a thirty-day period to attain the established goal, use the strategies to make instructional improvements, and then reconvene to monitor the goal's status at the conclusion of the thirty days. If the goal has been reached, the team establishes another goal. If the goal is still unmet, then additional refinements are implemented (Dobberteen, 2001, p. 4).

> "Instead of being discouraged by all that remains to be done, be encouraged by what has been accomplished by way of improvement resulting from your actions."
>
> —Fullan (1991, p. 106)

5.8 Change Masters Procure Resources

Culture Builder Exemplar Gabe Flicker received grants totaling over $600,000 from the Albertsons Foundation to establish a technology and distance learning center. During school days, the students of Grace Lutheran use the facility; the rest of the time the center serves as a teacher training site for technology in the state of Idaho. Gabe offers these observations regarding why the grant came to Grace Lutheran in the beginning and has been added to many times since:

> We were able to give the Albertsons committee an immediate answer when they explained the terms and details of the grant to us. Our streamlined decision-making process enabled us to avoid the red tape, permissions, and multiple signatures that were required in some schools. When Albertsons was ready to move on the decision, they wanted things to happen within the week and we were willing to drop everything and make sure that we had the space to house the center and get it up and running on their time lines. Charitable foundations have goals and needs, and we made ourselves able to meet them. We thought more in terms of how *we* could serve Albertsons than what *they* could do for us. We welcomed them with open arms and offered access and hospitality to any number of visitors with short notice at any time. A very important part of getting grants and finding outside funding for programs is to show appreciation. We never take any gift we receive for granted, and we go out of our way to make donors feel special and affirmed.

Change Masters aren't afraid to ask for what they need. From a pickup-truck-load of reading books to $600,000 worth of technology, and everything in between, they go for what they need to support the mission of their school.

5.9 Change Masters Trust Their Teams

Adhocracy is a term coined by Waterman (1990) to describe the formation of ad hoc teams to work on specific projects or to solve well-defined problems. Change Masters know the power of teams of all kinds and harness that power with spectacular results in their schools. Less effective principals form teams but do not know how to let go and get out of the way. They may be unwilling to take the time that is needed to develop teamwork and trust, or they may take the attitude that adults sometimes take when assigning a task to children: "I can do it faster by myself."

> "True ownership is not something that occurs magically at the beginning, but rather is something that comes out the other end of a successful change process. In successful change projects, ownership is stronger in the middle of the process than it was at the beginning and stronger still at the end."
>
> —Fullan (1992, p. 26)

Kathie Dobberteen's grade level teams have become highly skilled at identifying compelling monthly goals for their students, determining the strategies to meet those goals, and then developing assessments to measure progress toward reaching the goals.

They have their group process skills down pat and can usually complete the entire meeting in thirty minutes or less. La Mesa Dale's teams are textbook examples of Waterman's (1990) sage advice: (1) Take the emphasis off reports and put it on results, (2) stop studying it and get it done, (3) reward those who implement well, and (4) use a systematic method to measure results or make corrections (p. 94).

5.10 Change Masters Are Willing to Change Themselves

Change Masters know that "to lead change, [they] have to change" (Lynch & Werner, p. 7). Ineffective principals have extreme cases of what I call the Emperor's Syndrome, after Hans Christian Andersen's fairy tale, *The Emperor's New Clothes.* Emperor principals terrify their subordinates into ignoring their extreme nakedness and so they fail to realize the potential that comes from hearing the truth that what they are doing is ineffective.

Early in his career, Activator Exemplar Todd White took his teachers on an end-of-the-year retreat. At one point during the event, he asked

---

ROLL WITH THE PUNCHES

Communicator Exemplar Michelle Gayle, Middle School, Tallahassee, Florida

In my mind there is no such thing as an unsolvable problem. There are only challenges to be innovative, creative, and work together. I may not know how we're going to solve a problem, but we always do it. Last year we had some serious budgetary difficulties in our district. When the administrative meeting was adjourned, most everybody left with a "woe is me" attitude, but a group of us decided to take a different route. We looked at the budget shortfall as a challenge to get by on a shoestring and still be successful. My attitude really helped my faculty. You have to look at what you have and make that work.

---

them two questions: "What do I need to do to be a better principal?" and "What do I need to be in order for you to improve and change?"

Was it easy? Of course not. Todd confesses there were moments during the session when he felt like he was going to cry, but he kept things under control by imagining himself as a greeter at Wal-Mart. "It was the hardest thing I've ever done professionally," he says, "but the most rewarding in terms of my own personal growth as a principal." Experiences like these are routine for highly effective principals. They give others permission to tell them what's wrong and then they set about changing their own behavior before they prevail upon others to change theirs.

5.11 Change Masters Are Motivators

Change Masters can motivate. Some do it with flair and fanfare; others do it quietly and behind the scenes. Some do it one-to-one; others can fire up a group like a Methodist preacher at a camp meeting. Whatever their style, they are able to size up a situation and rally the troops behind them. They stand and then deliver—training, coaches, support, computers, celebrations, materials, encouragement, and even protection: protection of time, protection from paperwork, protection from parents, even protection from central office. Change Masters do not dictate or mandate. They facilitate and walk along beside. They roll up their sleeves and get their hands dirty. They work harder and longer and faster than anyone else. They are there in the morning when everyone arrives, and they are there in the evening when everyone leaves. And in many cases, they are still there on the weekends.

5.12 Change Masters Understand the Change Process

Educator Exemplar Alan Jones could write the book on change at the high school level. He says,

If I could point to one behavior that *I* had to change over the years, it would be paying attention to the details of a reform and patiently talking with all those personnel who could be affected by a new idea. When I first became a principal, I would force a reform because *I* had read the research on the issue. I did not spend time explaining or supporting teachers who would be implementing the reform nor did I understand and respect the goals or outcomes of the personnel who managed the systems that would be affected by the reform. As I became more experienced, I learned how to communicate (listen carefully and use their ideas) with all of the stakeholders. This approach resulted in reduced frustration on the part of all parties involved.

> "Process skills . . . are as important as knowledge of the problem under scrutiny . . . running a good meeting, setting schedules, keeping things on track, ensuring that work gets done between meetings, getting input from the whole team (rather than a few dominant members), and listening."
>
> —Waterman (1990, p. 35)

Change takes an enormous amount of energy. It is much easier to monitor current systems and send teachers to workshops. Deep structural reform occurs only when a principal is able to teach/explain/figure out how theory and practice will mesh together—and that means that all systems supporting the instructional innovation must be able to accommodate the change without extraordinary efforts.

SUMMING IT UP

Becoming a Change Master requires the ability to strike a balance between harried "hare brain" thinking and the more moderate pace of a "tortoise mind." Claxton (1997) advises that using a "hare brain" approach may well result in hurry-up-and-get-the-job-done thinking. While on-the-spot decision making is perfectly appropriate for day-to-day operational decisions, "[the kind of thinking that] takes place under the pressure to adopt one shallow nostrum, one fashionable idea after another, each turning out to have promised more than it was capable of delivering, [may result in winning the wrong race]" (Claxton, 1997, p. 214). On the other hand, the tortoise mind-set offers highly effective principals the opportunity to consider a diverse range of problems and issues without rushing, deal with ambiguity and uncertainty without panic, and resist the temptation to follow intuition or the crowd and wait for some solid research. Slow and steady often wins the change race.

Figure 5.1   Change Master Benchmarks

Trait Number 5: The highly effective principal is a Change Master—a flexible, futuristic, and realistic individual who is able to motivate as well as manage change in an organized, positive, and enduring fashion.

5.1   Change Masters can handle uncertainty and ambiguity.
5.2   Change Masters respect resisters.
5.3   Change Masters are futuristic.
5.4   Change Masters use a situational approach.
5.5   Change Masters know that the power is within.
5.6   Change Masters value the process.
5.7   Change Masters plan for short-term victories.
5.8   Change Masters provide resources.
5.9   Change Masters trust their teams.
5.10 Change Masters are willing to change themselves.
5.11 Change Masters are motivators.
5.12 Change Masters understand the change process.

NOTES

1. See the Facilitator's Guide for a Sample Force Field Analysis (Exhibit D.1) and a Force Field Analysis Worksheet (Form D.8).

2. See the Facilitator's Guide for samples of the forms used by Kathie Dobberteen and her teams (Form D.4 and Form D.5).

The Culture Builder

"It is not the teachers, or the central office people, or the university people who are really causing schools to be the way they are or changing the way they might be. It is whoever lives in the principal's office."

—Barth (1976, p. 10)

I write a weekly column for my local newspaper on education issues. Parents frequently send in questions regarding aspects of school life that puzzle them, and I give advice from my perspective. Questions regarding why principals do the things they do are not infrequent. For example, in a recent communiqué, a parent wondered why the principal of the elementary school in her neighborhood does not acknowledge parents when they speak to him in the hallways of his school. Actually, I had no easy answer for that question. We might be able to excuse this administrator's seemingly incomprehensible behavior if he were temporarily preoccupied with a problem, but since the writer of the question assured me that it was a pervasive problem, I can only assume he is oblivious and needs a crash course in culture building.

Could it be that this principal does not know that he is always on stage—serving as a role model for manners, decorum, and civility? Mothers and fathers, as well as foster parents and guardians, have entrusted their most valuable treasures to this individual's leadership capabilities. In their eyes, he is the captain of the ship, the leader of the band, and the coach of the team, all rolled into one. They want a principal who is caring and responsive, someone who greets parents by name

> "Culture . . . represents the accumulated learning of a group—the ways of thinking, feeling, and perceiving the world that have made the group successful [or unsuccessful]."
>
> —Schein (1999, p. 21)

when he encounters them, whether in the hallways of his school, at the supermarket, or on the soccer field. Parents are troubled, and rightly so, at the thought of having their children in a school where the leader doesn't greet them warmly or even acknowledge their presence. If the rude individual were the school's social worker or even the custodian, there would be reason enough to be distressed. But the principal *is* the chief executive in charge of culture building. His behavior sets the standard. Before long, others, if so inclined, will follow his lead, and soon the culture will begin to crumble.

Another parent wrote this to me:

My son has been attending a very good elementary school for three years—wonderful teachers, outstanding resource help, involved parents, and a terrific principal. Unfortunately, the principal was transferred last year, and the new principal has been extremely difficult. She seems to be single-handedly ruining the school atmosphere. She is imperious, a petty bureaucrat who micromanages the teachers and talks down to everyone—parents, teachers, and children. Speaking with her is like talking to a policy manual. I'm a pretty formidable person who can articulate my views logically, but many of the parents are cowed, confused, and angry. Teachers and other support staff are leaving en masse. Students are fearful, and the poisonous atmosphere is permeating the school.

John Locke (1690/1854) said, "The actions of men [or women] are the best interpreters of their thoughts" (p. 52). One can only speculate about what is going on in this principal's mind.

As you may have already discovered, there is a synergistic relationship between some of the traits. For example, principals cannot be Culture Builders unless they have a combination of three other traits—Communicator, Envisioner, and Character Builder. These three traits are the legs of the culture-building stool. Absent any one of them, principals will be unable to build positive and productive cultures. For example, principals who are missing the character leg of the stool are merely manipulators. They are selling the right vision for all the wrong reasons. Principals without the communication leg of the stool are unable to build relationships and therefore have a difficult time recruiting people for their missions. Or principals who are missing the vision leg of the stool can communicate well and create caring environments, but they have no worthwhile vision to inspire their schools.

I encounter all of these kinds of principals as I consult with school districts around the country. The clever manipulators say and do all the right things, but they are readying their résumés for the next step up the career ladder. They have no character. Then there are the numerous well-intentioned and high-principled individuals who do have a worthy vision but simply cannot figure out a way to get people to move on it. They cannot communicate or motivate. These folks keep saying they're going to do it; they turn in action plans and rehearse speeches, but when it comes right down to it, they are unable to convince their staff members that they are serious. The third and by far the largest category of principals are the Character Builders par excellence and Communicators without peer who have no vision for raising achievement. They prefer to let teaching and learning proceed without administrative interference—*teacher autonomy* and *creativity* are their bywords. They promote collegiality at staff parties, hold well-orchestrated special events for their students, and decorate their offices like extensions of their homes, but in many cases, their students are underachieving or not achieving at all.

The highly effective principal is a Culture Builder—an individual who communicates (talks) and models (walks) a strong and viable vision based on achievement, character, personal responsibility, and accountability.

> "What are the reasons why you should follow the lead of your supervisors? Because they know how to manipulate? Because they can meet your needs or provide you with other psychological payoffs? Because they are charming and fun to be with? Or because they have something to say that makes sense? Because their thoughts point you in a direction that captures your imagination? Because they stand on ideas, values, and conceptions that you believe are good for teachers, students, and the school?"
>
> —Sergiovanni (1992, p. 34)

CULTURE BUILDER EXEMPLAR: GABE FLICKER

Gabe Flicker, principal of Grace Lutheran School, has built a culture that has captured the imagination of parents, the community of Pocatello, Idaho, and numerous charitable foundations and organizations. Everyone is standing in line to be a part of this success story.

During his first week on the job, Gabe hung his school's purpose statement in the entryway.[1] You can't miss the four-inch-high red and blue letters that proclaim what the school is all about. When he gives an orientation tour to brand-new families, the first stop on the tour is always in front of the framed statement where he explains its meaning. He also makes sure that new staff and board members understand the school's purpose. And just to make certain they take him seriously, Gabe gives a little test every now and then during the school year. If newcomers don't pass his first test, they will definitely have the purpose statement memorized before the second test rolls around. A second stop on the orientation tour is the National Blue Ribbon School of Excellence Citation signed by the President of the United States. Grace Lutheran received the second one ever given in the state of Idaho. With these simple acts, Gabe is doing what organizational theorists call *purposing*—"engaging in a continuous stream of actions . . . which have the effect of inducing clarity, consensus, and commitment regarding the organization's basic purposes" (Vaill, 1986, p. 91).

> "When a school community feels it's really in control of its destiny, teachers, parents, and administrators are more inclined to do the hundreds of little things it takes to make their school work. When people are doing something they believe in, they do it better. There's more passion."
>
> —Manna (1999)

When difficult decisions need to be made, clarity is achieved by evaluating the issue in the light of the purpose statement. Gabe explains, "This process has given our school community a cohesive spirit and focus." Visitors to the Grace campus can see the purpose statement at work in the sixteen new classrooms that have been built and the eleven additional acres of prime land that have been acquired for expansion. They can see the culture Gabe has built reflected in the academic success of the students and the teamwork and leadership of the teachers. Achievement test scores average above the eighty-fifth percentile, and since Gabe first posted the purpose statement inside the front door, enrollment has grown from about 100 students to nearly 400. Gabe's culture building efforts aren't just confined to the walls of his school. Every third year, he takes the staff on a three-day retreat to a mountain lodge for team building. Training and group sessions are held during the day, and the staff hikes or bikes in the evenings. Gabe explains, "This is a great way for staff members to build quality professional relationships that lead to a positive work environment." When his new building was under construction, Gabe joined a group of church and family volunteers to do his part with a hammer and saw. He wasn't just building walls; he was building a strong and positive school culture.

"It's the little things that communicate to parents what the culture of a school is like," says Gabe. "For example, each spring we have daffodils blooming in the playground planter areas. The bulbs were planted by students.

Gabe was interviewing a new family and asked his usual question: "Why did you choose Grace Lutheran?" The mother's answer was a new one to him:

"Any school that can motivate kids to respect the spring flowers must have good learning and discipline."

Gabe observes, "As educators we often focus on the "big things," like our new building and the technology center. Parents, on the other hand, notice the little things, like the fact that our students are so proud of their school, they wouldn't dream of picking the daffodils."

You can be sure that the daffodil story will be told to teacher candidates, prospective families, and to the many individuals and groups from whom Gabe continues to solicit grants and funds to enhance the services at Grace Lutheran. It's a powerful story, and storytelling is a very important part of culture building.

Gabe is quick to point out that he doesn't have a built-in clientele or an automatic source of support. "Unless we have a culture that people *want* to be a part of, we won't have students or get paychecks. People contribute to the future of our school because they see a culture that supports both achievement and character."

How does one build a culture from scratch? Gabe can tell you. Hire the very best people you can find. Empower them to do what they do best. Provide a warm, loving, and secure environment. Be willing to serve your students, parents, and teachers in any way you can, whether it's providing hot cinnamon rolls and coffee before school or mopping up a spill in the entryway. Bring parents and community members into your school as valued partners. Settle conflicts and differences before the sun sets and definitely within twenty-four hours. Send out newsletters and newspapers; communicate with parents via a Web site and E-mail. But more important than anything, Gabe says, "Have a vision that is bigger than the Idaho wilderness—one that makes people's jaws drop when they first hear it."

> "Storytelling is one of the oldest ways in the world to convey the values and ideals shared by a community."
>
> —Kouzes and Posner (1999, p. 14)

These are the "big things." Gabe's most powerful communication and relationship-building techniques, however, are the "little things" he does regularly, like handing out kudos at staff meetings and expecting staff members to keep the positive comments flowing or being out in the hallway every morning and afternoon to greet students and parents with a cheery hello or a warm hug.

CULTURE BUILDER BENCHMARKS

School cultures are as varied as the tens of thousands of schools across our vast country. Visitors to some schools are greeted with chaotic classrooms, empty bulletin boards, and indifferent stares from passing staff members. In those schools, the culture hangs like a noxious cloud in the hallways. On the other hand, at the Noelani and Mitchell Road Elementary Schools or at Naperville Central High School, you can see the efforts of Culture Builders Clayton Fujie, Todd White, and Tom Paulsen at work. At the Noelani Elementary School in Honolulu, Hawaii, for example, a colorful wall mural featuring the colorful history of the island of Oahu greets you when you walk in the front door.

> **A CAN-DO CULTURE**
>
> **Kathie Dobberteen, Elementary, La Mesa Dale, California**
>
> Sometimes I think of my staff and school as "being full of itself," and I say that in a positive way. My teachers have a sense of accomplishment and esprit de corps that comes from having beaten the odds. We reached the point that we knew what we were doing, we knew how to set instructional goals and how to make continuous progress. If we had a problem, we knew that if we put our heads together, we could solve it.

At the Mitchell Road Elementary School, you'll receive a warm welcome from the "Friendly Fourth-Grade Greeters" who are showing some visitors through their school. At Naperville Central High School, you'll find the principal himself, Tom Paulsen, out in the hallway, talking to some of his students. You can be sure when he sees you, he'll wave you over for a hello and a handshake. Here are some of the other ways that Culture Builders work their magic:

6.1 Culture Builders Understand and Appreciate the Power of Culture

Culture Builders never underestimate the power of culture. Culture is, at once, deep, broad, and stable (Schein, 1999), and any attempts to manipulate, change, or toss it out completely are doomed to failure without appreciating its depth, width, and solid strength—whether for good or ill. Change guru Michael Fullan (1991) reminds principals to "assume that changing the culture of institutions is the real agenda, not implementing single innovations" (p. 107). Successful principals realize that adopting a single program or highly touted reform without simultaneously building collaborative work groups among teachers, inviting parents to be a part of the school community, or creating a safe and orderly school for students is like "trying to apply a Band-Aid underwater" (Childress & Senn, 1999, p. 7).

One of the metaphors I often use when talking to principals about changing the cultures of their schools is to compare it to redecorating a preowned home you have just purchased. Remember when you bought your first house and you absolutely despised the wallpaper with the black roses in the powder room? You declared in no uncertain terms that the *first* thing you were going to do when *you* moved in was to get rid of that nauseating wallpaper. Well, you moved in, and suddenly there were more urgent concerns that demanded your attention. A year went by, and the wallpaper with the black roses was still there. It didn't seem so disgusting anymore. In fact, you even bought some black towels to match the roses. You *were* a little embarrassed when you decided to sell the house after five years and listed it with the same realtor who sold it to you. You could read his mind when he looked into the powder room.

> "To truly change the [school], you need to change the culture."
>
> —Childress and Senn (1999, p. 7)

Building or changing aspects of a school's culture is one of those things that everybody talks about, especially when they begin a new job, but then, those considerations often get tabled when the day-to-day grind of the principalship kicks in. Once you have ignored a particularly unfortunate aspect of a school's culture for too long, you either get used to it and become an unwitting supporter of it, or you feel so guilty about the fact that you've ignored it, you are now too embarrassed to bring it up. Of course, you can't change everything at once, but Culture Builders assess and prioritize those areas of school culture that need immediate attention. The black roses in the powder room may not be a top priority, but the leaky roof, faulty electrical wiring, and broken sump pump do need to be fixed immediately. Then, strip off the roses.

6.2 Culture Builders Know What a Good Culture Looks Like

Whether they are building brand-new cultures, like Mary Ann Stevens in Mississippi, or changing unhealthy and unproductive ones, like Envisioner Exemplar Larry Fieber in New Jersey, Culture Builders know where they are headed. They can tell you what a good culture looks and feels like. Culture building is a more challenging assignment than you might think, since so much of what is included under the umbrella of culture is either unseen or unspoken: (1) the shared values of its members—the things people think are important or pay attention to, (2) the beliefs of its members—how they think things should be done, (3) the behaviors of its members—the habitual behavior patterns of teachers, students, and parents, (4) the heroes of its members—the people who personify the culture, and (5) the system—both the written and unwritten policies and procedures (Childress & Senn, 1999, p. 53).

Excellent principals watch, listen, ask questions, and become cultural anthropologists as they examine documents, interview informants, and observe behavior and listen to conversations in the teachers' lounge, in hallways, and in meetings. Their goal is to uncover and understand the cultures of their schools. Schein (1999) advises that a formal assessment of a school's culture is not usually worth the time and energy it takes. He suggests the best way to find out what's going on is through group interviews. He vetoes using surveys or questionnaires because "one does not know what to ask and cannot judge the reliability and validity of the responses" (p. 86).

It didn't take long for me to discover the "black roses" at Lincoln School. Unfortunately, they were all too obvious:

- Many students were not respected; a few teachers and lunchroom supervisors felt free to physically and verbally abuse them.
- Parents belonged to one of two groups—the "haves" or the "have-nots." The "haves" got the teachers they wanted for their children. The "have-nots" got the leftovers.
- Teachers closed their doors when they taught, and no one came in without an invitation, even the principal.
- Teachers felt powerless unless they had their union representative along with them.
- Red tape, regulations, and dozens of forms in different colors and sizes kept everybody in line.
- Meetings were designed to tell everybody things they already knew.

"Attempts at incremental change—'tweaking' the culture—ordinarily die for lack of energy. If you try to go slow, bureaucracy and resistance to change will cancel out your efforts. So get radical. Take action that turns heads. Let your opening moves leave no doubt that the old culture is incompatible with what's to come."

—Pritchett and Pound (1993, p. 6)

I didn't need Margaret Meade to interpret what these findings meant for reculturing. Dismantling a toxic culture and building a new one is complicated, messy, and even confrontational at times, but there can be no meaningful change without it. If Pritchett and Pound's (1993) philosophy of high-velocity culture change had been around in 1983, it would have been my handbook. I counseled with the abusive lunchroom supervisor until she resigned and then began vigorously observing, documenting, and conferencing with the abusive teacher. I opened my office doors—the one to the hallway that was nailed shut as well as the one to the outer office. I moved the new duplicating machine from the principal's office to the teacher's workroom, saw parents *whenever* they stopped by (not just when they made an appointment several days in advance), saw teachers *whenever* they needed to see me—not just by advance appointment, and began to visit every classroom every day. I asked the secretary to stop screening calls from parents with problems and to forward them directly to me. I listened to all of the parents who had concerns; if parents spoke Spanish, I tapped my migrant program teacher for translating.

Whenever I heard staff members, students, or parents speaking inappropriately to one other, I confronted their behavior immediately. I was kind but firm. I started handing out "goodies" to the teachers who had already caught a glimpse of the vision. I found money for more materials, release time for planning, and opportunities for staff development for the eager beavers. I began to go over the students' unit tests in math and reading with each grade level team. I let it be known that I wanted to hear the truth and that people would not be punished for telling it. Pritchett and Pound (1993) advise, "Significant culture change should start to occur in weeks or months. Not years. Start out fast and keep trying to pick up speed. *Leave skid marks*" (p. 44). At spring break, the hallways were

---

AN OPEN-DOOR CULTURE

Terry Beasley, Elementary, Fairhope, Alabama

When I arrived at my school, the culture was very unfriendly to parents. They were not allowed to go past the office. One of the first things I helped my teachers to understand and accept was that parents had to be welcomed into our school. Parental support and cooperation are essential to students' success. We agreed on a date that our "open classroom policy" would begin and from that day forward, parents were welcome to visit any classroom at any time without an appointment. Of course, we established some guidelines. Parents had to sign in and out at the office. They were not permitted to bring small children with them and were asked to refrain from talking with teachers, their children, or other students during the visit. We placed two adult chairs just inside the doorway of every classroom. The teachers who were confident (the vast majority) quickly realized the benefits of having an open-door culture. Those who needed to make some changes in classroom management or instruction (a small number) were quickly motivated to change. And teachers who thought that parents were an unwelcome interference (one or two) decided to move on. Parents now know that we have nothing to hide and consequently they are talking nonstop about the great things they see happening at our school.

painted a brand-new color, the union's grievance chairperson had lost her battle to save the abuser's job, and achievement was going up. I burned rubber.

6.3 Culture Builders Facilitate the Development of Core Values

Highly effective principals have solid and important core values but know better than to mandate or dictate that these values be adopted without discussion and debate. Culture Builders know the value of taking time to process and facilitate the development of mission, vision, purpose, or value statements.

Over a period of three years in the early 1980s, my staff and I developed learning outcomes in Reading, Mathematics, and Language Arts (Lincoln School, 1987). When I reflect on what we (a novice principal and a small staff) accomplished with no human or financial resources from central office, I am still amazed. It represented the first coherent statement of what students were expected to know and do that any of us had ever seen, and the fact that my staff suggested we publish it and give it to parents was even more remarkable. They wanted to include a set of behavioral expectations for parents and students in the booklet; I thought that was a fine idea but only if we also included a set of expectations for teachers.

The process of developing expectations for teachers turned out to be a lengthy and sometimes vocal process. The teachers took it very seriously and realized that by giving a copy of these expectations to parents, they were in essence promising to uphold them. They wanted to make certain that every word was parsed to its precise meaning. The list represented a quantum leap in our school's culture. Here's what the faculty promised the parents they would do:

- State clear expectations and desired outcomes for students.
- Communicate classroom and school rules to students and parents.
- Hold students accountable for following school rules and completing assignments.
- Provide quality instruction for students.
- Maintain discipline and control in the classroom.
- Provide a classroom environment conducive to learning.
- Evaluate and communicate student progress to parents and students.
- Present a positive role model to students and have neat personal habits.

6.4 Culture Builders
Communicate These Values Clearly

In my instructional leadership workshops for principals, we examine the many ways in which principals can communicate their core values to the school community. One way is to use what I call *refrains*. A refrain is the part of a song that is repeated after every verse—the chorus. A song may have five verses—each one different—but the refrain is always the same. It's what the singers come back to over and over to remind them and their listeners what the song is really all about.

I ask the workshop participants to share the phrases, words, epigrams, or ideas that they frequently repeat in their schools—the choruses, if you will, of their school's culture. Then we spend a few moments giving examples of where and how they have used these refrains—in graphic designs on hallway walls, on the school's letterhead, in cheers and chants, on bumper stickers and adorning T-shirts. Culture Builders repeat, explain, discuss, and illustrate their refrains to insiders (teachers, parents, and students) as well as outsiders (community members, taxpayers, foundations, and local businesses), in an ongoing effort to make sure that everyone gets the message.

During my conversations with the highly effective principals featured in this book, they inevitably articulated their core values to me with great clarity at some point. In most cases, we had not been talking more than five minutes before their values became clear. Gabe Flicker believes that students are more successful when they have strong, involved, empowered, and connected teachers. Eventually, I discovered the "big" things he has done to demonstrate his beliefs: hired an assistant principal to help teachers become more effective, organized leadership teams, awarded stipends to the leaders of these teams for their extra responsibilities, and budgeted for staff retreats and training. I also teased out the "little" things that happen regularly: kudos at staff meetings, veto power for the staff over any new hires, a staff huddle every morning to inform and inspire for the day, and a strong, visible presence by the principal.

While all outstanding principals have their students' intellectual development and academic achievement as a primary goal, each one approaches culture building from a slightly different perspective. There are cultures of sharing, caring, respect, community, growing, collaboration, inquiry, learning, problem solving, excellence, character, achievement, and equity. Gabe Flicker believes that learning is relational. Lola Malone, Tom Paulsen, and Patricia Hamilton believe that learning is character based. Kathie Dobberteen and Dale Skinner believe that learning is the result of knowing what to teach and teaching it well. Byron

Schwab believes that learning takes place when students and parents have choices about how and where to learn. Terry Beasley frames the culture of his school as an effort to capture both the hearts *and* heads of students. Jean Hendrickson believes that learning is dependent on a strong parent-school connection.

While they are all traveling to similar destinations, their routes, modes of transportation, and selected stopping-off places differ substantially. Saphier and King (1985) suggest twelve norms of school culture that impact school improvement: collegiality; experimentation; high expectations; trust and confidence; tangible support; reaching out to the knowledge base; appreciation and recognition; caring, celebration, and humor; shared decision making; protection of what's important; traditions; and honest, open communication (p. 67).

I was a new principal when I first encountered Saphier and King's (1985) norms of school culture. I naively assumed that I was responsible for doing it all. While highly effective principals play to their own strengths from the outset, they also identify the talents of their staff members and parents and use these abilities to assist them in building a strong school culture. Culture Builders not only communicate their values to students, parents, and teachers, they build cultures based on the collective strengths and values of every member of the school community.

6.5 Culture Builders Reward and Cheer Those Who Support and Enhance the Culture

High school principal Margaret Garcia-Dugan set out from the beginning to nurture teachers who enhanced the culture: "I cultivated a strong relationship with the teachers who were obviously producers and results-oriented individuals. They talked to me about ideas they had to increase student learning and suggested strategies to build teams of teachers to work collaboratively. As these teachers became leaders in their individual departments and produced increasingly positive results with their students, more and more of their colleagues became results oriented.

Those who were initially reluctant began to come to me frequently to discuss their instructional approaches. In my experience, teachers who are rowing the boat (increasing student achievement) do not have time to rock the boat (be whiners and complainers)."

Culture Builders know the power of affirmation and rewards when it comes to changing the culture and are always very clear about what matters most to them—results, effective instruction, collaboration, teamwork, creativity, caring for kids, and communicating with parents.

6.6 Culture Builders Build Cultures That People Choose

When I pulled up into the parking lot of Lincoln Elementary School to begin my first official day as principal, it never occurred to me that I was the only person that had a choice about what to do that day. I had chosen to be there because I believed I could make a difference. My other choice, the job I turned down, was a cultural continuum away from Lincoln.

I would shortly learn, however, that most families moved into the Lincoln neighborhood if they couldn't afford to live anywhere else. It was as if a sign had been posted over our front door: "Give us your

> **A CULTURE OF PRIDE**
>
> **Contributor Exemplar Lola Malone, Elementary, Springdale, Arizona**
>
> Lola Malone and her faculty hold a monthly "Tiger Pride" assembly to recognize and reward students who have exemplified the school's "character words" for that month. A variety of other awards are also given. The cafeteria manager hands out a "Marvelous Manners Silver Tray Award," the custodians present the "Golden Wastebasket Award" to the class that keeps the neatest and easiest-to-clean room, and each specialized teacher gives an award to the classroom that has demonstrated the best participation and behavior. If one class receives three of these awards in the same month, Lola throws a party just for them. Individual students who have practiced good citizenship and appropriate behavior for the month have a chance to win prizes like basketballs, footballs, Barbie dolls, and stuffed animals. Everyone looks forward to this monthly opportunity to celebrate and have fun together. There are cheers, songs, talent acts from faculty and students, and even a little craziness from the principal.
>
> Lola says, "I love that James Brown song, 'I Feel Good.' I play it over the intercom every now and then at the end of the day. The kids love it, and so now at the beginning of every assembly, I ask the question, 'How do you feel?' and the students respond in union: 'I feel good!' with great enthusiasm and joy."

exhausted and angry single mothers who have no money until the support check arrives; give us your immigrants who are hoping for a better way of life; and give us your unemployed and nearly homeless, and we will school their children." Oh, there was a determined core of homeowners who had not been seduced by the affluence of suburbia that surrounded them and rather liked the edgy counterculture atmosphere in

A CULTURE OF LEARNING AND LOVING

Activator Exemplar Clare Maguire, Elementary, Grover, Missouri

One of the things that I am proudest of as a principal is that the parents who were students here at Pond School during the days of court-ordered desegregation and busing are now choosing to send their own children here. They have options regarding where to send their children, and the bus ride is more than an hour each way. But these parents are so appreciative of the experiences they had here when they were growing up, they want the same ones for their own children. Our goal is to ensure success for every single child—whether they walk across the street or ride a bus to school.

the neighborhood. Their children rescued our achievement scores from total oblivion, but they were a very small minority. The most experienced teachers had come to believe that this was as good as it would get, and even parents arrived to register their students with an air of resignation and the strong belief that nobody cared. To build a school environment where parents would want to send their children—not a place where they were forced to come—became my goal.

You may not have to compete for your students yet, but as vouchers, charter schools, open enrollments, and other options become more available to parents, you could find yourself with a declining enrollment. Do you know what kinds of schools parents will choose for their children? Schools like Gabe Flicker's, where kids are learning, problems are solved, teachers care, daffodils are blooming, and the cinnamon rolls are hot. Larry Pollock knew he had "arrived" when he heard a parent make this comment about his school: "This used to be a school no one wanted to come to, and now it's a school that no one wants to leave."

6.7 Culture Builders Know the Small Stuff Is Really the Big Stuff

Do you have time for telling stories, impromptu celebrations, recognition for accomplishments, building traditions, and honoring the past? Do you have time to laugh and cry and hold hands? Some principals think of these cultural artifacts as unimportant or inconsequential time wasters. Culture Builders know that the "small stuff" is really the "big stuff" of which strong cultures are built.

SUMMING IT UP

Phillip Manna (1999) calls it a feeling: "What makes a good school has very little to do with how rich or poor the students are or the type of curriculum that's taught. It has very little to do with special programs,

Figure 6.1   Culture Builder Benchmarks

Trait Number 6: The highly effective principal is a Culture Builder—an individual who communicates (talks) and models (walks) a strong and viable vision based on achievement, character, personal responsibility, and accountability.

6.1 Culture Builders understand and appreciate the power of culture.
6.2 Culture Builders know what a good culture looks like.
6.3 Culture Builders facilitate the development of core values.
6.4 Culture Builders communicate those values clearly.
6.5 Culture Builders reward and cheer those who support and enhance the culture.
6.6 Culture Builders build cultures that people choose.
6.7 Culture Builders know that the "small stuff" is really the "big stuff."

expansive playing fields, huge endowments, snappy uniforms, celebrity alumni, or whether the school is wired to the Internet. What makes a good school, whether it's public or private, religious or nonreligious, charter or noncharter, is a feeling. A feeling shared by the entire staff [as well as parents and students] that their particular school is special. The feeling that their school really belongs to them" (n.p.).

The feeling of which Phillip Manna (1999) writes arises from the culture of a school—all of the attitudes, assumptions, values, purposes, feelings, beliefs, and behaviors that are taken for granted and routinely observed in the classrooms, hallways, playgrounds, playing fields, meetings, and offices of a school. Saphier and King (1985) posit the concept of "strong cultures" and call them the engines of school improvement. To build on that metaphor, I suggest that principals are the chief engineers. To be a Culture Builder is to engineer the development of a culture that has as its fuel, caring, concern, collegiality, humor, collaboration, communication, and character, combined with accountability, responsibility, and achievement.

NOTE

1. The Purpose of Grace Lutheran School is to Promote Excellence in Education and to Nurture Each Child in an Environment of Compassion, Reaching Out With the Love of Christ.

The Activator

7

"A person filled with gumption doesn't sit around dissipating and stewing about things. He's [she's] at the front of the train of his [her] own awareness, watching to see what's up the track and meeting it when it comes. That's gumption."

—Pirsig (1974, p. 303)

Gumption is an archaic word—one you seldom hear in conversation anymore, but it does portray the colorful behaviors of Activator principals quite accurately: "boldness of enterprise; initiative or aggressiveness; guts or spunk; common sense" (*American Heritage Dictionary*, 2000). As descriptive as *gumption* is, however, I opted for another word that is slightly less picturesque to describe the trait featured in this chapter: *activator*.

When the book, *Now, Discover Your Strengths* (Buckingham & Coffman, 2001), was first released, I bought it immediately and eagerly took the online assessment which identifies an individual's five major areas of strength based on their answers to a battery of questions. There are thirty-four possible strengths, and those who take the assessment are provided with their top five. I was not at all surprised to discover that one of my five strengths was called Activator.

Actually, my mother had me pegged for an Activator before I turned five. She uttered these words more than once in moments of intense frustration: "Please just go sit down and be quiet for a little while." I have been "activating" ever since. The profile I received after completing the StrengthsFinder survey had this, among other things, to say about activators: "'When can we start?' This is a recurring question in your life. You are impatient for action. . . . You must put yourself out there. You must take the next step. It is the only way to keep your thinking fresh and informed. The bottom line is this: You know you will be judged not by what you say, not by what you think, but by what you get done. This does not frighten you. It pleases you" (Buckingham & Coffman, 2001, p. 84).

One of the boldest and most "out there" things I ever did while an elementary school principal was to stand up in front of the Corridor Partnership for Excellence, a group of 200 educators and high-powered business leaders from the high-tech corridor in our county, and challenge the chairman, Carl Ball, to change places with me for a day. Carl, the CEO of Ball Seed Company, was at the podium pontificating about the need for increased understanding between business and education, and in an impulsive moment during the question and answer period, I raised my hand to suggest my own version of "trading places." It was one of those things that only an Activator principal would think about, much less do. To this day, if you asked me why I did it, I can only say that I was intensely curious about what went on in the modest-looking buildings and greenhouses located not far from our campus. Trading places would get me inside for a look around.

After the meeting adjourned, I went forward to meet Mr. Ball. If he thought I would vanish after my outrageous challenge, he was mistaken. He did appear slightly dazed at the thought of becoming an elementary school principal for a day, but I convinced him that we needed to model the kind of cooperation he had talked about earlier.

Before I left, we set a date and negotiated the terms. I learned that Carl's driver would not be at my disposal for the day, but I would have lunch in the corporate dining room after a session with all of the vice presidents. I told Carl that he would meet with my building leadership team and enjoy a free (or reduced-price) hot lunch in the cafeteria—corn dogs or tacos, no doubt. The day turned out to be a smashing success for both of us. I learned that Ball Seed Company produced the seeds from which three out of every four tomatoes in the world were grown. Carl learned about teacher tenure and union contracts.

I could not have predicted where my impulsive invitation to Carl would eventually lead. Our school-business partnership lasted for more than a decade. He encouraged the plant pathologists in his company to partner with my teachers to develop experimental research projects for our upper grade students. They regularly visited the greenhouses and research labs at Ball. Student teams prepared reports based on their research findings and presented them, complete with charts and graphs, to Ball's executives and scientists. The teachers became skilled horticulturists, and eventually we turned our classrooms into greenhouses for an annual Mother's Day plant sale. The students learned about growing, marketing, sales—and profit-and-loss statements. Carl provided the seed, soil, professionally constructed grow lights, fertilizers, and all of the technical assistance we needed.

We weren't the only ones who were learning. Carl figured out that schools operated nothing like his company. "Why, we'd go out of business in a heartbeat if we didn't spend big dollars on research and development," he told me. He read reams of education research for himself and was shocked by its poor quality in comparison to the tradition of experimentation he saw at work every day in his company. He invited education researchers from major universities to join him for roundtable discussions, paying what it took to buy their "brains" for the day. They came from Stanford, Columbia, and places in between, intrigued by this somewhat distractible, albeit brilliant, businessman who was obsessed with finding out all he could about how education research was funded, conceived, and disseminated. I was always invited to these roundtables where Carl would ask the questions and the researchers would tell him what they knew. Carl was frequently distressed by how little we really knew for certain in education.

Carl retired in order to spend more time with his new passion, education, and decided to take up teaching—substitute teaching, that is. I recommended a one-week student teaching experience under the tutelage of one of my master teachers, and Carl became our favorite substitute for any absences that we could schedule in advance with his secretary. When the district formed one of the first educational foundations in the county, I was asked to convince Carl to take a seat on the board of directors *and* make a sizable contribution to our coffers. Carl is now deceased, but his company still maintains the partnership we formed almost twenty years ago.

All of the highly effective principals I interviewed are Activators in their own ways. They are on the move, on the go, and quick to take advantage of any opportunity for advancing and enhancing their school's programs and reputations in the community. Tapping the talents of their teachers and parents, they collaboratively develop proposals, write grants, and design educational programs for parents, training for teachers, enrichment and acceleration opportunities for students, building improvements, and computer labs. Activators are indefatigable. They finish what they start, follow through on what they pledge to do, and quadruple their output by empowering and energizing others to work with the same degree of intensity and enthusiasm for their vision. Teachers, parents, and students find it difficult to say "no" to an Activator principal. For that matter, so do corporations, business leaders, foundations, and state departments of education.

The highly effective principal is an Activator—an individual with gumption (e.g., drive, motivation, enthusiasm, energy, spunk, and humor) enough to share with staff, parents, and students.

ACTIVATOR EXEMPLAR: CLARE MAGUIRE

Clare Maguire is an Activator. You met her briefly in Chapter 5 as an example of how to manage change, and there is no doubt that the Change Master and Activator traits are strongly dependent on one another. When Clare earned her master's degree in Educational Administration in 1976, she was the only woman in her class.

"I knew that if I were going to be successful in what was then a male-dominated field, I would have to work twice as hard and get twice the results. I will never forget the desolate feeling I had shortly after I received my first administrative position when I overheard someone in central office say, 'Don't expect too much. After all, she's young *and* she's a woman.'"

Those were fightin' words to an Activator principal like Clare, and they energized and motivated her to be the very best. Not that she needed any extrinsic motivation. For Clare is a bundle of energy and drive all on her own. She has her own definition of what it means to be an activator: "Activators are dynamic. They are persistent and outgoing. Frequently they are animated. They reflect and then act. They are able to blend their dreams with practicalities and common sense. They just do it. After decades of doing it, Activators say, 'It just happens.' Activating becomes as automatic as breathing. Consequently, it is difficult to pinpoint where one Activator benchmark begins and another ends. There is a continuous flow of striving to excel."

In one of her not infrequent outrageous moments, Clare arrived at a central office meeting to negotiate her upcoming budget wearing a general's helmet with two gold stars. Looking like a female version of General George Patton, she dramatized one of her favorite quotations from George: "Do something . . . lead, follow, or get out of the way." In another moment of zaniness, Clare showed up for a meeting with an associate superintendent to check out property lines in the woods dressed as Little Red Riding Hood.

But don't let Clare's sense of humor and fun-loving nature fool you. She is shrewd, smart, and all business when it comes to making it happen for her students. Her school is the only one in Missouri to have won two National Blue Ribbon of Excellence Awards, and she is constantly looking for ways to improve achievement and increase learning opportunities for students. She's willing to take risks and advocate for programs she believes in when others would play it safe.

Clare believed, after looking at the research, that elementary schools should have computers both in the classrooms *and* in a lab setting. Even though the local trend was to place computers in the classrooms, Clare knew it would be beneficial for her school to have both. The district only budgeted for television production studios at the secondary level, but Clare knew that TV production was the perfect way to challenge brighter students and give all students an opportunity to see how technology was used in the real world. She and her staff were convinced that media production would also help students develop writing and public speaking skills since they would write their own copy for the television announcements and deliver it.

Activators don't wait for central office to catch up with them. They just jump in and do it. Clare and her faculty found a way to fund computers for all of the classrooms, outfit a complete computer lab, *and* build a television production studio. Clare and her staff have received awards from the U.S. Department of Education, the state of Missouri, and CNN, and they've been featured on local television. But Clare doesn't really care about the awards. The most important outcome of the whole project is Pond School's achievement scores on the State MAP Test. Their Communication Arts score is consistently number one or two in the State of Missouri. Clare says, "If you want to raise achievement, it helps to take some risks and think outside the box."

Clare believes that motivating and energizing her teachers is one of her most important roles. "Unless I can motivate the staff to excel so that each child can reach their highest academic potential, I won't be successful. One of the most challenging things to do with a seasoned staff is to keep their youthful enthusiasm and zest for teaching alive, year after year. We have a spirit day and a casual day every week. Teachers love to wear comfortable clothes to work and save their clothing budget for other personal items. We have music in the halls every Friday morning. With a weekly bulletin and an open (principal's) door policy, faculty meetings are a rarity. They are only held when something important needs to be discussed and we need input from everyone."

Clare is up for anything that will motivate students and bring a little fun into school, especially if it's connected to golf. She sets up a mini golf course on Friday mornings and has a Hole In One Club for students who shine on her course. She has dressed as Dopey in the Seven Dwarfs play, because, as Clare explains, "You would never want a child to play a character named Dopey." If you need an Elvis impersonator, Clare is up for the role, but she confesses, "My personal favorite is wearing the glitter gown complete with a blue boa when some faculty members and I do our imitation of the Supremes." Clare may imitate the Supremes, but she really loves Pat Benatar best. Her favorite is "Hit me with your best shot. Fire away." Clare's version and her theme song: "Hit *it* with your best shot. Fire away. You just gotta go for it."

> "Two roads diverged in a wood, and I—
> I took the one less traveled by,
> And that has made all the difference."
>
> —Robert Frost (as quoted in Lathen, 1958, p. 105)

And going for it has been Clare's motto for twenty-five years. Yet she is still pushing forward. She recently analyzed her school's test data and found that the special education and African American students at Pond were not achieving as well as they had been in the past. She is reading, learning, attending workshops, thinking, and stirring up her faculty. Activators don't have time to rest on their laurels. There's another challenge just around the corner.

ACTIVATOR EXEMPLAR: TODD WHITE

When he was a kid, Todd White's teachers always recognized him as an Activator Exemplar. Here's what they've said about him: "We love having him in the classroom, but he can't stay in his seat." "He just can't let go of things sometimes." "He's a joy to work with, but he talks too much."

Growing up hasn't changed the way his teachers talk about Todd. They still describe him in similar terms: "If you don't grab him and hold on, he'll be gone." A hyperactive, highly creative, and energy-charged ten-year-old has become a highly successful and widely honored Activator principal. The little kid who colored outside the lines is now thinking outside the box. Well, not exactly. Todd would say, "What box? I didn't know there was a box." The man who confesses to writing eighteen billion sentences saying "I will not talk in class" is still hanging around schools stirring up trouble.

Fortunately for the students of South Carolina, Todd has channeled both his gumption *and* his penchant for saying the right things at the wrong time into raising student achievement—first in the two elementary schools where he has served as principal and then as Executive Director of the South Carolina Teacher Advancement Program. Along the way he has collected honors both for himself (National Outstanding Educator from the Milken Family Foundation and National Distinguished Principal from South Carolina) and his school (National PTA Parent Involvement Award and National Blue Ribbon School of Excellence Award).

In spite of all the certificates and plaques on his wall, Todd would scare some superintendents. "I don't see the world as a chain-of-command kind of thing," he explains. "If you hire me to do a job, I want you to get out of my way and let me do it. If I can't, then I want you to tell me about it. I don't follow rules real well, so if somebody wants all the rules followed, they need somebody else for the job." Of course, Todd doesn't scare teachers at all. He treats them just like *he* wants to be treated. He provides resources, forgives them when they make mistakes, and is there to pick up the pieces when they fail. But mainly Todd leaves them alone to do their jobs. His enormous optimism and energy are contagious.

"I never think about what could go wrong," he says. "I always see the glass as half full, and I try to get other people to see it the same way. I build safety nets under my teachers. They know that they can try something new, and if doesn't work, they won't get punished for failing."

Activators *can* sometimes wear you out, though. They're always up to something, and it's usually outrageous. Todd is no exception.

"My first year at Mitchell Road, I asked the faculty if they would put an act together for the all-school talent show. They flat out told me no. At that point, they were worried about maintaining their dignity."

As an Activator, Todd doesn't worry about things like that. He dressed up as Elvis that year and performed two songs. Of course, the kids loved it. Truth to tell, so did his teachers.

"That was a turning point for my teachers," Todd says. "They suddenly realized that it was OK to have fun at school."

> "In things pertaining to enthusiasm, no man [woman] is sane who does not know how to be insane on proper occasions."
>
> —Beecher (1887)

Todd loves to challenge his students to meet their reading goals by coming up with some wacky stunt he'll perform if they shine academically. On one occasion, he promised to jump into the community swimming pool (just a stone's throw away from the school) dressed in a suit, tie, shoes, and all the trimmings. Of course, his students kept their end of the bargain. What Todd didn't know was that his teachers had planned their own bit of wackiness. Before Todd had come up for air, ten fully clothed faculty members had jumped in to join him. If you can't change him, they had decided, you might as well join him!

Activators aren't all fun and games, however. Since Todd arrived at Mitchell Road, he has blended his brand of activation with accountability and responsibility, resulting in increased achievement for all students but especially poor and minority students. He leaves no stone unturned in tracking down the resources to support learning initiatives. One year his faculty gave him the Houdini Award for his ability to pull money out of his hat whenever it was needed for what they wanted to do.

The International Reading Association selected Mitchell Road for its Exemplary Reading Program Award in 2000. The program is designed to motivate students to set individual reading and achievement goals. "There are lots of carrots in our program," said Todd. "Incentives, goal setting, and accountability were the touchstones. Our students moved from reading below the fiftieth percentile on the state assessment to the mid-eightieth percentile in just five years."

Mitchell Road was the second ranked of fifty-four schools in Greenville County District, right behind the school with only 4 percent of its students receiving free or reduced-price lunch. At Mitchell Road, 40 percent of the students receive free or reduced-price lunch, and the transiency rate averages between 25 percent and 30 percent.

Todd's resolve and determination were tested when a central office administrator who did not share his fondness for "carrots" issued a directive banning them from the school's reading menu. Apparently, in this individual's opinion, "carrots" were "unhealthy" for children. Todd was understandably distressed but stood firm. "You can talk to me about this when I stop getting results. Otherwise, I don't want to hear about it." In situations like this, Todd relies on the wisdom of one of his favorite authors, Dr. Seuss. "Be who you are and say what you feel, because those who mind don't matter, and those who matter don't mind" (Seuss, 2002).

> "Nothing great was ever achieved without enthusiasm."
>
> —Ralph Waldo Emerson (as quoted in Cohen & Cohen, 1961, p. 154).

Where does Todd get all of his energy? He says, "From thinking about what can be. No matter how tired I am, if I'm thinking about what can be, there's something energizing and exciting about that. Even when I slow down and collapse on the sofa, I can't turn my mind off. So my periods of physical rest are actually times when I get a lot of thinking and planning done."

When Todd starts thinking and planning, his teachers, parents, and students get ready to leap into action. Since 1996, these are just a few of the things that have happened at Mitchell Road School:

- Parent volunteers have won awards from the South Carolina State Department of Education and the National PTA.
- The school has served as a demonstration site for technology and received reading awards.
- Todd has been recognized personally by the First Union Bank, the state of South Carolina, the Milken Family Foundation, and the National Association of Distinguished Principals.
- Four teachers have won Golden Apple Awards.
- Staff members have brought in grants totaling more than $250,000 to the school.

Activators have enough gumption left over at the end of every day to activate and motivate their teachers, parents, and students as well.

ACTIVATOR BENCHMARKS

Activators are definitely "high-maintenance" people. They never sit quietly in their offices shuffling papers. They are stirring things up; planning for the next big event; and motivating parents, teachers, and students who wouldn't have dreamed of raising their hands to volunteer for anything until they met their Activator principal.

7.1 Activators Mobilize People

Sergiovanni (1996) calls what Activators do *mobilizing people*. Activators are able to enlist parents and community members to their causes in amazing ways. Todd White started his mobilization efforts with a single house painter, and before long he had a whole crew of people renovating and repainting his building. Activator principals always have big dreams and plans about the things they want to see happen in their schools—interior decorating, technology, tutoring, day care, after-school programs, playground equipment, preschools, grant writing, newsletters, enrichment programs, landscaping, and library books. In the schools of Activator principals, parent and community volunteers routinely log 6,000 to 7,000 hours of volunteer service a year.

How do Activators persuade people to give up their valuable time and share their financial resources with their schools? Todd White could write the book on mobilization.

> You have to recognize the talents that people have and then put that knowledge together with the school's needs. Of course, that means taking the time to get to know people in more than just a superficial way. You have to get beyond the small talk and ask questions about their jobs, unique talents, interests, and hobbies. I used to keep that kind of information on a note pad in my pocket, but I ended up with so many note pads I had to turn them all over to a PTA committee. They developed a database with all of my information, and we eventually reached the point where we could identify a specific need and then pull up a list of people that fit that profile. This effort resulted in the Mitchell Road PTA winning the national PTA's parent involvement award in 2000. Ours was the only award given out that year. My teachers then began using parents in different ways, and our

"HIT THE GROUND RUNNING"

Sharon Beitel, "Rookie Principal of the Year," Elementary, Newtown, Connecticut

Stepping into the shoes of the formidable Dick Hoffman, who had successfully principaled Booth Free and Burnham Schools for over twenty-five years, was impossible. So I went to the shoe store and grabbed a new and different pair of cross training sneakers. With these sneakers, I could get between the two buildings quickly and effectively so that everyone would think that I could be at two places at once. I asked many reflective questions daily and throughout the year. I needed these sneakers to keep up with the staff as they answered my questions honestly and RAN with new ideas, direction, and enthusiastic focus. These cross trainers were also very good for all of the jumping up and down that I did cheering for the students and staff. My sneakers were also perfect for keeping my feet comfortable as I maintained a commitment to long, long days and nights. This comfort was important as I was then able to tap good humor and lots of laughter. These sneakers also allowed me to stay quick on my feet and focus our communities and board members on some serious needs that our facilities face.

As great as the sneakers were, an outstanding year could not have occured without 60 remarkable staff members, 265 wonder-full students, over 500 supportive parents, two cozy school facilities, and six wise administrative colleagues! Our accomplishments (at both schools) were many.

Overall, a renewed enthusiasm for continuous improvement and higher standards for all students and staff was bottom line. I stood by my vision of education and coached and supported the staff in realizing this vision.

parent involvement hours just skyrocketed. People love to help if you personally ask them to do something they can do successfully and then make them feel welcome and appreciated.

7.2 Activators Are Entrepreneurial

As an Activator principal in the early 1980s, I raised a few thousand dollars here and there, but the Activators of the twenty-first century have left me in the dust. Brenda Valentine, together with her faculty and parents, raised more than $500,000 in grants, donations, and in-kind contributions to build a state-of-the-art technology center. Gabe Flicker made home visits to ask for money, and with the help of others, raised $215,000 for a building expansion. Then he convinced a major foundation to place a $270,000 technology center in his school. Dawn Hurns procured grants totaling $300,000 for math instruction, technology, bilingual education, and educational support for immigrants. Jim Ratledge raised the funds to build a scenic nature trail through his school's twenty-two-acre campus that serves as an outdoor classroom. Larry Fieber has developed corporate partnerships that fund enrichment and learning support programs for his students. Terry Beasley developed community partnerships and secured funding that enabled him to convert previously unused locker rooms into well-equipped science and math labs. Byron Schwab, principal of Pilot Knob Elementary School in Eagan,

Minnesota, forged a partnership with Lockheed Martin that provided weekly mentors for students, volunteers who wired the building for Internet connections and instructed school staff in new technology, and funds for a portable planetarium program.

How do they do it? It's all about having big dreams and not being afraid to pick up the phone, knock on doors, write grant applications, and call on corporate sponsors. Todd says, "I always tell prospective donors, 'A contribution from you will make a difference for kids.'" He admits that people turn him down all the time. But that doesn't keep him from asking them again. Todd says, "Pretty soon, I know they'll start thinking, 'He's never going to quit until we give him something.' What they couldn't know was, once they gave me something, I'd be back asking for more."

Clare Maguire is very clear about the fact that she has always been absolutely legal in procuring funds for her school but says, "Sometimes a principal needs to find creative financing. I'm not shy about asking anybody for money. I've gone to the community for donations innumerable times. We got computers from companies that were upgrading to new ones. We've asked for donations from realtors who have made money from selling homes in the attendance area of our award-winning school, collected cans and coupons, and written grants. When all else falls through, we go to our PTA."

7.3 Activators Don't Wait to Be Told

Contributor Exemplar Lola Malone didn't wait for someone to mandate character education. She could see firsthand that discipline was taking more and more of her teachers' time, and that infractions were becoming more serious. Character education wasn't even being talked about in most schools in 1990, but Lola knew that with the way the world was going, somebody had to step in and teach children how to respect each other and work harder in school. So she and her staff designed a program they called Tyson Tigers . . . Children of Character. Lola's program had been up and running for about four years before anyone in central office heard about what she was doing. The Springdale school board went to the state school board convention where they heard a marvelous out-of-state speaker give a presentation on character education. Some of the board members were intrigued by the possibilities of doing something like it in their district. As they chatted with their fellow board members on the drive home, one of them, a father of students at Tyson, said, "Why, Lola's been doing that at Tyson for years."

> "The condition of the most passionate enthusiast is to be preferred over the individual who, because of the fear of making a mistake, won't in the end affirm or deny anything."
>
> —Thomas Carlyle, 1795–1881 (2000, n.p.)

When Activators see a need, they don't wait for all the lights to turn green. They get started immediately.

7.4 Activators Are Risk Takers

Activators don't think in terms of why something won't work. They only think of the reasons why it will. If Educator Exemplar Jean Hendrickson had listened to those who doubted her ability to establish the Core Knowledge curriculum in an inner-city school, the students of Mark Twain Elementary School would have missed a lifetime of learning. But she left her comfortable suburban school where success for all came effortlessly and took the risk.

Envisioner Exemplar Larry Fieber and Producer Exemplar Dale Skinner took the risks inherent in leaving their comfortable and predictable high school administrative positions to move to low-achieving elementary schools. What were they thinking? Certainly not that it wouldn't work. Activators are risk takers, but they do it with the supreme confidence that *they* will be able to make it work.

7.5 Activators Ask for Forgiveness Rather Than Permission

Activators are commonsense kinds of folks. Just make a rule that's silly, and they will find a way to circumvent it. Clare Maguire shares this example: "Recently it was recommended that parent communication be limited to twice-a-month newsletters. For seventeen years, the families in my school have received a weekly newsletter from me. My primary teachers have always published a weekly newsletter for parents, and the intermediate teachers send home a daily planner. The home-school connection and communication at our school is fantastic. In fact, 99 percent of the families responded during the most recent state inspection that they were happy with the home-school communication at Pond. I knew that suddenly limiting weekly newsletters at Pond was a grave mistake. So I just did not do it. I doubt if a principal would get fired for trying to enhance the home-school communication. Sometimes you just have to go for it."

7.6 Activators Run to Daylight

If you're not an "old-school" football fan, you might not be familiar with a play that Vince Lombardi, coach of the Green Bay Packers, used to shout out to his players on the field from time to time: "Run to daylight." According to Waterman (1990), Lombardi's command can be translated,

"Take advantage of an opportunity. Don't throw away the playbook, but don't blindly follow the rules if common sense tells you they won't work" (p. 25).

Activators "run to daylight" whenever they see an opportunity. One of Educator Exemplar Alan Jones's best runs concerned bilingual education, often a topic of controversy and consternation among educators.

Alan knew his program was in trouble, but he knew very little about bilingual education. So he found a guru in a neighboring district who was willing to give him a crash course.

Alan framed his problem for the guru this way: "Too many of our Hispanic kids are dropping out."

The guru just stared at him. "Jones, you're stuck in the old model of bilingual education," he said. "You're looking at all the wrong indicators. How many of your kids from Mexico are going on to college? How are they performing in postsecondary environments? That's what you should be looking at. The problem with your program is, you're not providing a content-rich environment. Start teaching your content areas in Spanish. How many kids do you have who *could* do calculus and geometry who are sitting in basic skills classes? What would *you* do if you were in those classes? Drop out, right?"

When the guru came up for air, Alan was speechless. As he described the experience to me, he said, "This man redirected my thinking from dropout prevention to the cognitive development of Hispanic students. The whole notion of teaching biology and calculus in Spanish kind of unnerved me in the beginning."

But the longer he thought about it, the more sense it made. For Alan, this was what Lombardi called an opportunity to "run to daylight." Throw away the playbook and go for the goal line. Don't look back. Alan went to his board of education and requested money, teachers, advanced classes taught by native Spanish speakers, and increased English learning opportunities with more ESL classes taught at increasingly challenging levels. He was very persuasive and went away with everything he requested. Whether you call it "churning and burning" as Alan does or "running to daylight" like Vince Lombardi, Activators take every opportunity to be out there in front of the pack.

THINK OUTSIDE THE BOX

Alan Jones, High School, West Chicago, Illinois

If your ideas are out-of-the box, you can be sure they will be in opposition to the systems and policies which support the organization. There is nothing inherently wrong with this situation. The systems were established to accomplish certain organizational goals (e.g., certification, documentation of state learning outcomes, assignment of teachers to classes, etc.). Large organizations require systems. However, effective leaders are able to find agreements or adjust systems so they support what is good for kids. They are activators.

7.7 Activators Don't Micromanage

Activators hate to be micromanaged and consequently they give their teachers as much freedom and autonomy as they need to make

> "I love being a principal! It's an action-packed job. I spend my days cheering, coaching, collaborating, visioning, questioning, developing, teaching, and empowering. How cool is that?"
>
> —Principal Sharon Beitel

things happen. Alan Jones just couldn't say no to the truant officer who wanted to design an alternative program. Clare Maguire advises, "Fire them up, trust them, and let them go and do their job. I personally have found that when my superiors micromanage me, I am not as successful." Doug Pierson gets out of his teachers' way. Brenda Valentine is emphatic: "I don't like micromanaging. I don't say, 'You can be in charge' and then pick everything to death."

7.8 Activators Make Things Happen

When Larry Pollock's special education teachers came to him with an idea for totally revising their workday, he was able to give them a positive answer before they left his office. Upper grade students were becoming increasingly reluctant to leave their classrooms for the intensive special help they needed. They hated the embarrassment of being "pulled out." The teachers came up with the incredibly sensible idea of starting a breakfast club called the Sunrisers for those students. They worked out the logistics of beginning their own school days earlier, and in a stroke of genius increased both their students' time on task *and* their motivation. A less effective principal would have bogged the project down with permissions, guidelines, regulations, forms, paperwork, contracts, and negotiations. Larry just said, "Yes, and what else do you need?" When staff members are willing to work harder, do more, and extend themselves for students, Activators empower and enable them.

7.9 Activators Are Outrageous

Todd White jumped into the community pool fully clothed. Clare Maguire sat on her roof and rode in on a motorcycle. My personal moment of outrageousness occurred when I promised my students I would jog around the building three times in my bathing suit for every classroom that met its reading goal. My secretary, slightly annoyed that I had once again charged off without consulting her about serious matters of this nature, told me in no uncertain terms that she would not be calling the newspaper photographer as she usually did when we planned a special event. "You're too old for this kind of nonsense," she said. "We can't have your picture in the paper in a bathing suit."

She assured me that she would think of something to get me off the hook, and sure enough, she did. It was a 1920s bathing ensemble, complete with modest ruffled bloomers, that covered the signs of aging on my thighs. All of my students were not as enthusiastic about the outfit as she was. "You're wearing your pajamas," said one disappointed sixth grader. "I thought you were going to wear a bikini," said another. "You mean I read all those books for this?" he said with disgust.

7.10 Activators Are Cheerleaders

Sharon Beitel taught first and second grade for eleven years before becoming the principal of two Connecticut schools in 2000. Her former principal, a special education expert, labeled Sharon ADHD, but Sharon disagreed with the diagnosis. "I'm certainly hyperactive," says Sharon, "but I'm also very focused." Sharon's activating philosophy can be summed up in one word: *Cheer.* The word appears on her license plate, and to her, it stands for spreading the word about the excitement of learning, celebrating the accomplishments of her staff, and even providing some exuberant cheerleading at a student assembly or two. Sharon definitely has cheerleading credentials. She was a varsity cheerleader for four years in high school and was hired to coach the team after she graduated. Sharon cheers for her faculty on a daily basis. Her excitement and enthusiasm for helping them "stay in the game," combined with her boundless energy, have enabled her to leap tall buildings with a single bound and provide leadership to two campuses at once. Activators just never seem to run out of energy and enthusiasm.

SUMMING IT UP

If you are more reserved than either Todd White or Clare Maguire, don't despair. All of the highly effective principals I interviewed have developed their own styles of activation, and you can too. You can still be an Activator, even if you don't do an Elvis impersonation. Activation has more to do with how you view your own ability to make things happen. If you are still waiting for all the answers before you begin to shake things up in your school, it's time to take a page out of Clare's or Todd's playbook and "run to daylight." If you are afraid it won't work, pair up with someone

Figure 7.1   Activator Benchmarks

Trait Number 7: The highly effective principal is an Activator—an individual with gumption (e.g., drive, motivation, enthusiasm, energy, spunk, and humor) enough to spare and share with staff, parents, and students.

    7.1   Activators mobilize people.
    7.2   Activators are entrepreneurial.
    7.3   Activators don't wait to be told.
    7.4   Activators are risk takers.
    7.5   Activators ask for forgiveness rather than permission.
    7.6   Activators run to daylight.
    7.7   Activators don't micromanage.
    7.8   Activators make things happen.
    7.9   Activators are outrageous.
    7.10 Activators are cheerleaders.

who will drag you into the pool with your clothes on. Identify the Activator Teachers on your faculty and ask them what three things they would change in your school if you gave them the green light. Then stop micromanaging and get ready to "churn and burn."

The Producer

"Do not mistake activity for achievement."

—Wooden (1997, p. 20)

In the late 1980s, my superintendent hired a management consultant to work with our administrative team. The word was that this high-powered expert had never consulted in education before, and we were highly suspicious of his ability to translate what worked in the corporate world to our small, suburban school district. We needn't have worried. Morris Shechtman was a master at nailing down culture and climate. "Call me Morrie," he said, as he poked, probed, and prodded us from top to bottom and inside out—personal interviews, focus groups, psychological testing, and a plethora of process activities. It quickly became evident that *our* bottom line was Morrie's bottom line: He had been hired to help us improve our "productivity"—a concept that scarcely mattered to most principals twenty years ago. Morrie's mantra, which he would later turn into a book, *Working Without a Net* (Shechtman, 1994), seemed bizarre to some of the old hands: "Be prepared for a loss of security and stability in your jobs and get ready for increased competition and accountability." In education? Those who had been planning on coasting to retirement felt the heat. More than a third of our team was gone by the following year.

"Activity"—pushing papers and implementing programs—was no longer acceptable. Productivity, accountability, and achievement were the new order of the day. Competition for students and accountability for their achievement are no longer far off in the future; they are facts of life for all administrators today.

Management guru Peter Drucker (2001) says, "Good intentions are no substitute for organization and leadership, for accountability, performance, and results" (p. 40), and highly effective principals enthusiastically embrace this philosophy. They do not abandon their altruistic motives to become cold-hearted number crunchers but rather combine caring with a sense of instructional relentlessness. They are as focused on achievement as a frenetic five-year-old at the candy counter. They don't give up until they get what they want! They recognize that academic achievement gives their students options and opportunities for the future.

The translation of high expectations, standards, and assessments into actual achievement is not an undertaking for the faint of heart. The inalterable demographic variables that for decades have been offered as excuses for low achievement (Bloom, 1980) do not miraculously lose their power to diminish teacher efficacy, depress student motivation, and destroy a school's culture and climate just because standards and assessments are mandated. The often-cited reasons for the achievement gap are as omnipresent and omnipotent as they have always been. However, highly effective principals, in concert with their staff members *and* parents, routinely find ways to do what Kathie Dobberteen calls "defying demographics."

The highly effective principal is a Producer—a results-oriented individual with a strong sense of accountability to taxpayers, parents, students, and teachers, who translates high expectations into intellectual development and academic achievement for all students.

PRODUCER EXEMPLAR: DALE SKINNER

Dale Skinner has been a Texas elementary school principal for nine years and his success at facilitating astounding academic success in challenging settings is no fluke. He has done it twice in less than a decade. When Dale became principal of the Loma Terrace Elementary School in the Ysleta School District of El Paso, there were skeptics on his faculty. After all, what could a former high school biology teacher and assistant principal in charge of discipline know about turning around a low-performing elementary school? The teachers were in for a huge surprise. Dale knew exactly what good instruction looked like, and he also knew that "good teaching is good teaching, no matter what the level."

The achievement data were depressing. Only 50 percent of the students passed the state reading assessment and slightly more than a third passed the mathematics test. The demographics were equally daunting. Ninety-two percent of the students were economically disadvantaged and nearly half were limited English proficient. The school's rating on the state's accountability system was Acceptable.[1] By the end of Dale's second year on the job, Loma Terrace had moved from Acceptable to Recognized status. Two years later, the school obtained the highest possible rating, Exemplary. It was an honor no other school in this huge urban district had ever received to that date, and their success was no flash in the pan. The school received three more Exemplary ratings under Dale's leadership before he relocated to San Antonio. The list of awards and recognition that came to the students and staff of Loma Terrace under Dale's leadership is impressive:

- Loma Terrace was named a Texas Title I Distinguished School for three consecutive years and was then honored in 1999–2000 as a national Title I Distinguished School (one of five in Texas and one of eighty-eight in the country).
- Just for Kids, a nonprofit watchdog group that monitors the percentage of high performing students in each school in Texas, ranked Loma Terrace first in the state in math for two consecutive years and third in reading, in its demographic category.
- The Disney Learning Corporation selected Loma Terrace as one of seven national finalists in 1999–2000 in its Spotlight School program.
- The Dana Research Center in Austin identified Loma Terrace as one of five Texas schools with an exemplary academic program for special education students and conducted research at the school regarding best practices.
- The American Institute of Research in Palo Alto, California, selected Dale Skinner as one of thirteen educators to serve on a committee to advise the U.S. Department of Education regarding the analysis of data to enhance student performance.

Dale is currently the principal at Eduardo Villarreal Elementary School (Northside Independent School District, San Antonio), where achievement zoomed from Acceptable to Exemplary in just one year, something no school in the Northside District had ever done. Other honors that have come to Villarreal include these:

- A Gold Performance Award in both reading and mathematics from the Texas Education Agency presented to schools in the top quartile of demographically comparable campuses in relation to the percentage of high-performing students
- A five-star rating from the National Center for Educational Accountability in recognition of Villarreal's standing in the top 20 percent of schools in Texas in its demographic category (i.e.,

percentage of low-income students, percentage of limited English proficient students, etc.)[2]

- A Successful Schools Award from the Texas Education Agency given in recognition of the number of students scoring in the top quartile for its demographic category[3]

To Dale, the astonishing success of his students at both Loma Terrace and Villarreal in the face of depressing demographics and a history of low achievement is no big deal—common sense, if you will. "It's just a matter of cause and effect," he explains. "Anybody can learn how to do it."

> "The litmus test for a good school is not its innovations but rather the solid, purposeful, enduring results it tries to obtain for its students."
>
> —Glickman (1993, p. 50)

It didn't take long for Dale to zero in on the critical attributes of raising student achievement: (1) a set of standards or learning outcomes and (2) a tool kit of effective strategies and methodologies to teach those standards to students. "I was fortunate to have a complete set of well-defined outcomes, the Texas Essential Knowledge and Skills, already in place," Dale explains. "I didn't have to figure out what needed to be taught. It was all right there in black and white."

What Dale did have to do, however, was to master the standards personally. He explains, "I took that binder home every night and read it and reread it until I knew exactly what my students were supposed to know and when they were supposed to know it. Then I looked at the test scores to determine our students' weaknesses. My next job was to determine the best possible way I knew to teach those particular standards. For example, I designed a lesson to teach 'summarization' because we had low scores in that area."

Less confident instructional leaders would no doubt blanch at Dale's next step—getting his teachers together and teaching his summarization lesson to the group. Not Dale, however. Producers like Dale know exactly where they want to be and aren't at all concerned about the fact that others aren't there yet. As Dale frequently says, "Only those that can see the invisible accomplish the impossible."

After teaching his lesson, Dale divided the teachers into small groups and encouraged each group to critique and fine-tune his lesson and then take turns teaching parts of the improved lesson they had developed to one another. Dale notes, "Eventually, we got to the point where we had a solid lesson that every teacher could use to teach summarization—one that got results." Other standards that Dale and his teachers have tackled with success include cause and effect, inference, estimation, and reasonableness. It all sounds so simple when you hear Dale explain it. But then, Dale sees the invisible.

Dale looked at the data from another perspective as well: How effective were individual teachers in getting results from their students? "If I have a teacher who is struggling," Dale explains, "I get a substitute for that person, and we work on teaching each other all day. I teach, the teacher teaches, we just play with instruction. I believe that I can help every teacher to be successful if I can work with them one-on-one like that." Dale rushes in where even angels fear to tread—and gets results.

He soon realized, however, that in order to spend the majority of his time on instructional improvement, he needed help with administrivia, the bane of every administrator's existence. He created a new job, an upper-level administrative clerk's position, to take care of the barrage of paperwork that threatened to bury him. "In order to get results, you have to think outside the box," advises Dale. Highly effective principals don't worry about obstacles. They simply find ways to remove them.

Dale and his staff recognize that achieving academic success with students is not like turning out a product on an assembly line. Student achievement is raised student by student. "We are relentless in making sure that no student falls through the cracks—tutoring, counseling, medical help—whatever it takes." At the beginning of the 2001–2002 school year, for example, Dale and the Villarreal staff identified approximately ninety students in Grades 3–5 (where the state assessments are given) as potentially at risk of not meeting the learning standards at their grade level. They set about to accelerate learning for them with individualized learning plans. At year's end, 290 of the 300 students passed the mathematics test, 273 of 293 passed reading, and all but one out of 82 students aced the fourth grade writing assessment. With the intensive efforts of Dale and his staff, more than seventy of the ninety at-risk students met the learning standards at their grade levels in all academic areas.

> "An emphasis on results is central to school improvement."
>
> —Schmoker (1999, p. 3)

Dale acknowledges, "It's a challenge to bring a student with an IQ of 75 to grade level, and when one of our students misses that cutoff, we take it personally, even if it's only by a point or two. But we do take great pride in knowing that there wasn't any intervention that we didn't try, not a stone we left unturned, to help those students succeed."

PRODUCER BENCHMARKS

Although Dale is the individual principal I chose to exemplify the Producer trait, all of the highly effective principals I interviewed focus on results and have a strong sense of accountability to their communities. Catherine Segura, principal of Avery Island Elementary School in Louisiana, speaks for her colleagues when she says, "I feel a deep commitment to this community. My children and grandchildren live near the school. Local businesses are committed to the school. I feel obligated to prepare the children of this area to be the very best they can be, not just academically but socially and morally. Perhaps it's because I have a vested interest in this community that effectiveness in this area is unquestionable for me. It is a necessity."

Although they are incredibly passionate about their work, highly creative in the ways they procure and deploy resources, and relentlessly driven by their individual visions and missions, Producer principals know that without systems, organization, structure, habits, and routine—"an integrated systems approach to school improvement" (Streifer, 2002, p. 10)—achievement doesn't just happen. Dale's story highlights three critical things that Producers do: (1) understand what students need to know and be able to do, (2) facilitate the development of strategies and methodologies to ensure that all students achieve, and (3) pay close attention to the academic needs of the students most at risk. Here are some other important ways in which Producers are able to raise and maintain academic achievement in their schools.

> **TAKE SMALL STEPS UNTIL YOU SEE SUCCESS**
>
> **Kathie Dobberteen, Elementary, La Mesa, California**
>
> In the beginning, teachers aren't sure they can do it [raise achievement]. But if you focus on meeting small but measurable incremental goals, student achievement goes up almost magically. When it happens, it energizes the whole school. In the spring of 2000–2001, 91 percent of our students were at or above grade level in reading. In June of 2002, we made it to 92 percent—a time for genuine celebration. [In 1996, when Kathie and her staff set their first reading goal, only 42 percent of their students were reading above grade level.] Ninety-eight percent of our fifth graders went on to middle school reading at or above grade level. All of our state standardized test scores (SAT9) are now in Stanines 6 and 7.

8.1 Producers Believe That Achievement Is the Bottom Line

A back-to-school article featuring "good" schools recently appeared in my local newspaper. The premise of the story was that achievement is not critical when defining a "good" school. The reporters described one particularly "good" school, noting that it had tidy halls, well-behaved students, caring teachers, and supportive parents—critical prerequisites to academic achievement, to be sure. However, the reporters went on to excuse the school's below-average achievement by noting that more than 80 percent of the students are eligible for free or reduced-price lunch and more than 30 percent are highly mobile, explaining, "many schools will never attain the high test scores that have become standard in wealthy districts. . . . There is more to a good school than test scores" (Chesnick & Bustamante, 2002, p. 4A). Highly effective principals know that "demographics don't have to define student performance" (Kathie Dobberteen), and they routinely prove it.

8.2 Producers Never Mistake Activity for Achievement

The phrase "Do not mistake activity for achievement" was heard frequently in the practices and games of retired UCLA basketball coach John Wooden during the years that he won ten NCAA championships. He could have been talking to a group of educators when he coined the phrase rather than to his championship teams. Educators are often guilty of promoting activity—programs, implementation, change, and innovation—over achievement, particularly achievement that is measured by standardized or mandated tests. I have heard the following timeworn phrases so often I have them memorized: "There's more to school than achievement." "You can't measure all that a child gets out of school from an achievement test." "Teachers just end up teaching to the test, and the test drives instruction." "What can one test on one day tell us about a child?" Of course, all of these statements and questions do contain grains of truth. However, when they become excuses for evading accountability, they are not acceptable.

> **FOCUS ON THE PRODUCT**
>
> **Jeanne Stiglbauer, High School, Columbia, South Carolina**
>
> I've been accused of being so focused on results that I couldn't celebrate, and I must admit I do often put in eighty-hour workweeks. But when it comes to students, my motto is, "Leave no stone unturned." If you ask most educators what the "product" of a school is, they will say "students," but at Dreher High School, "student work" is the product. I have focused from the beginning on the importance of students producing excellent work. Whether it's in the classroom, on the playing field, or in the technology lab, our emphasis is on a quality student product. In the beginning, it was hard to convince high school teachers to display student work in the hallways, but we've progressed to the point where we now have a lesson plan template in which the student product is defined and described in detail for every lesson. Teachers know before they begin a lesson or activity precisely what they want their students to be able to produce as a result of their instruction.

8.3 Producers Are Data Driven

Highly effective principals know that "if productivity is to be integrated into the organizational culture, a vehicle for monitoring progress, providing feedback, setting quantifiable objectives and evaluating [student] performance is a *sine qua non*" (Belcher, 1987, p. 51). Summative assessments, such as standardized tests or state assessments, are useful only to a point. They are generally inadequate when it comes to helping teachers monitor and plan for *daily* instruction. Summative tests do not provide the immediate and continuous feedback that is essential for making mid-course corrections *during* implementation. Monthly curriculum-based assessments are more relevant and serve to keep everyone focused on specific and measurable short-term goals. Without the knowledge regarding student progress that is gleaned from frequent "dipsticking," teachers are left to guesstimate the effects of their instruction.

In order to raise or maintain achievement, either schoolwide or in some subpopulation of students (e.g., girls in math classes, limited English proficient students in reading, incoming students from one particular feeder school), both longitudinal (summative) and current (formative) data are needed. Collecting data is relatively easy. Organizing it into a usable format is the point at which many principals hit a brick wall (Streifer, 2002).

Most schools have reams of data stacked in dusty storage rooms or hidden away on outdated hard drives. When student demographics are in one database, grades are located in another office, and test scores are found in still another set of files, it's impossible to do anything meaningful with the data. In the La Mesa-Spring Valley School District in California, one database houses SAT9 scores, district writing scores, and a variety of demographic variables that allow for the disaggregation of students by socioeconomic status, ethnicity, and gender. It also provides information for parents and teachers on the degree to which their students have met the California state standards.

Kathie Dobberteen and her staff regularly use the district's database in planning and decision making, but in their efforts to improve reading achievement and zero in on specific needs, they have also established a schoolwide reading database containing curriculum-based and

---

DON'T ACCEPT EXCUSES

Margaret Garcia-Dugan, High School, Glendale, Arizona

When I began my principalship, I would hear all kinds of excuses about why our students couldn't learn—their lack of ability, their socioeconomic status, their lack of English language proficiency, or their lack of a strong foundation from elementary school. I decided to keep focused on my goals: (1) achievement for all students and a belief that all students can and will learn and (2) a safe and orderly campus. Every meeting I had and every chance I got, I would dismiss excuses and tell teachers that it wasn't productive to spend time on excuses. Over and over I would say, "Our job is to find ways to get our students to the intended level of achievement—whatever it takes."

standardized assessment data over a six-year period. Kathie says, "Having comprehensive assessment data available for every student during grade-level planning meetings has enabled teachers to set performance goals with far more accuracy and specificity than had ever been possible in the past."

8.4 Producers Pay Attention to Individual Students

In *Bird by Bird: Some Instructions on Writing and Life*, Anne Lammot (1994) tells this story: "Thirty years ago my older brother, who was ten years old at the time, was trying to get a report on birds written that he'd had three months to write. [It] was due the next day. We were out at our family cabin in Bolinas, and he sat at the kitchen table close to tears, surrounded by binder paper and pencils and unopened books on birds, immobilized by the hugeness of the task ahead. Then my father sat down beside him, put his arm around my brother's shoulder, and said, "Bird by bird, buddy. Just take it bird by bird" (p. 19).

Producer principals recognize that even when the mission is a major one, it must be tackled "bird by bird." Every student counts, and the needs of individual students must be attended to with loving care and, in many cases, highly prescriptive programs. High school students who do not know how to read must be taught. If not now, then when? Special education and limited English proficient students need direct instruction and extended opportunities to learn. If not you, then who? There are too many transient students. If not here, then where? Achievement can only be raised student by student.

8.5 Producers Have Academically Focused Missions

At Dale Skinner's school, the mission is straightforward: "providing positive educational experiences which foster Academic, Social, and Personal Success for all our students, enabling them to become productive and responsible citizens in our multicultural society" (Villarreal Elementary School, 2002). Note that academic success comes first. It's not the *only* goal, but it is the *first* one. Producers know that a mission statement is only as meaningful as the principal who stands behind it.

LET THE DATA DO THE TALKING

Kathie Dobberteen, Elementary, La Mesa Dale, California

Data is irrefutable. It's not a matter of, "You're a bad teacher." I don't have to judge the teacher. I let the data do the talking. Teachers are either producing results or they're not, and the data tell the story. My role is one of meeting with a teacher as a colleague to look at the data and ask questions about what we see. The focus becomes, "How can we work together on this?" "What are we going to do for this child or for your class?"

8.6 Producers Make Research-Based Decisions

Some of us have had to learn the hard way that rushing to judgment and implementing programs that simply add more "activity" to the curriculum won't give us results. Dawn Hurns, of Palm Springs North Elementary School in Hialeah, Florida, says, "I've changed my approach over the past few years. I've become a far more discriminating consumer of information and research. *Before* we implement a new curricular approach schoolwide, we do it on a pilot basis and then evaluate its effectiveness by analyzing the data." Producers do not preside over what Bryk, Sebring, Kerbow, Rollow, and Easton (1998) call "Christmas tree schools," a phrase they coined to describe schools where "activity" has run amok: "There were many new programs—not just a few—and a great deal of activity and hoopla surrounded them. Some of these new initiatives may have some real strength and integrity. But, because they do not cohere as a group and may even conflict, their impact is minimal at best, and potentially negative" (p. 123).

Ignoring the seductive claims of consultants, salespersons, and articles in the popular professional journals is difficult, particularly when they are saying what you want to hear—that a particular program, curriculum, methodology, or policy is the answer to the achievement gap. To keep teachers focused on what works in the context of your school, rather than on what's popular in a neighboring district, takes backbone.

Tom Williams, principal of Walton-Verona Elementary School in Verona, Kentucky, has a mantra: "If it works, it works." He encourages teachers and instructional assistants to share ideas that have the potential to improve student achievement, but a focus on research-based instruction is paramount. Saying no to a program that lacks solid research to support it or to a methodology that conflicts with the school's mission, even if it's a gift from a generous donor or a publishing company, is part of what Producers do to stay on course.

PAY ATTENTION TO RESEARCH

Margaret Garcia-Dugan, High School, Glendale, Arizona

We look at the research and do not go off on irrelevant tangents. For example, starting the school day later and block scheduling were two of the most popular and persuasive organizational trends at the high school level. They are very expensive, time-consuming, and highly distracting. We said "no" to both of them because neither of them had the potential to contribute anything to our mission—increased student achievement and a safe and orderly environment for students. The research wasn't solid. Now on the other hand, a group of teachers came to me with an idea for using the reciprocal teaching cognitive strategy (Palincsar & Brown, 1989) and suggested we implement it in all of our content classes. We looked at the research and it was solid. So—we put together a plan, trained our teachers, and did it.

8.7 Producers Hold Teachers Accountable

Highly effective teachers thrive on accountability. Now retired and writing full-time, Johanna Haver taught English, foreign language, and English as a second language (ESL) in the Phoenix Union High School District for eighteen years. She has worked in schools with both high and low expectations. Which does she prefer? "I absolutely love teacher accountability, respect for instruction, and discipline," she asserts. "I have experienced what an enormous difference it makes to have a principal who visits my classroom frequently; conferences with me about my teaching; asks for evidence that I am notifying parents of students' progress and am teaching to clearly defined, educationally sound objectives; and expects to see lesson plans, tests, and examples of students' work. I think the solution to our crisis in education is to insist that all principals take control of their schools and produce results" (Haver, 1995, p. B7).

Producers recognize that effective teaching is the *sine qua non* of school improvement. The basis for Change Master Exemplar Marjorie Thompson's sustained achievement efforts at Kelso School was a powerful coaching model in which teachers were able to observe, practice, receive feedback, and continually fine-tune their instructional methods. Culture Builder Exemplar Gabe Flicker hired a part-time assistant principal to focus solely on instructional improvement and coaching; Dale Skinner had the expertise to personally coach his teachers; Jean Hendrickson trained her teachers in a totally new approach to curriculum; and Jeanne Stiglbauer restructured the school day to permit teachers to talk about teaching and learning.

> **TACKLE THE TROUBLE SPOTS**
>
> **Lorraine Fong, Elementary, Inglewood, California**
>
> If there are five teachers at the third grade level and only three of them are getting top-notch results with their students in a specific area, these three teachers and I have a responsibility to help the other two teachers figure out what to do differently, and we have to do it in a collaborative way. We're at the point in this process where our teachers are able to be up-front and honest with me and with each other. "My scores are lousy. What can I do? What did you do? How did you teach that lesson to get such good results?" My job is to facilitate that kind of dialogue.

Certainly, parent involvement, safe environments, and collegial staff relationships are foundational to meaningful change. But without effective teaching, the critical attribute that defines a school—learning—will be diminished, if not missing altogether. I have been in many schools where parent volunteers are tripping over each other, teachers are friendly and caring, and students are well behaved and mannerly. Unfortunately, the principals of these schools have failed to cultivate and facilitate effective

Figure 8.1

SHARE RESPONSIBILITY

Carol Schulte-Kottwitz, Elementary, Ellisville, Missouri

I was frustrated because whenever the district's writing scores were rank ordered, our school was at the bottom. My first inclination was to blame the fourth grade teachers [where the test is given] and ask them, "How are we going to solve this problem?" I tried that, and fortunately they came right back at me: "Why are you pointing your finger at us? What about third grade?"

They were absolutely right, and that's when we initiated our schoolwide writing project. We agreed as a staff that everyone in the school would be responsible for improving our students' writing. I'm not an expert in writing at all, but I will confess that the hardest thing as a principal sometimes is to let go of a project like this. After all, you're responsible. But you're not! Fortunately, I was able to let go.

Our goal was that all students would read and write at or above grade level every year. A staff committee put together a professional development program that has resulted in a significant increase in student achievement in writing that has been sustained over a three-year period. In addition to raising the writing proficiency of our students, we also received a U.S. Department of Education Professional Development Award, which was a real boost to our staff. (Kottwitz, 2000)

instruction. Crucial to student learning is the ownership by teachers of their students' achievement. Meaningful change in schools is only possible when teachers have a strong sense of efficacy regarding their personal ability to make a difference in the lives of students and when they are able to take both responsibility *and* credit for making it happen. Teacher empowerment is essential to getting results (Lee, Bryk, & Smith, 1993; Rowan, 1990). And it's the principal who can ensure that.

SUMMING IT UP

Ron Edmonds (1981) said, "We can, whenever and wherever we choose, successfully teach all children whose schooling is of interest to us. We already know more than we need to do that. Whether or not we do it must finally depend on how we feel about the fact that we haven't so far" (p. 53).

There are several possible responses you might have to reading about the successes of Producers like Dale Skinner, Kathie Dobberteen, Carol

Figure 8.2   Producer Benchmarks

Trait Number 8: The highly effective principal is a Producer—a results-oriented individual with a strong sense of accountability to taxpayers, parents, students, and teachers who translates high expectations into intellectual development and academic achievement for all students.

8.1 Producers believe that achievement is the bottom line.
8.2 Producers never mistake activity for achievement.
8.3 Producers are data driven.
8.4 Producers pay attention to individual students.
8.5 Producers have academically focused missions.
8.6 Producers make research-based decisions.
8.7 Producers hold teachers accountable.

Schulte-Kottwitz, Jeanne Stiglbauer, Nancy Moga, Catherine Segura, Michelle Gayle, Margaret Garcia-Dugan, and Lorraine Fong. All of the responses are quite predictable, and you may even experience all of them, albeit one at a time. One possible response is to feel that they are so unique and talented that you could never do what they have done.

Ah, but you *can* achieve your own version of success by incorporating their suggestions and ideas where they fit into your school and your style.

Another thought that may go through your mind, if you are at all human and the least bit honest with yourself, is to feel somewhat envious, a little like Gore Vidal, the bad boy author, who is quoted as saying, "Whenever a friend succeeds, a little something in me dies" (Farson, 1996, p. 115).

You are permitted a brief, but private, moment of immaturity, but then get to work on the task at hand. Your students, parents, and teachers are waiting for you.

A third response on your part might be an attempt to mandate or dictate what folks like Dale Skinner and Kathie Dobberteen have done, with no regard for the unique qualities of *your* staff, students, and community or for the importance of building trust and creating a culture to support high achievement at the same time that you are focusing on results.

Remember, being a Producer principal is never a solo act. It may take a village to raise a child, but it takes a community to nurture the intellectual development and raise the academic achievement of its students. Tap into the talents that you, your staff, and your parents bring to the task. Produce your own show!

NOTES

1. The Texas accountability system currently has four tiers: Exemplary, Recognized, Acceptable, and Low Performing. To receive an Exemplary rating, schools are required to have at least a 90 percent passing rate on the reading, writing, and math assessments. In addition, 90 percent of each ethnic group and 90 percent of economically disadvantaged students must pass the test. To receive a Recognized rating, schools must achieve a passing rate of 80 percent to 89 percent. Acceptable schools have a 50 percent to 79 percent passing rate. Schools below the 50 percent passing rate are considered Low Performing.

2. A complete description of the ratings can be found at the National Center for Educational Accountability Web site: www.ecs.org/html/offsite.asp? document=http://www.measuretolearn.org/

3. Villarreal is a Five Star, Gold Performance, Exemplary school, a distinction that takes into account both quantity and quality. Whether Villarreal is compared only with schools in its own demographic group or with all schools, it stands out as exceptional.

The Character Builder

*"Do not say things. What you are stands over you the while and thunders
so that I cannot hear what you say to the contrary."*

—Ralph Waldo Emerson (as quoted in
Douglas & Strumpf, 1998, p. 85)

Character, or the lack of it, is a hot topic in schools today. Educators
are desperate to create more humane and caring schools—not only
as an antidote to prejudice and violence from within but also to the hatred
and terrorism without. Character-building programs are more the rule
than the exception, and many states now mandate them. Some programs
are homegrown and unique, like the Value Pumpkin Walk that has
become a yearly October tradition at Legacy Elementary School in
American Fork, Utah (Utah State Department of Education, 2002) or the
Children of Character program at John Tyson Elementary School in
Springdale, Arkansas (Malone, 2002). Other programs, like Character
Counts™ (2002), have a nationwide presence and are used by coalitions
of schools, communities, and nonprofit organizations to teach the Six
Pillars of Character—trustworthiness, respect, responsibility, fairness,
caring, and citizenship—to students.

Do character education programs work? "If 'working' means improving students' academic achievement, behaviors, attendance and truancy
rates, school climate, and teacher morale, the answer is yes" (DeRoche &
Williams, 2001, p. 20). However, Lemming (1994) reports that more
effective than lectures, videos, codes, and pledges are "the nature of the

environment . . . the messages it sends to individuals, and the behaviors it encourages and discourages" (p. 57).

What do schools with character actually look like? Sergiovanni (1999) calls them *virtuous schools* and cites the bodies of research on school effectiveness (Brookover & Lezotte, 1979; Edmonds, 1979) and school culture (Deal, 1987; Sergiovanni, 1984) as evidence that character is a strong correlate of school success (p. 99). A 1990 RAND Corporation report, *High Schools With Character,* enumerates the following qualities found in secondary schools with character: high levels of school pride; commitment to a common cause; a willingness to accept responsibility; a mutual respect for one another on the part of students and teachers; an emphasis on honesty, reliability, and fairness; and a respect for individual rights but not at the expense of the school community (Hill, Foster, & Gendler, 1990).

> "Character is a compatible mix of all those virtues identified by religious traditions, literary stories, the sages, and persons of common sense down through history."
>
> —Novak (1986, p. 1)

How do schools become virtuous? The proliferation of character-building programs aside, the most powerful force for building character in schools is derived from the lives of the adults in that school and most particularly, from the life of the principal. Once, in a domestic moment that seemed to last forever, I labored over a counted cross-stitch of the well-known poem "Children Learn What They Live" (Nolte, 1972). I hung it in my office as a daily reminder of the impact that my words and actions had on students. If the principal's words are critical and hostile, similar words will soon become commonplace in classrooms, cafeterias, and playgrounds. If the principal is unfair, disrespectful, and discouraging, parents will grow angry and frustrated. If the principal gossips about families in the school community, speaks disparagingly of a student, or makes fun of a fellow administrator, everyone will soon feel free to follow the leader. The words and actions of the principal permeate a school.

Some have said that character is "what you are in the dark" (D. L. Moody, as quoted in Prochnow & Prochnow, 1962, p. 29) when no one is looking or "knowing what is right and doing it" (Telushkin, 1998, p. 59). More formally, character can be thought of as a "cluster of interlaced ideas and social virtues that includes morality, ethics, honesty, and human values" (Hawley, 1993, p. 129).

The highly effective principal is a Character Builder—a role model whose values, words, and deeds are marked by trustworthiness, integrity, authenticity, respect, generosity, and humility.

CHARACTER BUILDER
EXEMPLAR: TOM PAULSEN

Tom Paulsen is a Character Builder—an individual who is committed to what Glickman (1990) calls a "cause beyond oneself." It's an unusual role for a high school principal, particularly of a large, prestigious high school in an upscale suburb. Typically, principals in schools like these are too busy with politics and paperwork to worry about building character. After all, their students come from supportive families with high expectations where good manners are the norm and attending college is a given.

Tom has been the principal at Naperville Central High School in Illinois for thirteen years and was an assistant principal there for eight years prior. He has infused the building with his character—respect, humility, integrity, and trustworthiness—by modeling those traits every day. When asked about student achievement at Naperville Central, Tom responds almost apologetically: "We *are* up there academically. On most measures of academic success in a school, we do quite well. I will tell you, though, that what I am most proud of is hearing parents say that Naperville Central is a place where they and their children feel welcomed, accepted, and cared for. The fact that parents trust us is very important to me."

Tom asserts, "Knowing that we are shaping students' lives for the future means more to me personally than the academic or athletics successes of the school." He will tell you, if pressed, however, that his students have one of the top five ACT averages in the state of Illinois and that Naperville Central did win the state football championship the previous year. But he seems relatively unimpressed with these accomplishments that would have most high school principals waxing eloquent. Instead, Tom is focused on the speech he gives to graduating seniors every year. He chuckles softly when he explains, "Although I give a different speech every year, the message is always the same. 'If you really want to change the world, you have to put others before yourself.' Success for me is all wrapped up in building character. In fact, I think it's the most important job that a principal has."

What kinds of things does Tom do every day to build character in his school? He is constantly modeling humility, trust, respect, and integrity. Whether he's talking to his superintendent or to a frightened freshman— each one gets his undivided attention and respect. "Being disrespectful of others drives me crazy, but when that disrespect is shown by teachers to students, it's terrible. When students are put down and humiliated by teachers, it tears them apart. Of course, some young people do know how to get under adults' skins, but we have a responsibility to treat students with respect, even when we're calling them to task."

Whenever Tom hires new staff members, he looks for individuals who are as sensitive to their character-building roles as they are to the demands of their disciplines. "We want teachers who are as passionate about students and their development as human beings as they are about content." An ongoing program called RESPECT (responsibility, equality, sincerity, pride, empathy, communication, and trust) recognizes students and staff who demonstrate respect. "It's always difficult to measure the impact that a program like this has on a school as large and diverse as Naperville Central, but on the exit survey that we give to graduating seniors every year, they overwhelmingly tell us, 'Don't stop focusing on respect.'"

Listening to students is a big part of character building for Tom. He builds it into his calendar nearly every day. "I'm here early in my office with the door wide open so everyone knows right where to find me. Students and teachers don't hesitate to drop in when they have a problem. During passing periods, I'm out in the halls, interacting with students informally. I constantly put myself in places where I can listen to people. At lunchtime I head for the students' cafeteria, the teachers' lunchroom, or one of the departments where they're more apt to be talking shop over lunch."

> "To be persuasive we must be believable; to be believable we must be credible; to be credible, we must be truthful."
>
> —Edward R. Murrow (as quoted in Kouzes & Posner, 1987, p. 15)

When I asked Tom how it was possible for him to get to know all of his students in a school as large as Naperville Central, he admitted that it takes time. He could well delegate this job to his staff of nine administrators, but he believes that part of character-building is being a visible presence in his building—out there where students can see him and get to know him. Tom says, "If you ask any of the Naperville Central students if they know the principal, most of them would be able to say, 'Sure, I know who he is.' There are probably 300 students whom I know *very* well. Most of them are seniors, and I've developed relationships with them over their careers here. Those students all feel free to stop in and talk to me about anything. Often after a conversation I will refer them to a social worker, guidance counselor, or substance abuse prevention coordinator, but the fact that they were comfortable enough to come to me in the first place is what matters. There are probably another 600 students that I know by name, and I'm constantly working on getting to know more of them. I always pay a lot of attention to the freshman class (780 students) at the beginning of each year. When I sit down with a group of them at lunchtime, I can tell they're thinking: 'Who's he? What's he doing here?' But they soon learn what I am doing there. I want to get to know them. I really am interested in their lives, their plans, and their dreams."

Tom listens in other ways as well. He explains: "Several years ago when we started giving an exit survey to seniors, one of the areas that really came up short was our guidance department. The students talked about how friendly, welcoming, and caring their teachers were but reported that when they went to the guidance department, they felt like no one had the time to help them. 'My counselor doesn't know me,' was a frequent response. We took this feedback very seriously. We want every student to feel welcomed and respected everywhere in the school. We totally revamped the organization of the department as well as the expectations for the counselors, and our ratings have improved every year since."

If you follow Tom around on a given day, you might see him helping a custodian with a heavy load, opening a door for a teacher, or dropping his paperwork to focus his complete attention on a distraught student. These are small, and to some, insignificant, acts, but to Tom, they are the most important things he will do that day. Not only does he talk to students about putting others before themselves on graduation day each June—he also walks his talk on all of the other days of the school year.

CHARACTER BUILDER BENCHMARKS

Tom Paulsen isn't the only Character Builder among the highly effective principals I interviewed. Many of them put character at the top of their trait list in terms of importance. Terry Beasley believes that "a highly effective principal has to have a good heart." Jim Ratledge's definition of character is found in the Boy Scout Law (Boy Scouts of America, 2002), a powerful influence on his own character development as an Eagle Scout. Byron Schwab wraps up the character package this way: "Without character, the other nine traits could well be rather superficial, insincere, and very temporary."

9.1 Character Builders Are Human

In his essay *Help! How Do I Teach Character?*, Rabbi Steven Carr Reuben (1998) reminds us that nobody's perfect. "It takes character to teach character, but it also takes character to admit when you are wrong." Rabbi Reuben advises, "If we show our . . . [students and teachers] the courage and integrity to confront our own weaknesses as human beings, we will teach some of the most important lessons about true character" (p. 133).

The students at John Tyson Elementary School in Springdale, Arkansas, routinely interview Contributor Exemplar Lola Malone for their writing assignments. One of the questions they often ask is, "Have you ever failed a subject in school?" Lola shares, "I tell them the truth. I failed a subject, but I didn't fail life. It *was* one of the most humiliating and embarrassing experiences of my life, and I haven't forgotten a minute of it to this day, but it helped me become a more effective and empathetic teacher."

While Lola's failing grade in Spanish was a traumatic memory, her inability to speak Spanish didn't matter much. That is, until her school neighborhood began to change. In the past six years, the number of Spanish-speaking families in her school has grown from a handful to nearly half (45 percent). After all these years, Lola's failing Spanish grade has come back to haunt her.

"I could have kept my mouth shut about the whole thing," Lola said, "but I felt as though my failing grade in Spanish was a character flaw. I didn't have the perseverance and patience (two of the character words in the character education program at Tyson) that I expect from our students when *they* encounter something that's difficult for them." Lola decided that she needed to confess her failure to her Spanish-speaking parents. "It's humbling for me to tell that story," she says, "but it has built a bond between the parents and me. I don't take the position that it's easy to learn English as an adult or even as a child. I never feel superior when parents need a translator or speak to me in halting phrases. I admire and applaud them for any attempts they make, and I understand their reticence to expose their lack of knowledge to the principal. I was absolutely terrified when my Spanish teacher expected me to respond orally to a question."

Character Builders know they aren't perfect and are able to use their own failures to build bridges of understanding with parents, teachers, and students.

> **JIM RATLEDGE, K–8, MARYVILLE, TENNESSEE**
>
> I have always believed that we should love children more than adults in our business. By that I mean that children's interests should take precedence over staff interests. That position has not always been a popular one in my school, but I believe that people respect me for it and know where I come from.

9.2 Character Builders Are Trustworthy

Jack Lowe, Jr., is the president of TD Industries, a highly successful nationwide mechanical and electrical construction and service company. It can be found on a list of "fun companies to work for" on the Internet (Fun Companies, 2002). If you are wondering what construction and service have to do with the principalship, the answer is "a great deal if you're talking about trustworthiness." TD is organized and managed around the concept of "servant leadership," and its commitment to this concept has fostered an environment where employees trust leadership to listen to their thoughts and ideas. And the leadership team has learned to trust the judgment of the employees (TD Industries, 2002a).

Jack serves as a trustee on the Dallas Independent School District Board of Education and is committed to improving educational opportunities for the young people of the Dallas area. I asked him what advice he would give to principals who are faced with tough challenges in their communities. He said, "I would tell them to work on trust above and beyond anything else."

Jack knows what he is talking about. In *Trust in Schools: A Core Resource for Improvement*, Bryk and Schneider (2002) provide data correlating the trust levels in a school with its student achievement. They found that in schools where trust was high between faculty members, parents, and administrators, achievement was higher than in schools with low levels of trust, even controlling for factors like poverty and student mobility.

The values of TD Industries include concern for and belief in individual human beings, valuing individual differences, honesty, fairness, responsible behavior, high standards of business ethics, and building trusting relationships. Jack says, "We believe people react positively when trust and confidence are placed in them and when the best is expected of them. We try to reflect this belief in all our relationships." Not only is trust essential to the bottom line in business, it makes a huge difference to the bottom line in education.

> The Master has no mind of her own.
> She works with the mind of the people.
> She is good to people who are good.
> She is also good to people who aren't good.
> This is true goodness.
> She trusts people who are trustworthy.
> She also trusts people who aren't trustworthy.
> That is true trust.
> The Master's mind is like space.
> People don't understand her.
> They look to her and wait.
> She treats them like her own children.
>
> —Lao-Tzu (6th century BCE/1992, p. 49)

9.3 Character Builders Have Integrity

Integrity, according to Hawley (1993), "is having the courage to live by your inner truth" (p. 132). In *Good to Great: Why Some Companies Make the Leap and Others Don't*, Collins (2001) calls it being brutally honest about reality. He says, "It is impossible to make good decisions without infusing the entire process with an honest confrontation of the brutal facts" (p. 88). Although Collins is referring to the corporate world, the principle is equally applicable in education. Highly effective principal Terry Beasley explains the role that honesty has played in his principalship: "Principals are always 'supposed' to be on the side of teachers, but I

"Courage isn't the absence of fear; it's proceeding in spite of it. Not holding back something you know needs to be said, telling the truth in the face of peril and pitfall. It's being candid when it may be dangerous. It's going ahead and doing it or saying it even if it's uncomfortable."

—Hawley (1993, p. 133)

believe honesty is the best policy. You have to go home and put your head on the pillow at night. My wife tells me, 'You're too honest.' I ask her right back, 'How can you be *too* honest? The truth will set you free.' And the truth has set our school free—free from ineffective teachers who didn't care about kids and learning. I simply could not ignore them and hand out satisfactory evaluations to everybody just because that's the way it had always been done in the past." It takes great courage to face the truth and then do the right thing.

Bucking the status quo is a character-building experience for any principal. I hadn't been on the job very long before I encountered my first test of character. The dilemma called for wisdom like that of Solomon. I lay sleepless night after night as a nightmarish parade of witnesses took the stand to plead their cases in front of me: the teacher who was physically and verbally abusive to her students; one of her abused students who exacted retribution by spraying obscenities about her on the brick wall right outside her classroom window; his parents, who demanded that he be transferred to another classroom; the union grievance chairperson, who was sent to protect the rights of the teacher; the school district's lawyer, who was protecting the rights of the board of education; and my superintendent, who just wanted the whole fiasco to fade away.

Being a Character Builder is easy when all you have to do is buy an off-the-shelf program and hand out binders to the teachers. Being a Character Builder when you have to demonstrate integrity on a day-to-day basis is one of the biggest challenges of the principalship. I kept reminding myself that the bottom line was the student's welfare. Like Solomon, there was no way I could please everyone. In fact, I'm not sure that anyone walked away from the whole experience without a sense of loss. But I was able to sleep through the night again, once I had rendered my verdict.

I *was* able to give the student a fresh start in another classroom, with a teacher who was new to the building. The experienced teachers were somewhat suspicious and distrustful. In the eyes of many, I had given in to the parents. But truth to tell, mom and dad weren't that happy either. They wanted the abusive teacher fired on the spot. They believed that to allow her to spend one more day with a group of students was immoral. The teachers wanted the vandal shipped off to juvenile detention, but since he had been a model student to that point in his life, they did grudgingly agree that the district's discipline code must be followed. My superintendent wasn't happy because the union wasn't happy, and the board wasn't happy because the legal bills were mounting. Eventually everyone faced the brutal reality that kids can't learn from teachers who abuse them, and the teacher was quietly retired in the spring with a financial settlement.

9.4 Character Builders Are Authentic

We saw authenticity aplenty in Tom Paulsen's story. He gave the same kind of attention, respect, and kindness to everyone—parent, teacher, student, bus driver, or custodian.

Terry Beasley demonstrates authenticity in a similar fashion at the elementary level. Although Fairhope Elementary School is located in a largely middle- to upper-class neighborhood, nearly a quarter of the students receive free or reduced-price lunch. Terry knows what that feels like. He came from poverty, and he makes sure that students who struggle with keeping up (whether academically or any other way) get plenty of attention, respect, and kindness—especially from the principal.

"I saw a little girl the other day," he said, "and although she was ill-groomed and her clothes were wrinkled, there was something lovely about her. I walked up to her and said, 'Did your mother tell you how beautiful you were before you left for school this morning?' She beamed at me." Terry's words weren't false or empty. His inner reality is absolutely aligned with his outward expressions (Moxley, 2000, p. 126). As Terry says, "If the heart is pure, all of the other pieces fall into place."

> "Be the same person in every circumstance. Hold to the same values in whatever role you have."
>
> —Autry (2001, p. 10)

9.5 Character Builders Are Respectful

Persell and Cookson (1982), in their review of research on effective principals, found "a recurrent characteristic of successful schools concerns the amount of respect shown to all the participants" (p. 23). Respect is something that every human being craves. It consists of one or more of the qualities of consideration, courtesy, attention, esteem, and honor accorded to one individual by another. Respect can be a small social courtesy or a deep and passionate feeling. When someone is respectful of you, they care about what you think, listen to your concerns and opinion, do things that they think will please you, and even inconvenience themselves to make sure that you get what you need or want.

> "People won't believe the message if they don't believe the messenger. People don't follow your technique. They follow you—your message and your embodiment of that message."
>
> —Kouzes (1998, p. 323)

Giving respect to superiors, the people with power or individuals of note or importance in our lives, is something that we do routinely. We know where our bread is buttered and who signs our paychecks. The real test of character is how we treat subordinates, the poor and disenfranchised and those who have no influence or power over us.

When Educator Exemplar Jean Hendrickson arrived at Mark Twain Elementary School, she found that parents had previously received little attention or respect. PTA meetings were attended by no more than thirty people, of which only four or five were parents. The meetings were held immediately after school when most parents were unable to attend. When Jean queried her teachers about changing the time to early evening, they told her that the neighborhood wasn't safe after dark. "Oh," she answered, "I've been here every night this week so far, and there are people out everywhere—folks on front porches, people taking walks. I think it's very safe."

Jean knew that until the parents in her school community became involved and invested in Mark Twain and adopted her vision for a learning-centered school, the achievement of their children would not go up. She suggested a membership goal for PTA. The teachers once again had an answer for her: "Our parents are poor. They won't be able to afford the membership dues."

"Oh, really," Jean answered. "We'll see about that." She found a pizza company that agreed to offer a pizza party to every class with a 100 percent PTA membership. Then she organized an outdoor PTA roundup with free hot dogs, drinks, and door prizes. The parents packed the house. No one had ever invited them to dinner before. PTA membership doubled in the two subsequent years, approaching nearly 100 percent.

Despite the fact that nearly half of Mark Twain's students came from homes where Spanish was spoken, the school had no communication vehicles in Spanish. Jean found someone to donate two new signs—one in Spanish and one in English. The office began sending important information home in both languages.

When someone is respectful of you, they care about what you think, they listen to your concerns and opinions, they do things that will accommodate your needs and schedule. They may even inconvenience themselves to make sure that you feel welcomed and important. Character Builder principals know that the key to building a moral learning community is respect.

9.6 Character Builders Are Generous

Most of us have no problem being generous with our personal mone-
tary resources. We readily donate funds to charities or put together
baskets for needy families at Thanksgiving. We even give of our time to
volunteer for Meals on Wheels or Habitat for Humanity. Character
Builders are generous in a far different and deeper way, however. Covey
(1998) calls it "the abundance mentality—a deep sense of personal worth
and security [that] results in sharing recognition, profits, and responsibility" (p. 103). Having the abundance mentality when resources are tight,
praise is stingy, and competition is stiff takes character.

Brenda Valentine is the essence of generosity. As the story is told by
Brenda, she just happened to mentioned to some of her parents that she
needed a couple of new computers. Before she knew it, they had written a
grant, been awarded the money, and turned a vacant room into a new
computer lab, complete with carpeting, new furniture, and a teacher to
staff it. Brenda couldn't keep all those goodies for herself and her school, so
she began sharing them with others in her community—offering training
to teachers from the junior high schools and the
eleven surrounding elementary schools. The
state department of education awarded Brenda
and her staff a $280,000 technology grant, and
Brenda continued to share the wealth and
knowledge by offering summer technology
camps to children from all over the state. The
more recognition and money that came
Brenda's way, the more she shared with others.
To date, Kanawha City Elementary has received
over $350,000 in technology grants. According
to Brenda, she had absolutely nothing to do with
it. "I don't need all the glory, and I don't take the glory. This is not about me.
This is about my parents, my teachers, and my students working collaboratively." Brenda asked a parent recently why she put in so much time and
energy on grant writing and volunteering for the school, especially when
her children had already graduated. Her answer: "Because you let me."
That's what Brenda is all about—sharing power, recognition, and credit.

> "Until we get our kids'
> hearts, we will never get
> their heads. Once we
> have their hearts, their
> heads will be ours. If
> they don't want to be
> here, we will never
> reach them."
>
> —Principal Terry Beasley

9.7 Character Builders Are Humble

Ten percent of the student population at Holy Name of Jesus School
(K–8) in Indialantic, Florida, has special needs, not the typical enrollment
profile for a private school. Principal Lois Scrivener is proud of her school's

mission statement, especially the section that refers to meeting the individual needs of students in an inclusive setting. She readily admits, however, that she had no idea what this really meant on a daily basis until she had to spend some time with Jason. With an IQ that was barely measurable when he entered kindergarten and an array of obsessive-compulsive behaviors, meeting Jason's individual needs was almost a full-time job.

"My teaching experience is all at the middle and high school level, so substituting in the first grade is always a challenge for me. But the teacher went home ill, and I was it. Well, Jason loved sharpening pencils, so he was continually out of his seat, at the pencil sharpener, sharpening pencils until they seemed to vanish into thin air. He repeated these actions for the entire hour and a half I was in the room. I asked him to sit down. I begged him to stop, but he kept on sharpening more pencils. The next day I asked the teacher what she did when this happened, and she told me with a small smile on her face that she just unplugged the pencil sharpener. This was a most humbling experience for me. I had failed miserably." Lois seemed to have no difficulty sharing the story with me, even though it made her seem less than competent in the classroom. Character Builders are humble.

9.8 Character Builders Hire Staff Members With Character

Successful principals know that they cannot build character in students on their own. Every staff member plays a part. Tom Paulsen pays a great deal of attention to the character not only of the teachers he hires but also of the support staff. He wants individuals who share his values and goals for students. The same attention to hiring the "right" people can be seen at work in a variety of the highly effective companies that are featured in the popular book *Good to Great* (Collins, 2001). The author found that "good-to-great" companies "placed greater weight on character attributes than on specific educational background, practical skills, specialized knowledge or work experience" (p. 51). Leaders in these successful organizations believed that the technical aspects of the job could always be taught, while character was ingrained—an established habit, if you will, that would be very difficult to teach or change.

> "We are what we repeatedly do. Excellence, then, is not an act, but a habit."
>
> —Aristotle

9.9 Character Builders Are Consistent

Plutarch (as quoted in Fitzhenry, 1986, p. 56) said that character is "longstanding habit," and principals who are committed to building character in their students know that habits of character don't sprout up overnight. They require nourishing and tending—similar to growing grass the hard way: from seed. Once the seed is sown, there are endless days of sprinkling before the first fuzzy shoots of green appear. Even missing one day of watering can be disastrous to the germination process, and when the tiny shoots of green appear, daily moisture is still needed, lest the blazing sun burn up the tender plants. Unfortunately, moisture and fertilizer also stimulate the growth of weeds, necessitating even more tending. Growing grass from seed is a time-consuming and daily commitment—much like building character. One cannot let impressionable minds and tender hearts go unattended for even a day. Habits of character are only formed with frequent reminders and rehearsals.

Lois Scrivener knows well the Latin proverb "Repetition is the mother of studies," and she builds character (as well as culture) every morning of the school year. "We gather together each morning at opening exercises to pray; pledge; praise achievements; and celebrate our successes, birthdays, good behavior, good citizenship, random acts of kindness, Christian attitude, and best effort." Highly effective public school principals are no less fervent in their zeal to infuse their campuses with love, care, and respect.

Jim Ratledge knows that character is demonstrated in the little things. "One of my PTA officers found out that some of the other schools in the district were in violation of our board of education policy against having more than two fund-raisers during the school year. She wanted to follow their lead. I told her, 'We don't care what the other schools do. At Montdale School, we do what's right.' Kids know when we're inconsistent. They notice when our words and our actions don't match."

> "Repeat again what you hear; for by often hearing and saying the same things, what you have learned comes complete into your memory."
>
> —From the *Dialexis*

9.10 Character Builders Lead by Example, Not by Exhortation

I was very upset with Marion, my third grade teacher. She had used poor judgment in disciplining one of her students, losing her composure just outside my office. As if that weren't bad enough, the student's mother also happened along to overhear Marion's diatribe and proceeded to do unto Marion as Marion had done unto her daughter. Marion's class watched wide-eyed as mother and teacher exchanged angry accusations. I must admit that I was ready to give Marion a little of her own medicine when we finally had a chance to talk later in the afternoon. But Character Builders lead by example, so I remained calm, empathetic, but very firm.

Marion looked worried about the fallout from her lapse of judgment, but I told her that if she followed my lead, we could teach some valuable lessons to both parent and child. At the time I didn't have a clever name for what I suggested to Marion, but I've since discovered one: "Taking the A-Train" (Horn, 1996, p. 32). "Agree and apologize," I advised Marion: "Agree with mom that she has good reason to be upset with you. Agree that you used poor judgment in losing your temper and lashing out at her daughter. Then apologize for the embarrassment you caused her and her daughter *and* promise never to do it again." Marion looked a bit dubious about that part, but she agreed to follow my example.

The process took more than two hours. While Marion was taking the A-train, both mother and daughter also climbed aboard. Mom conceded that her daughter was a challenging child and that she was often driven to distraction by her behavior. She agreed that her own behavior was irresponsible and had only compounded the problem. She apologized to Marion. Her daughter agreed that Marion had reminded her several times to stop poking the student in front of her and that she had deliberately and defiantly ignored her. She apologized to Marion for being disrespectful. We accomplished quite a bit of character building in that two-and-a-half-hour meeting.

9.11 Character Builders Seek to Develop the Character of Students

Lola Malone has always been a Character Builder with high expectations for the behavior and lives of her students. However, a number of years ago, she began to notice that the job was getting much harder. Lola says, "It was a combination of things that affected the overall discipline and climate of the building. At the time, we had three self-contained special education classes, one of which enrolled many emotionally disturbed students. However, I can't put all of the blame on them. Society as a whole was changing. Parents didn't have the respect for teachers and administrators that they once had. We had problems with foul language from both parents and students. I became very frustrated by what was happening but didn't really have any idea about how to improve the situation."

It was at that point that Martha Walker, then a teacher at Tyson and later Lola's assistant principal, gave her an inspirational book titled *Silver Boxes: The Gift of Encouragement* (Littauer, 1989). "I read that book," reports Lola, "and a lightbulb went on in my brain. I realized that our problem with discipline was more than just the parents and the students. The problem was our approach. *We* weren't speaking nearly enough kind

Figure 9.1

THE THIRTY CHARACTER WORDS OF THE TYSON TIGERS

Responsibility: To be accountable for your behavior

Perseverance: Continuing to do something in spite of difficulties or obstacles

Kindness: A friendly, good-natured attitude toward others

Compassion: Feeling for another's need and helping that person without expecting anything in return

Dependability: Being trustworthy to do what I say I will

Work: Not being lazy in the tasks given to me

Generosity: Having an unselfish attitude, willing to share with others

Thankfulness: Being grateful and saying so

Friendliness: Knowing, liking, and accepting other people just the way they are

Manners: Ways of behaving which show good character

Determination: Continuing on, regardless of the circumstances

Obedience: Doing what you are told with a happy, submissive spirit

Forgiveness: Treating someone as though they never hurt you

Honesty: Truthful words and ways

Love: A great affection of the mind and heart

Orderliness: Neatness; tidiness; proper behavior; lawfulness

Patience: Waiting with a happy spirit

Contentment: Being happy with what I have

Optimism: A positive outlook that everything will turn out for the best

Thoughtfulness: Consideration of others; courtesy

Self-Control: Doing something even when I do not feel like it

Tolerance: Accepting others and their beliefs even when I do not agree

Courage: Standing up for what I believe in; bravery

Respect: A high or special regard; honoring one another

Enthusiasm: Strong positive excitement of feeling

Humility: Absence of pride or self-assertion; modesty

Punctuality: Being on time for the requirements of life

Attentiveness: Paying heed or care

Joyfulness: Delight, happiness, gladness

Confidence: Trust; a feeling of assurance or certainty

and caring words. *We* weren't modeling *and* teaching students the words and deeds that we wanted to see. *We* had not intentionally focused on the power of *positive* words to change and encourage children."

Lola explained the concept to her staff, and a parent volunteer made small mirrored boxes with magnets attached that were presented to each teacher at a schoolwide assembly. The boxes were then displayed prominently in each classroom to remind both teachers and students to speak kind and caring words to each other. That was the beginning of character development at Tyson School. The following year, the staff selected ten character words and focused on one per month. The first word was *responsibility*, and each month they added another word. The program was refined and expanded to another year, and soon visitors from other schools were coming to Tyson to see how just a few words could make such a huge difference in a school. "I believe that the character trait program our staff has developed is, without a doubt, the best thing that we have ever done. It has had a major impact on student behavior, student work habits, and achievement. It has become the icing on the cake of the good things that we were already doing. It has become the glue that gives stability and lays the foundation for everything we do. If we focus only on the academics, we will fall short of our goal of developing good, productive citizens.

"This is not a purchased program," Lola explains. "The thirty character words we ultimately chose are 'our words,' and they are the basis for everything we do in our school. The power of positive encouragement is amazing. I believe that one of the key reasons our achievement has remained high, even though our school population has enrolled increasing numbers of limited English proficient students (45 percent) and students on free and reduced lunch (55 percent), is that we use the "character words of *work, responsibility, determination, honesty,* and *perseverance* to explain to incoming parents and students the expectations that we have for them."

SUMMING IT UP

Stephen Covey (1998) believes that character is foundational to all that we aspire to be and do as educators: "Primary greatness is character" (p. 102). Make no mistake. None of the highly effective principals are paragons of perfection. They are real human beings with the same flaws and foibles that plague us all. What does distinguish them from ineffective principals, however, is the fact that they realize it. They know what Aristotle meant when he said, "If you would understand virtue, observe the conduct of virtuous men [and women]."

Figure 9.2   Character Builder Benchmarks

Trait Number 9: The highly effective principal is a Character Builder—a role model whose values, words, and deeds are marked by trustworthiness, integrity, authenticity, respect, generosity, and humility.

9.1   Character Builders are human.
9.2   Character Builders are trustworthy.
9.3   Character Builders have integrity.
9.4   Character Builders are authentic.
9.5   Character Builders are respectful.
9.6   Character Builders are generous.
9.7   Character Builders are humble.
9.8   Character Builders hire staff members with character.
9.9   Character Builders are consistent.
9.10 Character Builders lead by example, not by exhortation.
9.11 Character Builders seek to develop the character of students.

They recognize the power they have to mold and shape young people, encourage and empower teachers, and respect and affirm parents. They treat these responsibilities as a sacred trust. They recognize with Albert Schweitzer that their final report card will contain no mention of the curricular improvements, organizational restructuring, and budget balancing they so cleverly implemented but rather, it will contain only their deeds of kindness and respect.

"Of all the will toward the ideal in mankind, only a small part can manifest itself in public action. All the rest of this force must be content with small and obscure deeds. The sum of these, however, is a thousand times stronger than the acts of those who receive wide public recognition. The latter, compared to the former, are like the foam on the waves of a deep ocean" (Schweitzer, 1963, p. 74).

The Contributor

"The best test, and difficult to administer, is: Do those served grow as persons? Do they, while being served, become healthier, wiser, freer, more autonomous, more likely themselves to become servants?"

—Greenleaf (1977, pp. 13–14)

We are about to consider the final trait of the ten traits of highly effective principals: Contributor. At first glance, one might think that a Contributor is someone who gives generously to the United Way or volunteers for Habitat for Humanity. A Contributor principal, however, does far more than write an occasional check or volunteer time to a favorite charity. On the original list of thirty-seven traits (See Figure I.1 in the Introduction), the Contributor trait was called *a servant's heart.* It received only 15 votes; not the lowest vote getter, by any means, but very close to the bottom, nevertheless.

There are several possible reasons for this low standing: (1) Respondents were unfamiliar with the term as used in the leadership literature, (2) they did not believe that being a servant-leader was an important trait for highly effective principals to have, or (3) they believed that it was important but decided that another trait for which they had voted included the qualities of a servant. One former principal, now a central office administrator, believes that one of our chief difficulties in the profession is the lack of a servant's heart: "There are a lot of people in administration who don't listen to their followers and don't seem to believe that they need a servant's heart. They seem to care more about their careers than their students or teachers."

Although the respondents may have been unfamiliar with or disinclined to vote for the concept of principals as servant-leaders, the thirty-seven highly effective principals who contributed to the book were not. They knew exactly what having a servant's heart meant and assiduously cultivated the attitudes and behaviors associated with this perspective in their professional lives.

I find it fortuitous that by virtue of its low ranking in the vote total, the Contributor trait receives the honor of summarizing and concluding the book. Make no mistake, however; the Contributor trait is not the frosting on the cake. It is more like the baking powder that, though unseen, causes the cake to rise. Neither is servant-leadership like the last piece of the quilt to be put into place; rather, it is similar to the nearly invisible thread that holds the quilt together. Servanthood isn't about being the star of the show—it's about being a one-person supporting cast that makes the stars (teachers, parents, and students) shine. None of the ten traits is more critical to the actualization and realization of all of the other nine in the lives of highly effective principals than the Contributor trait.

If the concept of servant-leadership is new to you, here is a thumbnail sketch of its genius and genesis. Robert Greenleaf is acknowledged to be the modern father of servant-leadership, but the concept is ages old (Blanchard, 2002, pp. x-xi). After enjoying a distinguished forty-year career in management research, development, and education at AT&T, Greenleaf worked productively for twenty-five more years as a consultant to many institutions and charitable foundations. During this period, he experienced an epiphany of sorts while reading *Journey to the East*, a short novel by Herman Hesse (1968), in which a group of pilgrims takes a mythical spiritual journey. Greenleaf's epiphany: "True leadership emerges from those whose primary motivation is a deep desire to help others" (Greenleaf, 1977). The publication of Greenleaf's essay *The Servant as Leader* (1982) inspired a movement that would not only influence the work of many leadership theorists (Autry, 2001; Blanchard, 2001; Block, 1993; Covey, 1990; DePree, 1987; Senge, 1990; Spears, 1995; Wheatley, 1999), but also revolutionize the way many companies do business (Spears, 1995).

> "[Servant power] is used to create opportunity and alternatives so that individuals may choose and build autonomy. In [coercive power], individuals are forced into a predetermined path. Even if it is good for them, if they experience nothing else, ultimately their autonomy will be diminished."
>
> —Greenleaf
> (1977, pp. 41–42)

Forbes, the business weekly magazine, annually publishes a list of the 100 Best Companies to Work for in America (Levering & Moskowitz, 2002). As the title of the list implies, the choices are made from the employees' perspective, but make no mistake, profitability and productivity count. One company has been in the top five for four of the past five years, declining to enter the competition in 2002: Southwest Airlines. The business literature often cites Southwest Airlines as an example of the power of servant-leadership in the corporate world (Ruschman, 2002, pp. 130–133).

During the past four years, I have learned a great deal about this airline—not from an employee's perspective but from the customer's point of view. My husband and I fly SWA almost exclusively in our travels around the country. In fact, we have flown to fifty of the sixty cities that Southwest serves. One can learn a great deal about a company during 125 round-trip flights. Between April 1998 and October 2002, only one flight has been delayed because of mechanical failure. No flights have ever been cancelled. There have been no work stoppages or strikes. A good half of the flights have arrived early, and the rest have been on time or no more than a few minutes late. During this nearly five-year period, our luggage was only misplaced once. During all of those flights, we have encountered fewer than half a dozen employees who were less than top-notch. Since April 1998, I have rebooked our reservations dozens of times to accommodate an ever-changing workshop schedule. We have never had to pay a penalty or forfeit any money. In addition, Southwest fares are often from 50 percent to 70 percent less than other airlines for the same trips. The frequent flyer program is a study in simplicity. We have received dozens of free flights. How does Southwest do it?

> "Leadership doesn't depend on mystical qualities or inborn gifts but rather on the capacity of individual to know themselves, their strengths, and their weaknesses, and to learn from the feedback they get in their daily lives, in short, their capacity for self-improvement."
>
> —Kouzes and Posner (1999, p. 33)

In the Southwest family, all of the employees pitch in as needed: Pilots pick up trash and help passengers with baggage; flight attendants attend to passengers' needs nonstop through most flights; and everyone is unfailingly good-natured, friendly, down-to-earth, and sometimes just downright funny. These people don't take themselves seriously. What they do take seriously is customer service. "The company hires for attitude and behavior rather than skills, and recognizes and rewards achievement. Leaders of Southwest treat people as they would want to be treated, value people as individuals, and promote from within" (Ruschman, 2002, p. 131).

> "That's me. The servant-leader. I want everyone at the school—not just the students, but teachers and support staff as well—to be successful. I am personally responsible for facilitating their success."
>
> —Communicator Exemplar Michelle Gayle

I share this lengthy example in order to illustrate what servant-leadership actually looks like in action. It is not the newest wrinkle in a long line of management gimmicks to get more out of people for less but instead is a way of thinking and being that emanates from asking two questions of people: "What contribution from me do you require to make *your* contribution to the organization? When do you need this, how do you need it, and in what form?" (Drucker, 2001, p. 212).

Many of the characteristics of servant-leaders have already been explored in the context of describing the other nine traits. They include the abilities to listen, empathize, build consensus, support people, create communities, and dream big dreams (Burkhardt & Spears, 2002, pp. 226–227). So you might ask, why do we need another trait? Because it's the motive that makes the difference. Contributor principals do not merely listen, empathize, and build consensus in order to achieve their ends. Their motivations arise from a servant's heart.

The highly effective principal is a Contributor—a servant-leader, encourager, and enabler whose utmost priority is making a contribution to the success of others.

> "Ultimately, however, it is not just personality that counts. At least equally important is the leader's ability to establish a climate of trust and a sense of integrity in the ideas being proposed. Key to this effort is something worth following. Without ideas, values, and commitments, there can be no followership. Without followership, there can be no leadership. In this sense, the most basic principle of leadership is followership first, then leadership."
>
> —Sergiovanni (1990, p. 85)

CONTRIBUTOR EXEMPLAR: LOLA MALONE

Lola Malone can't keep from serving others—even when she's not on the job at John Tyson Elementary School in Springdale, Arkansas, where she has been the principal for seventeen of her twenty-four years in administration. She spreads her random acts of kindness throughout her community. For example, she frequently stops by the Braum's drive-through on her way to school to pick up a breakfast yogurt. Every now and then, she tells the clerk at the window that she is treating the person in the car behind her. "Just add the total to mine," she says. "It's my random act of kindness for the day." Lola could not know that on one morning, the person behind her was celebrating a birthday. She decided to publicly thank Lola by writing a letter to the editor: "This morning when I drove through Braum's to get breakfast to take to work,

I received an unexpected gift. The lady in front of me in the drive-through had paid for my breakfast. She could not have known it was my birthday and she gave me my first birthday gift of the day. I can only assume she does these "random acts of kindness" wherever she's at. What a boost in this day and time to find people still doing for strangers. I'll try to pass it on today to another" (Hoag, 1998).

Lola is always on the lookout for ways to serve others—sometimes to the chagrin of her husband, who doesn't always share her immense faith in humankind. "My husband and I were out for dinner at a popular local eatery one Friday night," she explains. "We were waiting to be seated, and I couldn't help but overhear an attractive young woman in a prom dress frantically talking to her grandmother on the pay phone. She had promised to pay for tickets to the prom and unless her mother materialized with the money very soon, she and her date, who only had enough money for dinner, wouldn't be dancing the night away.

"She could have been our daughter," Lola said. "How could I not help her?"

Lola gave her the money she needed along with her business card. Lola's husband was doubtful about the likelihood of repayment but supportive of Lola's generosity. Time passed, and just when Lola had forgotten about the incident, an envelope arrived in the mail with a prom picture and $30.00. The young woman had written a short thank-you note and included *her* name and number—"just in case Lola ever needed *her* help."

Greenleaf's test of servant-leadership is twofold: *Do those served grow as persons? Do they, while being served, become healthier, wiser, freer, more autonomous, more likely themselves to become servants?* It would seem so in the case of this young woman.

The teachers, parents, and students of John Tyson School have certainly grown as a result of Lola's contributions to their lives. One of her teachers recently wrote this note on the bottom of Lola's performance evaluation: "You set an example of very high standards in your personal life. I have watched you over ten years treat everyone (parents, students, and teachers) with utmost respect and kindness. I have seen your serving heart; you do many things that some principals might consider beneath them (checking for head lice; after-school duty). You are truly a ray of light in a sometimes very dark world. Thank you for being a motivator, an encourager, a wonderful example, and a true friend."

> "When teachers need things, the principal delivers. Resources are anything the principal can use to satisfy teacher needs: materials, student discipline, insulating teachers from parents, organizational maintenance."
>
> —Achilles, Keedy, and High (1999, p. 39)

Another teacher writes, "You have been my role model and mentor. Thank you!"

Lola is also a mentor to new principals in her district. She explains, "My goal is to help these beginners discover the needs of their teachers and then to explore with them how to meet those needs." Whatever Lola's teachers need, Lola's teachers get! Here are their needs as perceived and described by Lola:

My teachers *need* to be treated the very same way I wanted to be treated by my principal when I was a teacher. I ask myself several times a day—is this the way *I* would want to be treated?

My teachers *need* to know that I am willing to do anything that I ask them to do. I serve extra duties, just like my teachers. I am not beneath mopping up vomit or cleaning up a soiled child. I try to attend every major workshop that is required of my teachers. If we are going to adopt a new program, I need the same training that they do.

My teachers *need* to hear me ask these questions frequently:

- What can I do to help you do your very best job of teaching?
- What can I do to help you meet the needs of your students?

> "A non-servant who wants to be a servant might become a natural servant through a long arduous discipline of learning to listen, a discipline sufficiently sustained that the automatic response to any problem is to listen first. I have seen enough remarkable transformations in people who have been trained to listen to have some confidence in this approach. It is because true listening builds strength in other people."
>
> —Greenleaf (1977, p. 17)

Once I have asked these questions, I need to be prepared to deliver the training, resources, or answers they need to do their jobs well.

My teachers *need* to feel that I respect them as individuals and will protect their privacy. Everyone makes mistakes or uses poor judgment occasionally, and I will deal with these problems directly and privately in my office. I will never discuss faculty members or their problems by name in staff meetings or with other staff members.

My teachers *need* to be given credit for their ideas, creativity, hard work, and willingness to take on additional responsibilities. I will take great care to give credit where it is due, both privately and publicly, both orally and in writing.

My teachers *need* to know that I will always seek out the complete story before reacting to a situation. I will not act prematurely because one teacher or parent has drawn my attention to a problem. I will make sure to check with everyone. I will not jump to conclusions and make hasty decisions.

My teachers *need* a principal who is available and listens to them.

My teachers *need* to have reasons and explanations given when plans derail, problems occur, requests cannot be fulfilled, or promises are broken. They deserve to have all of the information and facts put on the table and to be apprised of what is happening in our school.

My teachers, collectively and as individuals, *need* to know that when decisions are made that affect them, they will be given ample opportunities for input and discussion.

My teachers *need* to know that I am fair and that I will not show favoritism to an individual or group.

My teachers *need* to know that I will keep an open mind when they advance ideas or make suggestions for changes.

My teachers *need* to know that they will always be a part of the team when parent and student problems are up for discussion and solution. I pledge to keep them fully informed and respect their needs and priorities when making decisions that involve them.

My teachers *need* to feel supported in their disciplinary decisions with students. A well-conceived and consistent schoolwide behavior plan is essential. Together we will persevere with a problem until it is resolved.

My teachers *need* to know that I will admit my mistakes, sincerely apologize when I am wrong, and then move forward.

My teachers *need* to know that I will always send parents to them first if there are questions or concerns about what they are doing in their classrooms.

My teachers *need* to know they can bring problems and concerns regarding my performance as a principal to my attention and that I will honestly, immediately, and positively address them.

My teachers *need* to know that I value their personal lives and will take their lives into consideration when making requests.

> "Humility comes naturally to the best leaders. They seldom take credit themselves but instead give credit to the group with which they have worked."
>
> —Farson (1996, p. 146)

CONTRIBUTOR BENCHMARKS

Many of the benchmarks that have been described in the context of other traits are benchmarks of Contributors as well. We will not discuss them again, but I include a brief list for consideration: listening (Communicator); supporting staff members (Facilitator); dreaming big dreams and having compelling visions (Envisioner); sharing the "power pie" (Facilitator); saying "we" instead of "I" (Facilitator); facilitating core values (Culture Builder); energizing people (Activator); and leading by example, not by exhortation (Character Builder). Also note that a complete list of all of the benchmarks for the ten traits can be found in Resource C.

10.1 Contributors Lead by Serving Others

The paradox of servant-leadership is not unlike the paradox of the Elijah effect discussed in Chapter 4. Recall the experience of the widow, who after she came to her senses and shared her last meager loaf with the prophet Elijah, found that her stores of oil and flour were freshly replenished each day. Inexplicably and just as miraculously, when one drops back to follow for a time, admits an inability to do and know it all, or gives up position power to another, far greater and grander goals are achieved than would ever have been possible through a posture of directing or mandating.

NOURISH THE SOUL

Margaret Garcia-Dugan, High School, Glendale, Arizona

I have always believed that my best work, both personal and professional, comes when the trinity of the body, soul, and mind are thoroughly and properly nourished. The most important aspect of that trinity for me is my soul. I nourish my soul through daily prayer, attending church, and my relationship with God and gain the strength I need to interact with people in a positive and a proactive manner.

10.2 Contributors Are Self-Aware and Reflective

An important but largely unseen aspect of being a Contributor principal is self-awareness. Self-awareness involves several mental processes: (1) an active inner thought-life that is likely to include a deep spiritual component, (2) a constant grappling with the tough issues of ethics and values in education through reflection and meditation, (3) the ability to think conceptually about the future, (4) the metacognitive ability to be part of the action (i.e., "in the game") while at the same time reflecting and critiquing what is happening (i.e., "on the sidelines"), and (5) the willingness to reflect often and deeply on one's personal effectiveness.

Self-awareness is what distinguishes highly effective principals from those who are merely going through the motions. Be forewarned that self-awareness is not necessarily a peaceful and contemplative state. Greenleaf (1997) notes, "Awareness is not a giver of solace—it is just the opposite. It is a disturber and awakener. Able leaders are usually sharply awake and reasonably disturbed. They are not seekers after solace. They have their own inner serenity" (p. 6). Many of the highly effective principals gain inner serenity through their spiritual lives. Patricia Hamilton says, "My faith helps center me. I would compare it to the bubble in a carpenter's level. By the weekends, when my emotions are drained, faith puts what really matters into perspective."

> "The cultivation of awareness gives one the basis for detachment, the ability to stand aside and see oneself in perspective in the context of one's own experience, amidst the ever present dangers, threats, and alarms."
>
> —Greenleaf (1977, pp. 27–28)

10.3 Contributor Are Good Stewards

Stewardship means "to hold something in trust for another" (Block, 1993, p. 237). It is the highest form of accountability. Contributors act as stewards—caring for, watching out for, and protecting the school as a community institution. They have its best interests at heart and rather than merely working for a school board, district, or superintendent, they see their role as one of nurturing and protecting the reputation of the school for the greater good of society. As Envisioner Exemplar Larry Fieber said about his work, "It's not a job. It's a way of life." The failure of a school to keep its covenant with the community is taken very seriously by Contributor principals. They feel a strong compulsion to step in to renew and rejuvenate the covenant when they find it has been broken or damaged.

Lois Scrivener is the principal of a Catholic school where stewardship and service are taken for granted. Lois teaches a graduate course for aspiring administrators, and she emphasizes the importance of serving the ideals of the organization to all of her students, not just to those who will work in private schools.

"It's easy for us in Catholic schools," says Lois. "My school's mission is to teach as Jesus did." Lois, however, offers the kind of love

> "[Contributors] provide the necessary oversight to ensure the school is meeting its commitments, and when it is not, find out why and help everyone do something about it."
>
> —Sergiovanni (1996, p. 89)

and service to parents and students that is even uncommon in most parochial schools, where placement tests and rigorous admittance standards often screen out those students who don't measure up.

At Holy Name of Jesus School, 10 percent of the students have special needs, many severe. They are welcomed, loved, and taught. "I really care about children, and parents trust us to both love and teach their children." Lois is committed to inclusive education and works tirelessly among her Catholic school colleagues to help them understand that if they really care about children, they must love and serve them all. "I have 575 children, and I care for each one," says Lois.

Lest you think that servant-leadership and stewardship are parochial school prerogatives, reflect on the contributions of Envisioner Exemplar Larry Fieber. He brought the ideals of servant-leadership alive in a public school community. "He took a relentless and most aggressive approach to help his school community come to life again. He effectively oversaw the construction of a new building while at the same time easing the community through the pain of losing their historic building. He was driven toward excellence and brought all parties on board. He began with a focused goal and kept all eyes on the target of education and social excellence." (Fieber, 2000). Larry never expected to work in an elementary school. All of his experiences prior to coming to Parkway were at the middle and high school levels, but he has found his true calling. He has a love of children and a joy for seeing them grow that is contagious. He has had offers to move to other communities, some more affluent, but he feels a loyalty and connection to his district and school. "I've never been one to jump from place to place," he says. "I have a sense of history and too many emotional connections to leave here."

Change Master Exemplar Marjorie Thompson, Elementary, Inglewood, California

It was unusual for me if a day went by without a child saying something amusing or refreshing. Their comments were always so frank. One new child told me in a very disapproving tone of voice: "You don't act like no principal." I asked him what a principal was supposed to act like. He responded: "They're supposed to sit in their office, shuffling their papers, not scrubbing no tables."

Figure 10.1   Contributor Benchmarks

Trait Number 10: The highly effective principal is a Contributor—a servant-leader, encourager, and enabler whose utmost priority is making a contribution to the success of others.

10.1   Contributors lead by serving others.
10.2   Contributors are self-aware and reflective.
10.3   Contributors are good stewards.
10.4   Contributors have strong wills.

10.4 Contributors Have Strong Wills

Some might associate the humility required to be a Contributor principal with a measure of weakness or meekness. Au contraire. In *Good to Great,* Collins (2001) describes individuals who have brought companies from being merely good to great and characterizes them as having a "paradoxical blend of personal humility and professional will" (p. 20). Contributor principals have the strength of character, personal focus, and determination that make them nearly invincible to the insecurities, self-doubts, and crises of confidence experienced by ineffective administrators. The missions and goals of Contributor principals do not revolve around career advancement, self-aggrandizement, or empire building. Their missions are centered in stewardship, empowerment, and service to others.

SUMMING IT UP

Contributor principals have learned the only lesson one really needs to master in order to make a true difference in education: *It's all about the teachers and the students and the parents.* To be a Contributor, one must understand this paradox: *You are essential to the life of a school only insofar as you make a contribution to the effectiveness of others.* If you are unable to do that, effectiveness will forever elude you. Barth (2000) observed, "A principal may comply with all 64 characteristics of an effective leader as seen by the state department of education, but if the teachers don't experience their principal as a leader [or a Contributor], then the principal isn't one" (p. x). You are only a Contributor when teachers, parents, and students experience you as one.

Conclusion

Personal Observations

Before we summarize what we have learned from our study of the lives of highly effective principals, I have some personal observations. They come as both good and bad news. The good news is that highly effective principals get amazing results as they empower, energize, and motivate staff, parents, and students. They habitually display the action and attitudes associated with the ten traits. On occasion, they even make it look easy. That is encouraging news for those of us who care deeply about education. The thirty-seven principals who are featured in this book have raised the effectiveness bar to a new level. They are *inspiring*, but they aren't the only ones. There are thousands more like them in districts around the country, many of them reading this book right now.

The bad news is that there aren't nearly enough of these highly effective principals to go around. Many schools aren't blessed with Contributors, Activators, Envisioners, and Producers. They're stuck with excuses, hostility, abuse, and low achievement (Blase & Blase, 2002). But there's more good news. Every principal has the potential to learn, grow, and change. *You* can go from good to great. These traits *can* be learned and practiced to the point of automaticity by principals at any point along the continuum, whether aspiring, novice, or even experienced principals who are weary of spinning their wheels and want to make a difference. If not now, then when?

All of the highly effective principals who contributed to this book believed they were works in progress and noted the many things they were doing to become more effective. Jim Ratledge said, "The more I learn about the job, the more I discover that I need to learn."

Patricia Hamilton agrees: "On any given day, I can tell you a multitude of areas in which I need to improve. I will never grow complacent and think that I no longer need training. I live by what my dad once told me: 'The more one learns, the more one needs to learn.'"

The successful principals who are profiled in this book also talked about turning points in their lives when they decided to do things differently and were able to move to a higher level of productivity. They did not achieve effectiveness by magic or inherit it at birth—they worked at it diligently over time. Some were fortunate enough to have coaches and mentors. Some learned by making mistakes or from listening to their staff members and parents. They realized that they didn't have to know it all and certainly didn't have to do it all on their own. They discovered that if they served people and enlisted them in a worthy endeavor, they could achieve far more in concert with others than they ever could on their own.

If you aspire to be highly effective, do it like these effective principals have done it and are continuing to do it, "the old-fashioned way," with determination and diligence. Just because you haven't done it yet is no reason not to begin tomorrow. Find a cause that is worthy of your efforts and get to work on achieving it right away.

If you teach, mentor, or coach aspiring or novice principals, encourage them to read, reflect, and revisit these stories often for direction and inspiration.

If you are working with principals who have more years of experience than years of effectiveness, encourage them to read and reflect on where they made a wrong turn. It is never too late to begin anew.

PROFESSIONAL CONCLUSIONS

There are always dangers in generalizing from a small, qualitative sample to the universe of highly effective principals or even more broadly, to principals in general. Therefore, I submit the following conclusions to readers as one of several possible ways to think about the principalship—certainly not the only or the most definitive way. Let these observations be a springboard for personal reflection as well as dialogue with other professionals. Refer to the Facilitator's Guide in Resource D.

All of the ten traits are essential to some degree in order to be a highly effective principal. While all of the ten traits need not be developed to the same degree of complexity and maturity, they must all be present to some extent for a principal to be highly effective. This conclusion may be debated hotly in discussion groups and administrative classes, but it is one that seems inevitable to me, based on my own experience as a principal, my interviews with all of the highly effective principals, and my experiences in hiring and supervising principals as a central office administrator. However, the key words to remember in this discussion are *to some degree.* No one principal has it all or will ever have it all, but without a few solid and very strong traits to lay a foundation, along with a basic understanding and commitment to listen and learn, the most pressing demands and challenges of today's principalship will go unmet.

Highly effective principals know themselves, and as has been said, they are works in progress. They have identified their strengths (the behaviors and attitudes that seem easy and natural to them) and use them to complement and enhance their less well developed traits (the behaviors and attitudes that take practice and discipline to achieve). In addition, successful principals know how to tap and develop the talents and strengths of parents, teachers, and other staff members to compensate for their own less well developed traits.

The ten traits interact with each other in synergistic and often inexplicable ways. The ways in which the ten traits interact with one another have become a fascination for me during the writing of this book. For example, as we noted earlier,

- To be a culture builder, one must also be a communicator, envisioner, and character builder.
- To be a contributor, it is necessary to be a facilitator, a communicator and a character builder.
- To produce, one must be an educator, an envisioner and an facilitator, and an activator.
- To be a facilitator, one must be a culture-building communicator.
- To be an envisioner, one must also be a communicator, and on the other hand, in order to be a communicator, one must have a worthy vision to communicate.

At times, a trait may play a starring role, as it were; at other times, it is supportive and facilitative in nature. Some very high profile traits, like Communicator, for example, can easily lose their power and punch without the other traits to give them substance, direction, and purpose. And the converse is true. Many supporting and facilitating traits totally disappear without the Communicator trait.

It is impossible to rank the ten traits or to identify one that is more critical than any other. I engaged in that exercise to no avail at several intervals during my writing. While I was working on a particular trait and describing its exemplar, I could easily convince myself that if I were a superintendent, I would hire no one but Contributors, or perhaps Producers, or perhaps some other combination or permutation of traits. I suspect that one *could* make a good case for any of these traits standing alone or being *the* most important trait. I did that to some extent with instructional leadership in my book *7 Steps to Effective Instructional Leadership* (McEwan, 2003b). Certainly, the servant-leadership theorists believe that their model is an all-encompassing one. Likewise, those who write about developing learning communities believe their thinking represents the most cohesive and useful paradigm (DuFour & Eaker, 1998). Similarly, those who focus on results have faith in the power of that model (Schmoker, 1999, 2001). The question for me is not which is the best model to describe highly effective principals' ways of being and doing but rather, how we can help all principals to become more effective.

Becoming a highly effective principal is definitely more of a process than a product. If the highly effective principals I interviewed felt a sense of arrival or overall effectiveness at any time, it usually occurred at a point where they or their schools were recognized for past achievements or when a major goal was achieved. However, the minute they began a new job or undertook a new initiative, the process started all over again. Highly effective principals recognize their need for improvement and growth, and they constantly seek to eliminate unproductive attitudes and behaviors while further enhancing their most productive ways of being and doing.

Highly effective principals are continually monitoring and adjusting their responses to the various schools, faculties, communities, and challenges they encounter. Highly effective principals are eager for feedback and use what they hear from teachers, parents, and students to make changes. They also know that the problems and the people are always changing (even in the same school from year to year), and they must be responsive and adaptive.

Highly effective principals are masters of timing. They have a sense of what attitudes and actions are most appropriate in which situations and can calibrate them to fit the occasion. One reader suggested that to be a highly effective principal, one must follow the advice found in Kenny Rogers's signature song, *The Gambler:* "You have to know when to hold and when to fold." Successful principals know when to activate and when to serve. They know when to lead and when to follow, and as fellow Corwin author Robert Ramsey (1999) *and* General George Patton have reminded us—they know "when to get out of the way."

Highly effective principals make a difference wherever they go. Many of the highly effective principals have duplicated their successes with different teachers, at different levels, in diverse neighborhoods and communities, and with unique challenges. Their visions, energy levels, learning curves, and intense needs to serve and contribute have enabled them to segue smoothly from elementary to middle school (Michelle Gayle), from high school to elementary (Larry Fieber and Dale Skinner), from middle to high school (Jeanne Stiglbauer), from Lake Woebegone to the inner city (Jean Hendrickson), and from nurturing 350 students to over 1,000 without missing a beat (Marjorie Thompson).

There may be occasions when a school or community *seems* to need a certain kind of principal with a definitive combination of traits, but as someone who has helped to hire and supervise building principals, I have found matchmaking to be a perilous and highly frustrating undertaking. Thankfully, the superintendent who hired Larry Fieber (looking for a disciplinarian to subdue an out-of-control school) got an Educator, who was an Envisioner as well as a Culture Builder. I have worked with teacher selection committees and superintendents who were so focused on not getting what they had and didn't like in a former principal that they failed to recognize that what they really needed was someone who was more balanced overall—not someone who was the complete opposite of what they had had.

Highly effective principals are emotionally, physically, and spiritually healthy individuals. They know what they need to do to maintain a high efficiency level. Of course, they have doubts, fears, failures, and not a few flaws, but they do know there is life after school, and they live it to the fullest. They bike, golf, run marathons, and climb mountains. They enjoy their friends, their spouses, their children, and their grandchildren. They read, go to movies, study, learn, and grow. They eat well, pamper themselves when they need to, and rely on their faith to get them through the tough times and crises of confidence.

All principals, including the thirty-seven highly effective ones featured in this book, possess totally unique combinations and permutations of the ten traits. I always read the evaluations I receive from workshop participants, looking for ways to improve my presentations. There are invariably one or two people in every group who scribble this comment at the bottom of the instrument: "You didn't tell us how to do it." These individuals want easy answers—a blueprint, formula, or prescription to take back to their schools and replicate. In fact, there are doubtless some readers who may be thinking the same thing as they finish reading this book. If you were merely looking for novel activities to implement in your school, you are doubtless disappointed. There is nothing new under the sun. This book was about how principals can change their attitudes and behaviors to be more responsive to teachers, parents, students, and taxpayers—not about providing another list of activities and programs to implement. Every school's problems are unique, and so are the individuals who are called upon to solve them. All of the highly effective principals would tell you that they have had to "do their own thing" in response to the situations in which they found themselves. I encountered this advice from Andre Gide while reading Peter Block's (1996) *Stewardship: Choosing*

Service Over Self-Interest, and I commend it to you in closing: "Look for your own. Do not do what someone else could do as well as you. Do not say, do not write what someone else could say, could write as well as you. Care for nothing in yourself but what you feel exists nowhere else and out of your self create, impatiently or patiently . . . the most irreplaceable of beings" (p. 237).

HOW CAN YOU USE THIS BOOK?

There are several ways that you can apply the ideas in this book to your own professional growth: (1) Choose a trait that you or your staff members have highlighted for improvement and focus on developing the benchmarks of that trait as habitual actions and attitudes. (2) Choose an area of strength and make it even stronger by identifying the one or two benchmarks that need fine-tuning and improvement. (3) Use the ten traits as a template for gathering input from your teachers, parents, or students about your personal performance. Or (4) form a study group to explore how you and the members of your team can increase your effectiveness and support each other in your uniqueness.

Be sure to consult the Facilitator's Guide (Resource D) found in the shaded section following the References. I have included process activities, questions for dialogue, suggested Rapid Rewards Goals, and reflective writing assignments for each chapter, as well as the Introduction and Conclusion.

If you have questions or comments regarding the book or would like to schedule a workshop in your school or district, please contact me at *emcewan@elainemcewan.com.* If you are interested in other books I have written or the availability of online seminars for continuing education credit, visit my Web site, *www.elainemcewan.com.*

Resource A
List of
Contributing
Highly Effective
Principals

The following addresses were correct at the time of publication.

Sandra Ahola
Pomfret Community School (K–8)
20 Pomfret Street
Pomfret, CT 06259

Terry Beasley
Fairhope Elementary School
2 N. Bishop Road
Fairhope, AL 36532

Sharon Beitel
12 Susan Lane
Newtown, CT 06470

Regina Birdsell
Academy Elementary School
4 School Street
Madison, CT 06443

Kathie Dobberteen
Highland Ranch Elementary School
14840 Waverly Downs Way
San Diego, CA 92128-3702

Laurence Fieber
Parkway Elementary School
446 Parkway Avenue
Ewing, NJ 08618

Gabe Flicker
Grace Lutheran School (K–8)
1350 Baldy Avenue
Pocatello, ID 83201

Lorraine Fong
Bennett-Kew Elementary School
11710 S. Cherry Avenue
Inglewood, CA 90303

Clayton Fujie
Noelani Elementary School
2655 Woodlawn Drive
Honolulu, HI 96822

Margaret Garcia-Dugan
Glendale Union High School District #205
Director of Curriculum
7650 N. 43rd Avenue
Glendale, AZ 85301

Michelle Gayle
Griffin Middle School
800 Alabama Street
Tallahassee, FL 32304

John Giles
Hinckley Elementary School
1586 Center Road
Hinckley, OH 44233

Patricia Hamilton
Arbuckle Elementary School
701 Hall Street
Arbuckle, CA 95912

Jean Hendrickson
Mark Twain Elementary School
2451 W. Main
Oklahoma City, OK 73107

Dawn Hurns
Palm Springs North Elementary School
17615 NW 82nd Avenue
Hialeah, FL 33015

Alan Jones
Assistant Professor
St. Xavier University
3700 West 103rd Street
Chicago, IL 60655

Mark Kern
New Palestine Elementary School
POB538
4801 S. 500 W.
New Palestine, IN 46163

Clare Maguire
Pond School
17200 Manchester Road
Grover, MO 63040

Lola Malone
John Tyson Elementary School
1067 Chapman Avenue
Springdale, AR 72762

Nancy M. Moga
Callaghan Elementary School
4018 Midland Train Road
Covington, VA 24426

Tom Paulsen
Naperville Central High School
404 Aurora Avenue
Naperville, IL 60540-6266

Douglas Pierson
Hamilton Elementary School
25 Salisbury Avenue
North Kingston, RI 02852

Larry Pollock
Juanita Elementary School
9635 NE 132nd Street
Kirkland, WA 98034

Jim Ratledge
Montvale Elementary School
3128 Montvale Road
Maryville, TN 37803

Kathy Schneiter
Roselle Middle School
500 S. Park Street
Roselle, IL 60172-2298

Carol Schulte-Kottwitz
Ridge Meadows School
777 Ridge Rd.
Ellisville, MO 63021

Byron Schwab
Pilot Knob Elementary School
1436 Lone Oak Road
Eagan, MN 55121

Lois Scrivener
Holy Name of Jesus School (K–8)
3060 N. Hwy A1A
Indialantic, FL 32903

Catherine Segura
Avery Island Elementary School

Hwy. 329 Avery Island Road
Avery Island, LA 70518

Dale Skinner
Villarreal Elementary School
10311 Country Vista
San Antonio, TX 78240

Mary Ann Stevens
East Jones Elementary School
108 Northeast Drive
Laurel, MS 39443

Jeanne Stiglbauer
Dreher High School
701 Adger Road
Columbia, SC 29205

Marjorie A. Thompson
26819 Via Desmonde
Lomita, CA 90717

Brenda Valentine
Kanawha City Elementary School
3601 Staunton Avenue S.E.
Charleston, WV 25304

Todd White
Executive Director for the South Carolina Teacher Advancement Program
1027 Altamont Road
Greenville, SC 29609

Tom Williams
Walton-Verona Elementary School
15066 Porter Road
Verona, KY 41092

Steve Wilson
Centura Elementary School
POB 430
201 North Highway 11
Cairo, NE 68824

Resource B
Ten Traits of
Highly Effective
Principals

Trait Number 1: **The Communicator**

The highly effective principal is a Communicator—a genuine and open human being with the capacity to listen, empathize, interact, and connect with individual students, parents, and teachers in productive, helping, and healing ways, as well as the ability to teach, present, and motivate people in larger group settings.

Trait Number 2: **The Educator**

The highly effective principal is an Educator—a self-directed instructional leader with a strong intellect and personal depth of knowledge regarding research-based curriculum, instruction, and learning who motivates and facilitates the intellectual growth and development of self, students, teachers, and parents.

Trait Number 3: **The Envisioner**

The highly effective principal is an Envisioner—an individual who is motivated by a sense of calling and purpose, focused on a vision of what schools can be, and guided by a mission that has the best interests of all students at its core.

Trait Number 4: **The Facilitator**

The highly effective principal is a Facilitator—a leader with outstanding human relations skills that include the abilities to build individual relationships with parents, teachers, and students; collaborative teams with staff members and parents; and a schoolwide community of leaders.

Trait Number 5: **The Change Master**

The highly effective principal is a Change Master—a flexible, futuristic, and realistic leader, able to motivate as well as manage change in an organized, positive, and enduring fashion.

Trait Number 6: **The Culture Builder**

The highly effective principal is a Culture Builder—an individual who communicates (talks) and models (walks) a strong and viable vision based on achievement, character, personal responsibility, and accountability.

Trait Number 7: **The Activator**

The highly effective principal is an Activator—an individual with gumption (e.g., drive, motivation, enthusiasm, energy, spunk, and humor) enough to share with staff, parents, and students.

Trait Number 8: **The Producer**

The highly effective principal is a Producer—a results-oriented individual with a strong sense of accountability to taxpayers, parents, students, and teachers who translates high expectations into intellectual development and academic achievement for all students.

Trait Number 9: **The Character Builder**

The highly effective principal is a Character Builder—a role model whose values, words, and deeds are marked by trustworthiness, integrity, authenticity, respect, generosity, and humility.

Trait Number 10: **The Contributor**

The highly effective principal is a Contributor—a servant-leader, encourager, and enabler whose utmost priority is making a contribution to the success of others.

Resource C
Complete List of
Benchmarks

Trait Number 1: The highly effective principal is a Communicator—a genuine and open human being with the capacity to listen, empathize, interact, and connect with individual students, parents, and teachers in productive, helping, and healing ways, as well as the ability to teach, present, and motivate people in larger group settings.

1.1 Communicators attend.

1.2 Communicators listen.

1.3 Communicators empathize.

1.4 Communicators disclose themselves to others.

1.5 Communicators get the whole story.

1.6 Communicators ask the right questions.

1.7 Communicators say what they mean and mean what they say.

1.8 Communicators can accept criticism.

1.9 Communicators can give correction.

1.10 Communicators communicate creatively.

1.11 Communicators can disagree agreeably.

1.12 Communicators always pay attention to parents.

1.13 Communicators connect emotionally and professionally with staff.

1.14 Communicators communicate with students.

1.15 Communicators can talk to the boss.

1.16 Communicators connect in productive, helping, and healing ways.

1.17 Communicators care enough to send the very best.

1.18 Communicators know how to schmooze.

1.19 Communicators write, speak, and teach.

Trait Number 2: The highly effective principal is an Educator—a self-directed instructional leader with a strong intellect and personal depth of knowledge regarding research-based curriculum, instruction, and learning who motivates and facilitates the intellectual growth and development of self, students, teachers, and parents.

2.1 Educators believe that all students can learn, and they develop programs to help them succeed.

2.2 Educators provide training and support for teachers.

2.3 Educators create cognitive dissonance.

2.4 Educators establish, implement, and achieve academic standards.

2.5 Educators focus on instruction.

2.6 Educators model continuous learning.

2.7 Educators develop teacher leaders.

2.8 Educators pay attention to what matters most.

2.9 Educators create learning communities.

Trait Number 3: The highly effective principal is an Envisioner—an individual who is motivated by a sense of calling and purpose, focused on a vision of what schools can be, and guided by a mission that has the best interests of all students at its core.

3.1 Envisioners are hedgehogs.

3.2 Envisioners feel called.

3.3 Envisioners have resolve, goals, and lifevision.

3.4 Envisioners can see the invisible.

3.5 Envisioners know where they are headed.

3.6 Envisioners have compelling visions.

3.7 Envisioners can articulate their visions and make them happen.

Trait Number 4: The highly effective principal is a Facilitator—a leader with outstanding human relations skills that include the abilities to build individual relationships with parents, teachers, and students; collaborative teams with staff members and parents; and a schoolwide community of leaders.

4.1 Facilitators bond people into a community of leaders.

4.2 Facilitators tap the potential of people.

4.3 Facilitators say "we" instead of "I."

4.4 Facilitators favor people over paperwork.

4.5 Facilitators build up emotional bank accounts.

4.6 Facilitators cultivate their own well-being.

4.7 Facilitators value diversity.

4.8 Facilitators share the "power pie."

4.9 Facilitators accentuate the positives.

4.10 Facilitators promote parental involvement.

4.11 Facilitators celebrate.

4.12 Facilitators spend time with students.

Trait Number 5: The highly effective principal is a Change Master—a flexible, futuristic, and realistic leader, able to motivate as well as manage change in an organized, positive, and enduring fashion.

5.1 Change Masters can handle uncertainty and ambiguity.

5.2 Change Masters respect resisters.

5.3 Change Masters are futuristic.

5.4 Change Masters use a situational approach.

5.5 Change Masters know that the power is within.

5.6 Change Masters value the process.

5.7 Change Masters plan for short-term victories.

5.8 Change Masters provide resources.

5.9 Change Masters trust their teams.

5.10 Change Masters are willing to change themselves.

5.11 Change Masters are motivators.

5.12 Change Masters understand the change process.

Trait Number 6: The highly effective principal is a Culture Builder—an individual who communicates (talks) and models (walks) a strong and viable vision based on achievement, character, personal responsibility, and accountability.

6.1 Culture Builders understand and appreciate the power of culture.

6.2 Culture Builders know what a good culture looks like.

6.3 Culture Builders facilitate the development of core values.

6.4 Culture Builders communicate those values clearly.

6.5 Culture Builders reward those who support and enhance the culture.

6.6 Culture Builders build cultures that people choose.

6.7 Culture Builders know that the "small stuff" is really the "big stuff."

Trait Number 7: The highly effective principal is an Activator—an individual with gumption (e.g., drive, motivation, enthusiasm, energy, spunk, and humor) enough to share with staff, parents, and students.

7.1 Activators mobilize people.

7.2 Activators are entrepreneurial.

7.3 Activators don't wait to be told.

7.4 Activators are risk takers.

7.5 Activators ask for forgiveness rather than permission.

7.6 Activators run to daylight.

7.7 Activators don't micromanage.

7.8 Activators make things happen.

7.9 Activators are outrageous.

7.10 Activators are cheerleaders.

Trait Number 8: The highly effective principal is a Producer—a results-oriented individual with a strong sense of accountability to taxpayers, parents, students, and teachers who translates high expectations into intellectual development and academic achievement for all students.

8.1 Producers believe that achievement is the bottom line.

8.2 Producers never mistake activity for achievement.

8.3 Producers are data driven.

8.4 Producers pay attention to individual students.

8.5 Producers have an academically focused mission.

8.6 Producers make research-based decisions.

8.7 Producers hold teachers accountable.

Trait Number 9: The highly effective principal is a Character Builder—a role model whose values, words, and deeds are marked by trustworthiness, integrity, authenticity, respect, generosity, and humility.

9.1 Character Builders are human.

9.2 Character Builders are trustworthy.

9.3 Character Builders have integrity.

9.4 Character Builders are authentic.

9.5 Character Builders are respectful.

9.6 Character Builders are generous.

9.7 Character Builders are humble.

9.8 Character Builders hire staff members with character.

9.9 Character Builders are consistent.

9.10 Character Builders lead by example, not by exhortation.

9.11 Character Builders seek to develop the character of students.

Trait Number 10: The highly effective principal is a Contributor—a servant-leader, encourager, and enabler whose utmost priority is making a contribution to the success of others.

10.1 Contributors lead by serving others.

10.2 Contributors are self-aware and reflective.

10.3 Contributors are good stewards.

10.4 Contributors have strong wills.

References

Achilles, C., Keedy, J., & High, R. (1999). The workaday world of the principal: How principals get things done. In L. Hughes (Ed.), *The principal as leader* (pp. 25-58). New York: Macmillan.

American Heritage dictionary of the English language. (2000). Boston: Houghton Mifflin. Retrieved August 15, 2002, from education.yahoo.com/reference/dictionary/

Anderson, T. D. (1998). *Transforming leadership: Equipping yourself and coaching others to build the leadership organization* (2nd ed.). Boca Raton, FL: St. Lucie.

Andrews, R., & Soder, R. (1987). Principal leadership and student achievement. *Educational Leadership, 44*(6), 9-11.

Aspy, D. N., & Roebuck, F. N. (1977). *Kids don't learn from people they don't like.* Amherst, MA: Human Resource Development Press.

Association for Supervision and Curriculum Development. (2001). *How to produce results* (Results video series). Alexandria, VA: Author.

Aubrey, C. A., II, & Felkins, P. K. (1988). *Teamwork.* Milwaukee, WI: ASQC Quality.

Autry, J. A. (2001). *The servant leader: How to build a creative team, develop great morale, and improve bottom-line performance.* Roseville, CA: Prima.

Autry, J. A., & Mitchell, S. (1998). *Real power: Business lessons from the Tao Te Ching.* New York: PenguinPutnam.

Barth, R. (1976). A principal and his school. *The National Elementary School Principal, 56,* 9-21.

Barth, R. (2000). Foreword to the second edition. In J. Blase & J. Blase. *Bringing out the best in teachers* (pp. x-xi). Thousand Oaks, CA: Corwin.

Beecher, H. W. (1887). From *Proverbs from Plymouth pulpit.* Retrieved January 27, 2003, from http://www.thinkexist.com/English/Author/x/Author_3093_8.htm

Belcher, J. G., Jr. (1987). *Productivity plus: How today's best run companies are gaining the competitive edge.* Houston, TX: Gulf.

Bennis, W. (1989). *Why leaders can't lead: The unconscious conspiracy continues.* San Francisco: Jossey-Bass.

Bennis, W. (2002). Become a tomorrow leader. In L. C. Spears & M. Lawrence (Eds.), *Focus on leadership: Servant-leadership for the twenty-first century* (pp. 101-109). New York: John Wiley.

Berlin, I. (1970). *The hedgehog and the fox: An essay on Tolstoy's view of history.* New York: Simon & Schuster.

Blanchard, K. (2001). *Empowerment takes more than a minute.* San Francisco: Berrett-Koehler.

Blanchard, K. (2002). The heart of servant-leadership. In L. C. Spears (Ed.), *Insights on leadership: Service, stewardship, spirit, and servant-leadership* (pp. ix-xii). New York: John Wiley.

Blase, J., & Blase, J. (1994). *Empowering teachers: What successful principals do.* Thousand Oaks, CA: Corwin.

Blase, J., & Blase, J. (1998a). *Handbook of instructional leadership.* Thousand Oaks, CA: Corwin.

Blase, J., & Blase, J. (1998b). *How really good principals promote teaching and learning.* Thousand Oaks, CA: Corwin.

Blase, J., & Blase, J. (2002). *Breaking the silence: Overcoming the problem of principal mistreatment of teachers.* Thousand Oaks, CA: Corwin

Blase, J., & Kirby, P. (2002). *Bringing out the best in teachers: What effective principals do* (2nd ed.). Thousand Oaks, CA: Corwin.

Block, P. (1993). *Stewardship: Choosing service over self-interest.* San Francisco: Berrett-Koehler.

Bloom, B. S. (1980). The new direction in educational research: Alterable variables. *Phi Delta Kappan, 61,* 382-385.

Boy Scouts of America. (2002). *Boy Scout Oath, Law, Motto, and Slogan.* Retrieved February 10, 2002, from www.scouting.org

Brice, J. (2002, September 25). High-poverty schools that succeed share common teaching programs. *San Francisco Chronicle.* Retrieved September 29, 2002, from www.sfgate.com

Brookover, W. B., & Lezotte, L. W. (1979). *Changes in school characteristics coincident with changes in school achievement.* East Lansing: Michigan State University, Institute for Research on Teaching.

Bryk, A. A., & Schneider, B. (2002). *Trust in schools: A core resource for improvement.* New York: Russell Sage Foundation.

Bryk, A. S., Sebring, P. B., Kerbow, D., Rollow, S., & Easton, J. Q. (1998). *Charting Chicago school reform: Democratic localism as a lever for change.* Boulder, CO: Westview.

Buber, M. (1958). *Hasidism and modern man* (M. Friedman, Trans. & Ed.). New York: Horizon. (Original work published 1948)

Buckingham, M., & Coffman, C. (1999). *First break all the rules: What the world's greatest managers do differently.* New York: Simon & Schuster.

Buckingham, M., & Coffman, C. (2001). *Now, discover your strengths.* New York: Free Press.

Building Champions. (2002). *What is coaching.* Retrieved September 24, 2002, from www.Buildingchampions.com

Burkhardt, J., & Spears, L. C. (2002). Servant-leadership and philanthropic institutions. In L. C. Spears (Ed.), *Insights on leadership: Service, stewardship, spirit, and servant-leadership* (pp. 223-243). New York: John Wiley.

Carlyle, T. (2002). *The great quotations by Thomas Carlyle to inspire you to achieve your dreams.* Retrieved January 27, 2003, from www.cyber-nation.com/victory/quotations

Character Counts™. (2002). Retrieved August 21, 2002, from www.character-counts.org

Chesnick, J., & Bustamante, M. (2002, August 16). Creativity, faith in children can transform D's into A's. *Tucson Citizen,* pp. 1A, 4A.

Childress, J. R., & Senn, L. E. (1999). *The secret of a winning culture: Building high-performance teams.* Los Angeles: Leadership Press.

Claxton, G. (1997). *Why intelligence increases when you think less.* London: Fourth Estate.

Cohen, J. M., & Cohen, M. (Eds.). (1961). *The Penguin dictionary of quotations.* New York: Penguin.

Collins, J. (2001). *Good to great: Why some companies make the leap and others don't.* New York: HarperBusiness.

Covey, S. R. (1990). *The seven habits of highly effective people.* New York: Simon & Schuster.

Covey, S. R. (1993). *Principle-centered leadership program workbook.* Provo, UT: Covey Leadership Center.

Covey, S. R. (1998). Growing great children. In M. S. Josephson & W. Hanson (Eds.), *The power of character: Prominent Americans talk about life, family, work, values, and more* (pp. 99-106). San Francisco: Jossey-Bass.

Cox, A., & Liesse, J. (1996). *Redefining corporate soul: Linking purpose and people.* Chicago: Irwin.

Deal, T. E. (1987). The culture of schools. In L. T. Scheive & M. B. Schoenheit (Eds.), *Leadership: Examining the elusive* (pp. 3-15). Alexandria, VA: Association for Supervision and Curriculum Development.

DeBono, E. (1999). *Six thinking hats.* Boston: Little, Brown.

DePree, M. (1987). *Leadership is an art.* East Lansing: Michigan State University Press.

DeRoche, E. F., & Williams, M. M. (2001). *Character education: A guide for school administrators.* Lanham, MD: Scarecrow.

Diekman, J. R. (1979). *Get your message across: How to improve communication.* Englewood Cliffs, NJ: Prentice-Hall.

Dobberteen, K. (2001). *Second Annual Chase Change Award: Essay.* La Mesa, CA: La Mesa Dale Elementary School. Unpublished document.

Douglas, A., & Strumpf, M. (Eds.). *Webster's new world dictionary of quotations.* New York: Macmillan.

Drucker, P. F. (1999). *Management challenges for the 21st century.* New York: HarperBusiness.

Drucker, P. F. (2001). *The essential Drucker.* New York: HarperBusiness.

DuFour, R., & Eaker, R. (1998). *Professional learning communities at work: Best practices for enhancing student achievement.* Bloomington, IN: National Educational Service.

Edmonds, R. (1981). Making public schools effective. *Social Policy, 12,* 53-60.

Edmonds, R. R. (1979). Effective schools for the urban poor. *Educational Leadership, 37*(2), 15-18, 20-24.

Educational Research Service. (2000). *The principal, keystone of a high-achieving school: Attracting and keeping the leaders we need* (prepared for the National Association of Elementary School Principals and National Association of Secondary School Principals). Arlington, VA: Author.

Faber, A., & Mazlish, E. (1990). Liberated parents, liberated children: Your guide to a happier family. New York: Avon Books.

Farson, R. (1996). *Management of the absurd: Paradoxes of leadership.* New York: Simon & Schuster.

Fieber, L. (1999). *New Jersey principal of the year program: Rewarding visionary leadership* (application form). Unpublished document.

Fisher, G. (1989, June 8). *Expectations of a leader.* Unpublished speech. Schaumburg, IL.

Fitzhenry, R. I. (Ed.). *The David and Charles book of quotations.* London: David & Charles.

Flesch, R. (Ed.). (1957). *The new book of unusual quotations.* New York: Harper & Row.

Fox, M. (1992). *Sheer joy: Conversations with Thomas Aquinas on creation spirituality.* San Francisco: Harper.

Frost, R. (1958). The road not taken. In E. C. Lathen (Ed.), *The poetry of Robert Frost* (p. 105). New York: Holt, Rinehart & Winston.

Fullan, M. (1991). *The new meaning of educational change* (2nd ed.). New York: Teachers College Press.

Fullan, M. (1992). *Successful school improvement.* Buckingham, UK: Open University Press.

Fullan, M. (2001). *Leading in a culture of change.* San Francisco: Jossey-Bass.

Fun companies: TD Industries. (2002). *Graduating Engineer Online.* Retrieved August 11, 2002, from www.graduatingengineer.com

Gardner, H. (1983). *Frames of mind: The theory of multiple intelligences.* New York: Basic Books.

Gardner, H. (1999). *Intelligence reframed: Multiple intelligences for the 21st century.* New York: Basic Books.

Glickman, C. D. (1990). *Supervision of instruction: A developmental approach* (2nd ed.). Boston: Allyn & Bacon.

Glickman, C. D. (1993). *Renewing America's schools: A guide for school-based action.* San Francisco: Jossey-Bass.

Goodnough, A. (2002, August 29). Schools chief names top aides and hints at his main priorities. *New York Times.* Retrieved August 29, 2002, from www. nytimes.com

Greenleaf, R. K. (1977). *Servant leadership: A journey into the nature of legitimate power and greatness.* Mahwah, NJ: Paulist.

Greenleaf, R. K. (1982). *Servant as leader.* Peterborough, NH: Greenleaf Center.

Hallinger, P., & Heck, R. (1996a). Reassessing the principal's role in school effectiveness: A review of empirical research. *Educational Administration Quarterly, 32*(1), 5-44.

Hallinger, P., & Heck, R. (1996b). The principal's role in school effectiveness: An assessment of methodological progress, 1980-1995. In K. Leithwood, J. Chapman, D. Corson, P. Hallinger, & A. Hart (Eds.), *International handbook of educational leadership and administration* (pp. 723-783). Dordrecht, The Netherlands: Kluwer.

Haver, J. (1995, October 12). Central High shows how schools should work. *Arizona Republic,* p. B7.

Hawley, J. A. (1993). *Reawakening the spirit in work: The power of dharmic management.* San Francisco: Berrett-Koehler.

Heck, R. H., Larsen, T. J., & Marcoulides, G. A. (1990). Instructional leadership and school achievement. *NASSP Bulletin, 77*(5), 20-28.

Heifetz, R. A. (1994). *Leadership without easy answers.* Cambridge, MA: Harvard University Press.

Hesse, H. (1968). *The journey to the east* (H. Rosner, Trans.). New York: Farrar, Strauss & Giroux.

Hill, P. T., Foster, G. E., & Gendler, T. (1990). *High schools with character.* Santa Monica, CA: RAND.

Hoag, N. (1998, November 11). Letter to the editor. *The Morning News of Northwest Arkansas,* p. 8.

Horn, S. (1996). *Tongue fu! How to deflect, disarm, and defuse any verbal conflict.* New York: St. Martin's Griffin.

Institute for Educational Leadership. (2000). *Leadership for school learning: Reinventing the principalship.* Washington, DC: Author.

Johnson, D. W., & Johnson, F. P. (1982). *Joining together: Group theory and group skills.* Englewood Cliffs, NJ: Prentice Hall.

Joyce, B., Hersh, R., & McKibbin, M. (1983). *The structure of school improvement.* New York: Longman.

Juanita School. (2002). *Mission statement.* Retrieved February 11, 2003, from www.jua.lkwash.wednet.edu/

Kanter, R. M. (1983). *The change-masters: Innovations for productivity in the American corporation.* New York: Simon & Schuster.

Katzenbach, J. R., & Smith, D. K. (1993). *The wisdom of teams: Creating the high-performance organization.* Boston: Harvard Business School Press.

Kingsolver, B. (1995). *High tide in Tucson.* New York: HarperCollins.

Knowles, E. (Ed.). (1997). *The Oxford dictionary of phrase, saying, and quotation.* Oxford, UK: Oxford University Press. (Original work published in 1849)

Kosmoski, G. J., & Pollack, D. R. (2000). *Managing difficult, frustrating, and hostile conversations: Strategies for savvy administrators.* Thousand Oaks, CA: Corwin.

Kossan, P. (2002, September 30). Schools fear public labels of "failing." *The Arizona Republic,* pp. B1-2.

Kotter, J. P. (1996). *Leading change.* Boston: Harvard Business School Press.

Kotter, J. P. (1999). *What leaders really do.* Cambridge, MA: Harvard Business School Press.

Kottler, J. A., & McEwan, E. K. (1999). *Counseling tips for elementary school principals.* Thousand Oaks, CA: Corwin.

Kottwitz, C. (2000). *Application for National Awards Program for Model Professional Development.* Unpublished document.

Kouzes, J. M. (1998). Finding your voice. In L. C. Spears (Ed.), *Insights on leadership: Service, stewardship, spirit, and servant-leadership* (pp. 322-325). New York: John Wiley.

Kouzes, J. M., & Posner, B. Z. (1987). *The leadership challenge: How to get extraordinary things done in organizations.* San Francisco: Jossey-Bass.

Kouzes, J. M., & Posner, B. Z. (1999). *Encouraging the heart: A leader's guide to rewarding and recognizing others.* San Francisco: Jossey-Bass.

Kuczmarski, S. S., & Kuczmarski, T. D. (1995). *Values-based leadership.* Englewood Cliffs, NJ: Prentice Hall.

Labovitz, G., & Rosansky, V. (1997). *The power of alignment: How great companies stay centered and accomplish extraordinary things.* New York: John Wiley.

Lamott, A. (1994). *Some instructions on writing and life.* New York: Anchor.

Lao-Tzu. (1963). *Tao te ching* (D. C. Lau, Trans.). New York: Penguin. (Original work published in the 6th century BCE)

Lao-Tzu. (1985). *Tao te ching* (R. Wilhelm, Trans.). London: Arkana. Translated into English by H. G. Ostwald. (Original work published in the 6th century BCE)

Lao-Tzu. (1992). *Tao te ching: A New English Version.* New York: HarperPerennial. (Original work published in the 6th century BCE).

Learning Research and Development Center. (2002) *The learning walk: A signature tool of the Institute for Learning.* Retrieved February 11, 2003, from http://www.lrdc.pitt.edu/. Available as a PDF file.

Lee, V., Bryk, A., & Smith, J. (1993). The organization of effective secondary schools. *Review of Research in Education, 68,* 241-270.

Leithwood, K., Begley, P., & Cousins, B. (1990). The nature, causes, and consequences of principals' practices: An agenda for future research. *Journal of Educational Administration, 28*(4), 5-31.

Lemming, J. S. (1994). Character education and the creation of community. *The Responsive Community, 4*(4), 49-57.

Lerner, H. (2001). *The dance of connection.* New York: HarperCollins.

Levering, R., & Moskowitz, M. (2002, February 4). Best companies to work for: How we pick the 100 Best. *Fortune.* Retrieved September 29, 2002, from www.fortune.com/lists/bestcompanies/faq.html

Lewin, T. (2002, August 31). Educator has accomplishments and enemies. *New York Times.* Retrieved August 31, 2002, from www.nytimes.com/2002/08/31/education/31LAM.html and www.nytimes.com/2002/08/31/nyregion/31BIOB.html

Lezotte, L. W. (1992). *Creating the total quality effective school.* Okemos, Michigan: Effective Schools Products.

Littauer, F. (1989). *Silver boxes: The gift of encouragement.* Dallas: Word Publishing.

Locke, J. (1854). *An essay concerning human understanding and a treatise on the conduct of understanding.* Philadelphia: Hayes & Zell. (Original work published in 1690)

Los Angeles Unified School District. (2002). *Learning Walk PowerPoint Presentation.* Retrieved February 11, 2003, from www.lausd.k12.ca.us/

Lynch, R. F., & Werner, T. J. (1992). *Continuous improvement: Teams and tools.* Atlanta, GA: QualTeam, Inc.

Malone, L. (2002). *Character Words Program.* Unpublished document. Springdale, AR: John Tyson School.

Manasse, A. L. (1982). Introduction. In National Association of Secondary School Principals (Ed.), *The effective principal* (pp. vii-viii). Reston, VA: National Association of Secondary School Principals.

Manna, P. (1999, November 17). Hooked on a feeling. *Education Week.* Retrieved September 9, 2002, from www.edweek.com

Maurer, R. (1996). *Beyond the wall of resistance: Unconventional strategies that build support for change.* Austin, TX: Bard.

McEwan, E. K. (1985, November). When students assess the principal. *Principal,* 17-20.

McEwan, E. K. (1997). *Leading your team to excellence: How to make quality decisions.* Thousand Oaks, CA: Corwin.

McEwan, E. K. (1998). *How to deal with parents who are angry, troubled, afraid, or just plain crazy.* Thousand Oaks, CA: Corwin.

McEwan, E. K., & Damer, M. (2000). *Managing unmanageable students: Practical solutions for administrators.* Thousand Oaks, CA: Corwin.

McEwan, E. K. (2002). *Teach them all to read: Catching the kids who fall through the cracks.* Thousand Oaks, CA: Corwin.

McEwan, E. K. (2003). *7 steps to effective instructional leadership* (2nd ed.). Thousand Oaks, CA: Corwin.

McEwan, E. K. (forthcoming). *Brain-based reading: Cognitive strategies that boost student achievement.* Thousand Oaks, CA: Corwin.

McKechnie, J. L. (Ed.). (1983). *Webster's new universal unabridged dictionary* (2nd ed.). New York: Simon & Schuster.

Morse, J. (2001, May 21). Let them lift us up. *Time*, pp. 75-76.

Moxley, R. S. (2000). *Leadership and spirit: Breathing new vitality and energy into individuals and organizations.* San Francisco: Jossey-Bass.

Nanus, B. (1992). *Visionary leadership.* San Francisco: Jossey-Bass.

National Association of Elementary School Principals. (2001a). *Honoring America's national distinguished principals.* Alexandria, VA: Author.

National Association of Elementary School Principals. (2001b). *Leading learning communities: Standards for what principals should know and be able to do.* Alexandria, VA: Author.

National Association of Secondary School Principals. (2001). *Priorities and barriers in high school leadership: A survey of principals.* Reston, VA: Author.

Newstrom, J. W., & Scannell, E. E. (1980). *Games trainers play: Experiential learning exercises.* New York: McGraw-Hill.

Niebuhr, R. (1951, February 13). To be abased and to abound. *Messenger,* p. 7.

Nolte, D. L. (1972). *Children learn what they live.* Retrieved August 27, 2002, from www.empowermentresources.com/info2/childrenlearn-long_version.html

Novak, M. (1986, Spring/Summer). Crime and character. *This World,* pp. 1-5.

Olson, L. (2000, January 12). Policy focus converges on leadership. *Education Week.* Retrieved October 20, 2002, from www.edweek.com

Palincsar, A. S., & Brown, A. L. (1989). Instruction for self-regulated reading. In L. B. Resnick & L. E. Klopfer (Eds.), *Toward the thinking curriculum: Current cognitive research* (pp. 19-39). Alexandria, VA: Association for Supervision and Curriculum Development.

Parkhurst, W. (1988). *The eloquent executive: A guide to high-impact speaking in big meetings, small meetings, and one-on-one.* New York: Times Books.

Persell, C. H., & Cookson, P. W., Jr. (1982). The effective principal in action. In National Association of Secondary School Principals (Ed.), *The effective principal* (pp. 22-29). Reston, VA: Editor.

Pirsig, R. (1974). *Zen and the art of motorcycle maintenance.* New York: William Morrow.

Pritchett, P., & Pound, R. (1993). *High-velocity culture change: A handbook for managers.* Dallas: Pritchett.

Prochnow, H. V., & Prochnow, H. V., Jr. (Eds.). (1962). *A dictionary of wit, wisdom, and satire.* New York: Harper.

Providence Schools. (2002). *Rekindling the dream: A framework for reform in the Providence Schools.* Retrieved October 15, 2002, from www.providenceschools.org/rkd_lwalks.cfm

Public Agenda. (2001). *Trying to stay ahead of the game: Superintendents and principals talk about school leadership.* New York: Author.

Ramsey, R. D. (1999). *How to say the right thing every time: Communicating well with students, staff, parents, and the public.* Thousand Oaks, CA: Corwin.

Reuben, S. C. (1998). Help! How do I teach character when I'm still questioning my own. In M. S. Josephson & W. Hanson (Eds.), *The power of character: Prominent Americans talk about life, family, work, values, and more* (pp. 126-133). San Francisco: Jossey-Bass.

Richard, A. (2000, November 1). Panel calls for fresh look at duties facing principals. *Education Week.* Retrieved October 20, 2002, from www.edweek.com

Rogers, C. R. (1957). The necessary and sufficient conditions of therapeutic personality change. *Journal of Consulting Psychology, 21,* 95-103.

Rowan, B. (1990). Commitment and control: Alternative strategies for the organizational design of schools. *Review of Research in Education, 16,* 353-389.

Ruschman, N. L. (2002). Servant-leadership and the best companies to work for in America. In L. C. Spears & M. Lawrence (Eds.), *Focus on leadership: Servant-leadership for the twenty-first century* (pp. 123-139). New York: John Wiley.

Safire, W. (Ed.). *Lend me your ears: Great speeches in history.* New York: Norton.

Saint-Exupéry, A. (1943). *The little prince* (K. Woods, Trans.). New York: Harcourt, Brace & World.

Saphier, J., & King, M. (1985, March). Good seeds grow in strong cultures. *Educational Leadership, 43,* 67-74.

Sawyer, R. K. (2001). *Creating conversations: Improvisation in everyday discourse.* Cresskill, NJ: Hampton.

Scearce, C. (1992). *100 ways to build teams.* Palatine, IL: IRI/Skylight.

Schein, E. (1999). *The corporate culture survival guide: Sense and nonsense about culture change.* San Francisco: Jossey-Bass.

Schmoker, M. (1999). *Results: The key to continuous school improvement* (2nd ed.). Alexandria, VA: Association for Supervision and Curriculum Development.

Schmoker, M. (2001). *The results fieldbook: Practical strategies from dramatically improved schools.* Alexandria, VA: Association for Supervision and Curriculum Development.

Schweitzer, A. (1963). *Out of my life and thought.* New York: New American Library.

Scott, S. (2002). *Fierce conversations: Achieving success at work and in life, one conversation at a time.* New York: Penguin Viking.

Seldes, G. (Ed.). (1999). *The great quotations.* New York: Lyle Stuart.

Senge, P. M. (1990). *The fifth discipline: The art and practice of the learning organization.* New York: Doubleday.

Sergiovanni, T. J. (1984). Leadership and excellence in schooling. *Educational Leadership, 41*(5), 4-14.

Sergiovanni, T. J. (1992). *Moral leadership: Getting to the heart of school improvement.* San Francisco: Jossey-Bass.

Sergiovanni, T. J. (1996). *Leadership for the schoolhouse: How is it different? Why is it important?* San Francisco: Jossey-Bass.

Sergiovanni, T. J. (2000). *The lifeworld of leadership: Creating culture, community, and personal meaning in our schools.* San Francisco: Jossey-Bass.

Sergiovanni, T. J. (2001). *The principalship: A reflective practice perspective.* Boston: Allyn & Bacon.

Seuss, Dr. (1940). *Horton hatches the egg.* New York: Random House.

Seuss, Dr. (2002). *BrainyQuotes.* Retrieved October 14, 2002, from www.brainyquote.com

Sharan, S., Shachar, H., & Levine, T. (1999). *The innovative school: Organization and instruction.* Westport, CT: Bergin & Garvey.

Shechtman, M. R. (1994). *Working without a net: How to survive and thrive in today's high risk business world.* Englewood Cliffs, NJ: Prentice Hall.

Spears, L. C. (1995). *Reflections on leadership: How Robert K. Greenleaf's theory of servant leadership influenced today's top management thinkers.* New York: John Wiley.

Stowell, S. J., & Starcevich, M. M. (1998). *The coach: Creating partnerships for a competitive edge.* Sandy, UT: Center for Management and Organization Effectiveness.

Streifer, P. A. (2002). *Using data to make better educational decisions.* Latham, MD: Scarecrow.

Stricherz, M. (2001, April 18). Leadership. *Education Week,* p. 5.

TD Industries. (2002). *Servant leadership.* Retrieved August 11, 2002, from www. tdindustries.com/AboutUs/ServantLeadership.asp

Telushkin, J. (1998). The power of words. In M. S. Josephson & W. Hanson (Eds.), *The power of character: Prominent Americans talk about life, family, work, values, and more* (pp. 58-66). San Francisco: Jossey-Bass.

Thomas, R. M. (2002). *Overcoming inertia in school reform.* Thousand Oaks, CA: Corwin.

Utah State Department of Education. (2002). *Legacy Elementary Value Pumpkin Walk.* Retrieved August 15, 2002, from www.usoe. k12.ut.us/curr/char_ed/ districts/alpine/pmpwlk.htm

Vaill, P. B. (1986). The purpose of high-performing systems. In T. J. Sergiovanni & J. E. Corbally (Eds.), *Leadership and organizational culture: New perspectives on administrative theory and practice* (pp. 85-104). Urbana: University of Illinois Press.

Villarreal Elementary School. *Mission Statement.* Retrieved August 2002, from www.nisd.net/villaww/

Waterman, R. H., Jr. (1990). *Adhocracy.* New York: Norton.

Wheatley, M. J. (1999). *Leadership and the new science: Discovering order in a chaotic world.* San Francisco: Berrett-Koehler.

White, T. (1999). *Palmetto's Finest* (Application form). Carolina First Bank and the South Carolina Association of School Administration. Greenville, SC. Unpublished document.

Wolcott, H. F. (1973). *The man in the principal's office: An ethnography.* New York: Holt, Rinehart & Winston.

Wooden, J. (with Jamison, S.). (1997). *Wooden: A lifetime of observations and reflections on and off the court.* Chicago: Contemporary Books.

Ziglar, Z. (1986). *Top performance: How to develop excellence in yourself and others.* New York: Berkley Books.

Index

Facilitator's Guide

WHO SHOULD USE THIS GUIDE?

The facilitator's guide for *Ten Traits of Highly Effective Principals: From Good to Great Performance* is designed to be used by the following individuals and groups:

- College and university teachers who wish to use in-depth studies of the ten traits as part of their courses on the principalship
- Leaders of districtwide study groups of principals who wish to notch up the performance of their principals through staff development and group interaction
- Facilitators of ad hoc study groups of principals who desire to motivate discussion and pursue issues and problems with regard to the principalship
- Individual principals who want to enhance their own personal effectiveness regarding one or more of the ten traits
- Individual principals who are engaged in reflective self-study as part of personal goal-setting or evaluation processes
- Mentors or coaches of individual principals or small groups of principals who wish to develop and encourage the principals with whom they work to become more effective

While all of the exercises and activities in this guide have been designed with practicing principals in mind, facilitators who are working with aspiring principals can readily adapt the activities to meet their specific needs in one of three ways:

- Participants can adapt the exercises or activities to their unique job situations (e.g., classroom teacher, assistant principal, or media specialist).

- Participants can examine the traits of administrators with whom they currently work and evaluate or describe their attitudes and actions.
- Participants can *imagine* themselves on the job as administrators and hypothesize what they *might* do in specific instances.

HOW IS THE GUIDE ORGANIZED?

The guide contains twelve instructional modules—an introductory module, ten modules that correspond to the ten traits, and a concluding module. There are several possible ways to configure your small-group meetings:

- Hold twelve sessions.
- Hold just two sessions using only the introductory and concluding modules.
- Choose selected modules or combine modules, editing the activities to fit your specific time frame.

Each of the trait modules stands alone and contains the following components: (1) an energizer to introduce the trait and engage participants in group interaction, (2) a group process activity that explores the trait in more depth, (3) a set of questions to inspire dialogue among group participants, (4) a reflective writing activity to be logged into the participants' Ten Traits Journals, (5) suggested Rapid Rewards Goals to be implemented between meetings, and (6) a reading assignment for the upcoming unit. This guide is designed so that you can select the exercises and activities that best fit the needs of your group, the time you have available, and your own personal facilitation style.

WHAT MATERIALS ARE NEEDED?

Materials for Facilitators

Copy of *Ten Traits of Highly Effective Principals: From Good to Great Performance*

Name tags for participants

Chart paper and markers

Pushpins, masking tape, or sticky chart paper

Overhead projector for transparencies

Copies of the forms, figures, or exhibits for participants in various modules (noted at the beginning of each module)

Miscellaneous materials for the various exercises (noted at the beginning of each module)

Materials for Participants

Copies of *Ten Traits of Highly Effective Principals: From Good to Great Performance*

Bound journals in which participants will record reflective writing assignments and notes

STUDY MODULES

Introduction

Materials Needed

Sticky-backed name tags (to be completed by participants)

Magic Markers

Copies of Resource B for participants if desired

Assignment to be completed *before* first meeting

Participants should have read the Preface and Introduction to *Ten Traits of Highly Effective Principals: From Good to Great Performance* before the first meeting. If desired, suggest that participants use the Questions for Dialogue in this module as a focus for their reading. If you plan to schedule only two sessions, keep in mind when choosing your meeting dates that participants must read Chapters 1–10 between the first and second meetings.

Energizer for Groups Whose Members Do Not Know Each Other: What's My Name?

One aspect of being a highly effective principal (especially a Communicator or a Facilitator) is learning the names of everyone (staff, parents, and students) in the school community. One way to do that is to combine alliterative adjectives with people's first names. Give participants blank name tags and ask them to choose an alliterative adjective (for their first name) that is descriptive of their attitudes or actions as a principal. Request that participants not wear their name tags until all of the introductions have taken place. Then ask participants to introduce themselves either to the whole group (if a relatively small one) or to the individuals at their table (if a very large group). For example, "I'm Energetic Elaine (Loquacious Lou, Empathetic Ed, Reflective Raymond)." Once all participants have introduced themselves, ask for volunteers to repeat as many names of their group members as they can remember. Then have participants put on their name tags.

Alternate Energizer for Groups That Are Well-Acquainted: Two Truths and a Lie

In Two Truths and a Lie, individuals share two statements about themselves that are true and one that is not. Other members of the group try to determine which of the statements is not true. Ask participants to write down three statements about themselves, two of them true and the third false. When all participants have completed their statements, ask for volunteers to read their statements, and have group members decide which one is false. The object of this "game" is to fool the participants with an outrageous truth and a very sensible and commonplace untruth.

Process Activity: What Are My Strengths?

Ask participants to choose a partner for this activity. Direct the participants' attention to the complete list of Ten Traits found in Resource B or provide photocopies of this list to save time. Ask participants to refresh their memories regarding the ten traits by silently reading the list. Next, ask participants to choose the *two* traits that they believe to be their *major* strengths.

Then ask participants to write the traits they have chosen, one per page, in their Ten Traits Journal. Then direct participants to write one specific thing they do regularly that is related to this trait. Encourage participants to focus on behaviors that provide direct evidence to others of the presence of this trait in their lives. Ask participants to share this information with their partners.

Debrief with the whole group using the following questions:

1. Did you feel uncomfortable with this activity?

2. Why is it important to know what your strengths are?

3. Were you honest with yourself or did you choose a trait(s) that might make you seem less "boastful" when you shared the information with your partner?

4. Do you think that your staff members would identify the same two traits that you chose as your strengths? How about your colleagues or family members?

5. Did you find it difficult to specify an attitude or action that was evidentiary in nature for the traits you chose? Why?

6. Have you ever asked staff members to provide feedback about your strengths or needs for improvement?

7. If yes, were you surprised or did you disagree with their findings? How could this discrepancy have occurred?

8. Consider some reasons for the differences between their perceptions and reality. Or your perceptions and reality.

If time permits (or in place of the debriefing), ask participants to arrange themselves in numerical order according to the traits they chose. Note the most "popular" traits and speculate with the group why so many participants chose those traits.

Questions for Dialogue

Remind participants that a dialogue is somewhat different from a discussion. The goal of a dialogue is not to reach a resolution, compromise, synthesis, or closure. The goal is to understand the concepts and ideas more completely. In a dialogue, listening is a form of participation; all participants are asked to listen carefully and to refrain from sideline discussions.

1. Do you agree with the author's choices for the ten traits? Why? Why not?

2. If you could add another trait to the list, what trait what would it be? Why? What trait would you give up in exchange?

3. If you believe that it is possible for people to change their behavior and attitudes, give personal examples to support your belief.

4. In the Introduction, the author quotes Max DePree, who says, "In some sense, every reader 'finishes' every book according to his or her experiences and needs and beliefs and potential." What are some possible ways you might "finish" this book?

5. Jeanne Stiglbauer, the first high school principal mentioned in the Introduction, refers to herself as "a warrior on a steed," but the author chose the metaphor of a basketball player to describe Jeanne. What

metaphor best describes how you see yourself in the principalship? Why did you choose that metaphor?

6. The author suggests that the term "effectiveness," as used in describing principals, means getting a desired result from a set of behaviors and attitudes. What results are you looking for as a principal?

7. In the Preface, an anonymous principal is quoted as saying, "When I started in this business, my job was to manage the school and keep the parents and teachers happy. Now, to be considered effective, I need to get results." Reflect on this paradigm shift and what it means for the principalship today. What are some things you have had to do differently?

Rapid Rewards Goals

A Rapid Rewards Goal, as its name suggests, will provide immediate and positive feedback from teachers, students, and parents to principals as they engage in the behaviors specified in their goal. Participants write and then implement one Rapid Rewards Goal for each of the ten traits, adding one per week, while continuing to implement the prior week's goal activities. The purpose of these goals is to create habits of thinking and being (attitudes and actions) that will lead to increased effectiveness on the part of the participants. The guide provides two suggested Rapid Rewards Goals for each trait, but participants are free to choose another goal that is related to one or more of the trait's benchmarks or a current job goal.

Remind participants that their Rapid Rewards Goals must be both compelling *and* measurable in some way (e.g., by surveying faculty members or parents or charting specific behaviors). Encourage participants to think about possible goals as they read Chapter 1 or to engage in the following activity prior to the next meeting, for the purpose of identifying possible weekly goals based on staff input.

Participant Instructions: Gaining Input From Faculty

Hold a short meeting with your faculty for the purpose of giving you input regarding the ten traits. Pass out copies of two items to your faculty members: (1) Resource B, Complete List of the Ten Traits, and (2) Form D.1, Ten Traits Questionnaire for Staff. Ask staff members to carefully read the list of ten traits. Then ask them to complete the questionnaire and return it to a staff member you have chosen ahead of time. This individual will collate all of the votes and comments and then sit down with you to summarize them. This step is necessary to avoid the possibility of handwriting recognition on your part. Complete anonymity is important for this exercise. Choose someone to collect the faculty's input whom you trust, and gain their agreement ahead of time that they will hold the survey results in confidence.

Form D.1   Ten Traits Questionnaire for Staff Members

1. Read the attached list of ten traits and descriptors. Choose the trait that you believe to be your principal's strongest trait and write it on the line below:

_____

Cite some specific things that your principal regularly does that made you choose this particular trait:

_____

_____

_____

_____

_____

2. Choose the trait that you believe is most in need of "work" by your principal:

_____

Cite some specific things you would like to see your principal do that he or she is not currently doing that, in your opinion, would strengthen this trait:

_____

_____

_____

_____

_____

Reflective Writing Activity: What I Want to Know

Ask participants to list the questions they would like to have answered as they read *Ten Traits of Highly Effective Principals: From Good to Great Performance.*

Assignment for Next Meeting

Read Chapter 1. Each module covers one chapter that must be read in advance of a scheduled meeting. Vary the focus or approach of the reading assignments by suggesting that participants use one of the following formats or a format that you suggest:

Participant Directions: Reading Assignment Strategies

1. Use the dialogue questions from the upcoming module as a focus during reading. Record your observations in your journal as you read.

2. Use the Sticky Arrow Strategy while you read the chapter (see Figure D.1). Purchase a package of different-colored sticky arrows to use during your reading. Be prepared to discuss the confusions, connections, mental images, and feelings that reading the chapter evoked.

3. Develop five thought-provoking questions to ask the members of your small group in the warm-up session. Jot them down in your journal.

Trait Number 1: The Communicator

The highly effective principal is a Communicator—a genuine and open human being with the capacity to listen, empathize, interact, and connect with individual students, parents, and teachers in productive, helping, and healing ways, as well as the ability to teach, present, and motivate people in larger group settings.

Materials

A set of 3×5 cards for the Process Activity

Energizer: Alliterative Adjectives

Repeat the energizer from the first meeting, asking any newcomers to introduce themselves with an alliterative adjective and testing all participants regarding how well they remember each other's names (and traits).

Figure D.1 The Sticky Arrow Reading Strategy

Purchase a package of sticky arrows of different colors from an office supply store. Use four of the colors to stand for four different reactions you may have to the text that you are reading: (1) confusion, (2) connections, (3) mental images, or 4) strong feelings.

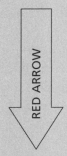

Confusion: If you don't understand something you read and need clarification or explanation to help you understand, put a red sticky arrow there.

Connections: If you can connect what you read to something you already know, put a green sticky arrow there.

Mental Images: If you can picture in your mind what you read, put a blue sticky arrow there.

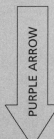

Feelings: If you have strong feelings about what you read, put a purple sticky arrow there.

Process Activity: Table Topics

Principals are often called upon to speak extemporaneously (e.g., answer questions at school board meetings, say a few words at an assembly, or speak to students when visiting a classroom). This exercise is called Table Topics and has been adapted from *Games Trainers Play* (Newstrom & Scannell, 1980, p. 97).

Prepare a series of 3 × 5 cards on which you have written various topics from Chapter 1 (e.g., attending, listening, empathy, self-disclosure, telling the truth in love, reality therapy, schmoozing). Recruit volunteers to stand up and give sixty-second impromptu talks. Give each volunteer one of the prepared topic cards, and give them ten seconds to collect their thoughts. If participants are reluctant to volunteer, ask them what this reluctance implies for their ability to meet the constant demands of the principalship for extemporaneous speaking.

If participants are still reluctant to volunteer, break the group into several small groups and have a set of cards prepared for each group. Debrief after several participants in each group have spoken extemporaneously in their small groups: (1) How did this exercise make you feel? (2) How can you become a more confident extemporaneous speaker? (3) How *have* you become a more effective extemporaneous speaker?

Questions for Dialogue

1.   The author suggests that communication isn't effective unless the individuals who are communicating with one another are able to achieve understanding. How much of the "communication" in your school would qualify as effective using this definition? What might improve this situation?

2.   What do you find is the most serious communication problem among your staff members? Staff members and parents? You and your staff members? What have you done (are you doing) to remediate communication difficulties? What might be done?

3.   If you were the coach or mentor of the principal with the inability to listen who is described at the beginning of Chapter 1, what advice would you give that individual? How might you help him?

4.   Do you believe it is possible to change one's communication style? Give an example of a bad habit that you have changed and explain how you accomplished it.

5.   Do you agree with Zig Ziglar's (1986) statement that is quoted in Chapter 1: "I'm convinced that with commitment and persistence you can find *something* good about any person, performance, or situation" (p. 53). Can

you think of someone for whom you currently have (or have had) a difficult time "goodfinding"? Describe how you are handling or have handled this situation. What might you do differently in the light of Ziglar's advice?

6. What are some schoolwide activities or initiatives that principals and teachers could undertake if confronted with an overabundance of angry and hostile parents in their community? Consider some probable causes for the hostility.

Reflective Writing Activity

Ask participants to use Susan Scott's six-step process described in Chapter 1 to compose a sixty-second monologue for use with a staff member whose inappropriate behavior needs to be confronted. Ask participants to have their monologues ready to deliver to a partner at the beginning of the next session.

Rapid Rewards Goals

Ask participants to identify one Rapid Rewards Goal to be implemented during the upcoming week. Two goals are provided, but participants can also identify their own goals if they relate to one or more of the Communicator Benchmarks.

Participant Instructions

• Use Communicator Exemplar Michelle Gayle's practice of phoning parents to ask them what they appreciate about your school (see Chapter 1). Use the feedback you receive from parents to make changes as appropriate. Your Rapid Rewards Goal is to make six such phone calls. Ask your secretary to randomly choose the six names to avoid the temptation of choosing "easy" parents. Describe the results in your Ten Traits Journal.

• If you have never solicited input from your faculty relative to your personal effectiveness as a principal, use an upcoming faculty meeting to do just that. Divide the faculty into small groups and give them these three questions: (1) What do I do that you value? (2) What do I do that you don't appreciate? (3) What else would you like to share with me that will help me grow as a professional? Ask a trusted faculty member to collate the results and share them with you.

Assignment for Next Week

Read Chapter 2.
Implement the Communicator Rapid Rewards Goal.

Trait Number 2: The Educator

The highly effective principal is an Educator—a self-directed instructional leader with a strong intellect and personal depth of knowledge regarding research-based curriculum, instruction, and learning that motivates and facilitates the intellectual growth and development of self, students, teachers, and parents.

Materials Needed for Educator Module

At least four to five pieces each of several kinds of bite-sized candies for the Candyland Process Activity

A chart, transparency, or slide containing the questions for the Reflective Writing Assignment

Energizer: Sixty-Second Confrontation

Ask participants to find a partner and trade off giving their sixty-second monologues developed in their reflective writing assignment. Debrief by asking if any participants used their monologues with staff members and, if so, what happened. Find out if anyone has plans for using the monologue, and if so, how.

Process Activity: Candyland Brainstorming

Divide the group into several smaller groups by using different varieties of individually wrapped candies. First divide the total number of participants by the number of people you want in each group. For example, thirty-six participants divided by four people in each group will result in nine groups. Purchase four pieces each of nine different types of candy at the supermarket bulk candy counter. Put an assortment of candy pieces in the middle of each table. (Instruct people not to eat the candy until after their groups have been formed.) Ask participants to choose one piece of candy and then find the other participants in the group who have the same variety of candy.

Once the small groups are formed, tell participants that they will be doing a brainstorming activity. Remind them of the basic rules of brainstorming: (1) Quantity of ideas, not quality, is the goal; (2) be freewheeling and creative; (3) make no critical comments or evaluative remarks; and (4) accept all suggestions.

Advise participants that their brainstorming goal is to develop a list of actions and attitudes that would demonstrate to observers that they (or any group of principals) *truly* believe that all students can learn, as stated in Benchmark 2.1.

Inform the participants that they have three minutes to generate their lists of characteristics. The facilitator will serve as timekeeper, but each group must choose its own recorder to write down the brainstormed items. When the groups have completed their brainstorming, post the lists of behaviors around the room. Give participants time to walk around and look at the lists.

Use the following questions to debrief: (1) What was most difficult about brainstorming regarding your vision of what schools can be? (2) What was most difficult about coming up with attitudes and actions that would give solid evidence of your belief in the ability of all students to learn? (3) What are the implications for making statements like this or having them as part of your mission or vision and not following through with behaviors that give evidence of that belief?

Questions for Dialogue

1. Recall the statement made by the Broad Foundation director regarding being "agnostic" about the power of instructional leadership (see Chapter 2). Are you an atheist, agnostic, or a believer with regard to the impact of instructional leadership on the performance of students and teachers? Explain the reasons for your answer.

2. Carl Glickman says that cognitive dissonance is a characteristic of effective schools. (See Chapter 2.) Give some examples of how you personally create cognitive dissonance in your school and how you have used it to create a Learning Community.

3. According to the vignettes in this chapter, Alan Jones wasn't always the easiest principal to work for *or* the easiest to supervise. Why do you think the author chose him as the Educator Exemplar?

4. What questions or observations would you have for Alan and Jean (the Educator Exemplars) if they were a part of this discussion group?

5. Sandra Ahola says, "My philosophy is to play to people's strengths. I do not believe in spending 90 percent of my time trying to fix, change, or improve 10 percent of the staff. Instead I spend 90 percent of my time with 90 percent of my teachers, and I 'feed the leaders.' I encourage, enable, empower, find funds, give release time, and provide praise." Comment on this approach. What are some possible outcomes of developing teacher leaders?

Rapid Rewards Goals

A Rapid Rewards Goal, as its name suggests, will bring you positive and immediate feedback from parents, staff, and students when you accomplish it. You can choose your own goal, but here are two Educator goals that will bring rapid rewards:

- Take an experimental Learning Walk with three teachers. Visit the Web sites on which Learning Walks are described before you plan one in your own school. See Providence Schools (2002) and Los Angeles Unified School District (2002).

- Visit every teacher in your school during the coming week. Shortly after the visit, send that individual a short note in which you offer specific and descriptive praise regarding some aspect of instruction.

Reflective Writing Activity: What Am I Living For?

This activity has been adapted from *100 Ways to Build Teams* (Scearce, 1992, p. 30) and is designed to elicit the values and beliefs that participants have about their jobs. Write the following questions on a piece of chart paper and ask participants to copy them into their Ten Traits Journals.

- Why did I become (or why do I want to become) a principal?
- What is the most important aspect of my job to me?
- What do I like about my job?
- What would I change about my job if I could?
- What is my definition of success in the principalship?
- Have I ever wanted to quit my job? What changed my mind?

These questions will serve as the Dialogue Questions for next week.

Assignment for Next Meeting

Read Chapter 3.
Complete the Reflective Writing Assignment: What Am I Living For?
Implement the Educator Rapid Rewards Goal.

Trait Number 3: The Envisioner

The highly effective principal is an Envisioner—an individual who is motivated by a sense of calling and purpose, focused on a vision of what schools can be, and guided by a mission that has the best interests of all students at its core.

Materials

Copies of Forms D.2 and D.3 for participants

Form D.2   Wanted . . . For

My name is _____

And I am wanted for _____

Always being _____

Having strong needs for _____

Greatly valuing _____

Living by the slogan _____

Energizer: Wanted . . . For

The Wanted . . . For process is designed to encourage participants to think about their own personal values. Although these posters won't be appearing on the walls of the post office in the near future, they could well be used as advertisements to fill your shoes when you retire. Prepare a copy of Form D.2, Wanted . . . For, for every group member (McEwan, 1997, pp. 18–19).

Process Activity: The Hedgehog

Ask participants to give their interpretation of the following statement: "The fox knows many things, but the hedgehog knows one big thing." See Form D.3, The Hedgehog. Pass out a copy of the form to each participant. Ask participants to spend a couple of minutes in reflection about their "one big idea" and then ask them to write it on the form. Display the forms so that participants can read them all (e.g., spread out on tables, taped to the backs of the participants with masking tape). Debrief with these questions: (1) What surprised you about the various big ideas? (2) Did you see any big ideas that you felt were more worthy of hard work and effort than others? (3) Do you still like *your* "big idea"?

Questions for Dialogue

Use the Reflective Writing Activity from the last module for this dialogue.

Form D.3   The Hedgehog

My one big idea is _____

_____

_____

_____

_____

_____

_____

_____

_____

- Why did you become (or why do you want to become) a principal?
- What is the most important aspect of your job to you?
- What do you like about your job?
- What would you change about your job if you could?
- What is your definition of success in the principalship?
- Have you ever wanted to quit your job? What changed your mind?

Rapid Rewards Goals

The Rapid Rewards Goals for this module are reflective rather than active in nature.

- Use the three definitions of the word *purpose* (resolve, goals, and lifevision) that are suggested by the author in Chapter 3 as the basis for a short written response to each of the following questions: (1) What are the issues or values that you have or would stand up for against opposition from faculty, the board of education, or your superintendent? (2) What specific goals are you working on in the areas of career, education, family, spiritual life, and recreational life? (3) What is your "lifevision?" What would you like to be noted or remembered for as an administrator?

- Write a short, reflective essay titled "How to Be a Hedgehog: What I Learned From the Choosing One Big Thing Exercise." Use your answers to the following questions to help you in your writing: (1) What surprised you about the other people's big ideas? (2) Did you see any big ideas that you felt were more worthy of hard work and effort than others? (3) Do you still like your "big idea"? (4) Is your big idea "big" enough? How can you tell?

Reflective Writing Assignment

Pay special attention to the Facilitator Benchmarks (see Figure 4.1 for a complete list) as you read Chapter 4. Choose two of the benchmarks, and write a brief description of at least two ideas, activities, attitudes, or actions in which you regularly engage that specifically accomplish these two benchmarks.

Assignment for Next Meeting

Read Chapter 4.
Do the reflective writing assignment.
Complete the reflective Rapids Rewards Goal.

Trait Number 4: The Facilitator

The highly effective principal is a Facilitator—a leader with outstanding human relations skills that include the abilities to build individual relationships with parents, teachers, and students; collaborative teams with teachers and parents; and a schoolwide community of leaders.

Materials

No special materials needed

Energizer: The Name Game

This energizer is adapted from *100 Ways to Build Teams* (Scearce, 1992, p. 9). Ask participants to list the first names of ten of their teachers. Make sure they include two of their star teachers, two average teachers, and two they find difficult to work with. Once they have these six teachers, they can pick four more at random. Then ask participants to come up with two positive, descriptive words that begin with the same letter as each of those teachers' first or last names. For example, "Franco is fun loving and focused. Diane is direct and daring. Eleanor is eager and energetic."

Process Activity: Facilitator Pair and Share

Ask participants to take out their Ten Traits Journal for a "pair and share" activity. Ask participants to pair off and share their ideas for relationship building they developed for the reflective writing assignment with each other. Swap partners and repeat the process with another set of ideas. Swap partners a third time and share another idea, if time permits. Encourage participants to make notes regarding the ideas that are shared, as they will easily be forgotten. Also encourage participants to write down names and telephone numbers of the people from whom they received the ideas in case they want to implement them in the future and need more information.

Questions for Dialogue

The following questions in their original form appeared in a Gallup survey and were adapted for inclusion in Chapter 4. They have been adapted yet again for purposes of this dialogue.

- In what ways do you give recognition or praise to teachers for effective instruction, their caring attitudes toward students, or special attention and service to parents?
- How do you show that you personally care about staff members as people?

- How do you encourage and facilitate the personal and professional development of staff members?
- How do you make sure that the opinions of all staff members count when important decisions are made?
- Give examples of how the mission of your school makes staff members feel as though their work is important?
- Does every staff member have a best friend at school? How would you determine the answer to this question? Why do you think a positive answer to this question is so important?
- How do your staff members have opportunities to learn and grow through the work they do in your school?

Rapid Rewards Goals

You can choose your own goal, but here are two goals related to the Facilitator Trait that will bring rapid rewards.

- Choose a parent with whom you have a "personality clash" or with whom you have failed to make a communication connection. Does this parent threaten you in some way? Does he or she show signs of disrespect? Or, does he or she make you feel guilty because you can't meet his or her needs? Reflect on the benchmarks of Facilitators and choose two actions/attitudes that you will intentionally take/show to demonstrate respect, caring, and appreciation for that parent.

- Plan an individual coaching/teaching session with two of your teachers—one highly effective and supportive teacher and one challenging and less supportive teacher. Teach a lesson while the teachers observe you and then schedule a time for you and the teacher to talk about how *you* could improve *your* lesson.

Reflective Writing Activity

Write up the results of your Rapid Rewards Goal answering the following questions: (1) What is your goal statement? (2) What actions have you taken to meet your goal? (3) What did you expect would happen as a result of your activities? (4) What did happen as a result of your activities? (5) How do you plan to follow up and incorporate these actions and attitudes into your daily habits?

Assignment for Next Meeting

Read Chapter 5: Change Master.
Bring enough copies of your school's current goal statements so that everyone in the group can have a copy. Remove any identifying information

regarding the district or the school on the statements before making the copies.

Trait Number 5: The Change Master

The highly effective principal is a Change Master—a flexible, futuristic, and realistic leader who is able to both motivate and manage change in an organized, positive, and enduring fashion.

Materials

Two small prizes for the Energizer

Chart, slide, or transparency of Characteristics of Good Goals (see the Process Activity)

Copies of Forms D.4, D.5, and D.6.

Energizer: Are You on Innovation Overload?

Ask participants to list the number of major innovations or implementations they currently have going on in their schools. Have a small prize ready to give the individual with the most site-based innovations, curricular changes, or supplementary programs. Next, ask participants to list the changes that have been imposed upon them from the outside (e.g., boundary line changes, organizational changes, budget cuts, budget increases, etc.). Be ready to hand out another small prize to the individual with the most imposed changes. Last, ask participants how many things the average person is able to retain in working memory at one time. There is no prize for the correct answer: 5 to 9 items. Briefly discuss the implications for teachers, principals, students, and parents when too much is happening simultaneously.

Process Activity: Do You Know What a Good Goal Looks Like?

Project the following statements on a screen or write them on chart paper.

- Goals should be specific.
- Goals should be measurable.
- Goals should be results centered.
- Goals should be realistic.
- Goals should be challenging.
- Goals should be flexible.
- Goals should be limited in number (Aubrey & Felkins, 1988, p. 94).

Ask participants to place the copies of their schools' goal statements on a long table so that participants can easily pick up one copy of each. Divide into groups of three and ask participants to evaluate the goals using the statements you have posted. Give one point for every statement that is applicable. Superior goals will receive a total of seven points. Adequate goals will receive a total of between four and seven points. Goals that receive fewer than four points need reworking.

(If you are uneasy or feel that problems could arise from evaluating "real" goal statements, develop several imaginary goal statements that will serve the purpose of this activity or provide goal statements you have gathered anonymously from various districts and schools. Web sites of schools and districts are good sources for goal statements. Simply remove any identifying information before distributing the goals to the participants.)

Ask participants to spend a few minutes considering the following questions:

- What conclusions have you drawn about the goal statements?
- What are the implications of this activity for the goal-setting process?
- What might you do differently in terms of setting goals in the future?

Questions for Dialogue

1. Is Diana Lam, the individual described at the beginning of Chapter 5, a Change Master? Give your reasons for answering yes or no. What lessons can you learn from individuals like Diana Lam?

2. Principal Patricia Hamilton carries this recipe for change around in her daily planner: "One portion each of collaboration, cooperation and communication; 1 large cup of trust; 1 dash of risk-taking; and 1 T of responsiveness to customer needs." Who are our customers? How much responsibility do we have to be responsive to their needs?

3. *"Change is one thing, progress is another"* (B. Russell, as quoted in Seldes, 1999, p. 605). What does this quotation mean for education? Give examples of change without progress. Give examples of progress without change.

4. If you have held principalships in more than one school, contrast the approaches you took to bringing about change in different settings.

5. Alan Jones says that the real work of the leader is helping people to understand and fully implement a program or innovation. How does

Alan's approach differ from the usual approach to implementation? What kinds of actions and attitudes might someone like Alan exhibit during the implementation of a new program or curriculum?

6. What is the Emperor's Syndrome? What can principals do to keep from getting it?

7. Is change good or bad?

Rapid Rewards Goals

You can choose your own goal, but here are two suggested goals related to the Change Master trait that will bring rapid rewards.

- Select a grade level (team or department) in which to pilot the 30 Day/30 Minute Rapid Results Goal Setting format used by Kathie Dobberteen. Meet with the teachers to formulate a simple goal based on assessment results and samples of student work. Use Form D.4, for Grades K–1, Form D.5 for Grades 2–5, and Form D.6 for Grade 6 and higher. Agree on a pre- and posttest, set a thirty-day period to attain the established goal, determine the strategies that all teachers will use to make instructional improvements, and then reconvene to monitor the goal's status at the conclusion of the thirty days.

- Choose a process activity that has been used during previous meetings of this study group or find a new one to use in a team or faculty meeting to develop teamwork, set goals, plan for implementation, or generate ideas (McEwan, 1997).

Reflective Writing Activity

Ask participants to write a short essay in which they argue for more change in education *or* less change in education. Ask them to specify what kind of changes they would recommend if more change is needed or to note what kinds of changes they would eliminate if less change is called for. Encourage participants to use personal examples and to be prepared to share their essays in the next session.

Assignment for Next Meeting

Read Chapter 6. Do Reflective Writing Activity on change.
Implement Rapid Rewards Goal.

Trait Number 6: The Culture Builder

The highly effective principal is a Culture Builder—an individual who communicates (talks) and models (walks) a strong and viable vision

Form D.4   30-Minute/30-Day Rapid Results Meeting Agenda Grades K–1

Timekeeper _____   Recorder _____   Facilitator _____

> Purpose of this meeting: To set a 30-day team-level reading goal.

List all of the grade-level team's concerns about your students' reading or readiness to read based on running records, Brigance scores, teacher perceptions, other assessments. (5 minutes)

_____

_____

Rate the concerns in order of importance from highest to lowest. (4 minutes)

_____

Write a clear, measurable, attainable, and compelling goal for what your students should be able to do for the one area you have chosen as most important. (5 minutes)

_____

Brainstorm possible solutions to reach this goal. (8–10 minutes)

_____

List the best ideas from the brainstorming session. **Describe** how they will be measured. **Set priorities** based on which are perceived to be most effective. (8 minutes)

Best Ideas	Measure	Priority

Team Members Present at Meeting: _____

_____

> Next team meeting is on _____ to share results and set a new goal. The recorder is to give a copy of this completed form to principal and team members today. Thank you.

Reprinted by permission of Dr. Christopher Quinn. San Diego County Office of Education.

Form D.5   30-Minute/30-Day Rapid Results Meeting Agenda Grades 2–5

Timekeeper _____   Recorder _____   Facilitator _____

> Purpose of this meeting: To set a 30-day team-level reading goal.

Rank the grade-level team's reading scores (word study skills, vocabulary or comprehension) on the SAT-9 *Mastery List Summary* from the highest to lowest using National PR (percentile). (2 minutes)

_____

_____

Identify the lowest score on the *Group Report* (each teacher has one by name) in the *reading* category listed in the first step. List other areas of concern in reading from other assessments, teacher perceptions, and so on. (4 minutes)

_____

Write a clear, measurable, attainable, and compelling goal for what your students should be able to do for the one area you have chosen as most important. (5 minutes)

_____

Brainstorm possible solutions to reach this goal. (8-10 minutes)

List the best ideas from the brainstorming session. **Describe** how they will be measured. **Set priorities** based on which are perceived to be most effective. (8 minutes)

Best Ideas	Measure	Priority

Team Members Present: _____

_____

> Next team meeting is on _____ to share results and set a new goal. The recorder is to give a copy of this completed form to principal and team members today. Thank you.

Reprinted by permission of Dr. Christopher Quinn. San Diego County Office of Education.

Form D.6   30-Minute/30-Day Rapid Results Meeting Agenda Grades 6–12

Timekeeper _____   Recorder _____   Facilitator _____

Purpose of this meeting:

Rank the students on a teacher-made, standardized, or state-mandated assessment.

_____

_____

Identify the students who are most in need of extra help or the outcome or standard that is the lowest overall for the class.

_____

Write a clear, measurable, attainable, and compelling goal for what your students should be able to do for the one area you have chosen as most important. (5 minutes)

_____

Brainstorm possible solutions to reach this goal. (8–10 minutes)

List the best ideas from the brainstorming session. **Describe** how they will be measured. **Set priorities** based on which are perceived to be most effective. (8 minutes)

Best Ideas	Measure	Priority

Team Members Present: _____

_____

Next team meeting is on _____ to share results and set a new goal. The recorder is to give a copy of this completed form to principal and team members today. Thank you.

Reprinted by permission of Dr. Christopher Quinn. San Diego County Office of Education.

based on achievement, expectations, character, personal responsibility, and accountability.

Materials

Copies of Form D.7 for participants

Energizer: What's Your Refrain?

The author suggested in the chapter you read for this meeting that one way Culture Builders communicate core values to their school communities is by means of refrains—the "choruses" they keep coming back to over and over again to remind the "singers" what the song is really all about. You might also call a phrase or idea that is repeated over and over again a mantra. Direct participants to jot down their refrain or mantra—the phrases or sayings that epitomize what they believe are (or should be) the core values of their schools. Each participant should be prepared to share his or her refrain or mantra with the group.

Process Activity: Changing Your School's Culture

Divide the large group into small groups of from three to five individuals. Assign one of Saphier and King's norms of school culture referenced in Chapter 6 to each of the small groups. Use the Norms of School Culture Worksheet (Form D.7) to focus the small-group discussion of the assigned norm. Each group should choose a reporter to summarize its findings and conclusions for the large group.

Questions for Dialogue

1. Pritchett and Pound (1993) advise, "Significant culture change should start to occur in weeks or months. Not years. Start out fast and keep trying to pick up speed. *Leave skid marks*" (p. 44). Comment on this sentiment from your own perspective.

2. Recall Terry Beasley's "open-door culture." Consider this practice from your own perspective. What advantages do you see? What potential problems might you anticipate?

3. If parents in your community had a choice, would they choose your school? Why? Why not? What might you do in the short term to influence their decisions?

4. How important are "the daffodils"? Why?

5. What makes a good school, in your opinion?

Form D.7   Modified Norms of School Culture Worksheet

Norm: _____

1. What practices or conditions in our school currently strengthen this norm?

2. What practices or conditions in our school weaken this norm?

3. What is your vision of what this norm would look like at its best?

4. What specific recommendations would you make to the principal for improving this norm?

5. What would *you* be willing to do to improve this norm?

6. Would you send your children or grandchildren to your own school? Why? Why not?

7. What was the first thing you set about to change in your current school? Do you have any black roses still hanging around your school? Why?

Rapid Rewards Goals

Here are two suggested goals related to the Culture Builder trait that will bring rapid rewards.

- Administer the Norms of School Culture Worksheet to your faculty and use the information to plan for change:

Choose one aspect of culture in your school that (in your opinion) needs work. Write the norm along with a brief definition on a copy of the worksheet and make enough copies for your faculty members. Pass out a copy of the worksheet to all faculty members and ask them to complete it. After each individual has completed the worksheet, divide the large group into small groups of three to five members each. Divide the number of people in the group by the number you want in a group and use that total to count off your faculty. Place all of the 1's into a group, the 2's into another group, and so on. This strategy will ensure heterogeneity and result in a livelier and more balanced discussion. After each group forms, ask the members to choose a recorder to record and collate their information into a single sheet and a reporter to share the information with the large group and collate it into a schoolwide summary. Then schedule a meeting to make plans regarding what to do with the information.

- Use the Norms of School Culture Worksheet with your PTA board or a group of randomly selected parents.

Reflective Writing Activity

Write a brief essay on the topic "If My School Were . . . " (McEwan, 1997, pp. 15–16). Imagine that your school is one of the following: a movie, a book, a car, a song, a sports team, a food, or a soap opera. Pay attention to the aspects of culture discussed in Chapter 6. Be prepared to share your paragraph with the group during the next meeting. Certificates will be awarded for the best essays.

Assignments for Next Meeting

Read Chapter 7.
Complete Reflective Writing Activity to share.

Trait Number 7: The Activator

The highly effective principal is an Activator—an individual with gumption (e.g., drive, motivation, enthusiasm, energy, spunk, and humor) enough to spare and share with staff, parents, and students.

Materials

Certificates for three essay winners (humorous, poignant, and inspirational)

Energizer: Two Truths and a Lie

If you did not use this activity earlier, use it here. If you have already used this activity, combine the Energizer and Process activities for this module.

Process Activity: If My School Were . . .

Ask participants to pair up and read their "If My School Were . . ." essays. Ask participants to nominate particularly outstanding essays in these three categories: (1) humorous, (2) poignant, and (3) inspirational. Ask participants to vote (by ballot or applause, whichever you prefer) and give out certificates you have prepared ahead of time.

Questions for Dialogue

1.   What do you think of Todd White and Clare Maguire? Would you hire them for your district if you were a superintendent? Why? Why not?

2.   Should principals aspire to become activators if they are not? Why or why not?

3.   What does it mean to be entrepreneurial?

4.   Is there anything in education worth losing your job over?

5.   What really makes an activator an honest-to-goodness activator in your opinion?

6.   Would you advise aspiring principals to emulate Todd and Clare? Why? Why not?

Rapid Rewards Goals

You can choose your own goal, but here are two goals related to the Activator trait that will bring rapid rewards.

●   If you are *not* an Activator (in your opinion), become one this week. Let your hair down. Wear casual clothes. Do something that is totally out of character for you. If you need courage, ask one or more of your Activator faculty members for help or moral support.

• If you *are* an Activator, spend the week in quiet reflection and do more listening to what others have to say. Ask people for their opinions, probe for their concerns, and let others speak first.

Reflective Writing Activity

Write a short, reflective essay on what you learned by varying your activity levels during the past week.

Reading Assignment for Next Meeting

Read Chapter 8.

Trait Number 8: The Producer

The highly effective principal is a Producer—a results-oriented individual with a strong sense of accountability to taxpayers, parents, students, and teachers who translates high expectations into intellectual development and academic achievement for all students.

Materials

Student Performance Statement on a slide, transparency, or chart

Agree, Strongly Agree, Disagree, Strongly Disagree signs

Copies of the Force Field Analysis Charts for participants (Exhibit D.1 and Form D.8).

Energizer: Agree or Disagree

Write the following statement on chart paper, overhead projection, or a slide and post or project it where everyone will see it when they enter the room: *Student performance is a measure of teacher performance.* Write *Agree* and *Strongly Agree* on pieces of chart paper and post them in the corners of one side of the room. Write *Disagree* and *Strongly Disagree* on pieces of chart paper and post them in the corners on the opposite side of the room. Ask participants to read and consider the statement and choose a corner of the room in which to stand. Then tell them to break into groups of three to five people, talk about their choice, and derive a summary statement as to why they chose the position they did. Ask a reporter from each group to summarize their position for the whole group.

Process Activity: Force Field Analysis

To produce results, principals must marshal and engage all possible facilitating forces toward clearly stated achievement goals, while at the same time diminishing, reducing, or eliminating the restraining forces that are standing in the way of improving student achievement. The Force Field Analysis process described in Chapter 5 is an ideal way to identify the facilitating and restraining forces that impact the achievement of a specific goal (McEwan, 1997, pp. 100–102). A sample Force Field Analysis is shown in Exhibit D.1. Distribute copies of Form D.8 for use as a worksheet. Explain the process to participants and give them sufficient time to discuss and identify the forces. Once the forces have been identified, cross off the restraining forces that are inalterable (e.g., student demographics). Ask participants to choose one restraining force that is particularly powerful and brainstorm ways to solve that problem or minimize that force.

Questions for Dialogue

1. What are your reactions to what Dale Skinner did in his school?

2. What does accountability mean to you?

3. Comment on Dale's statement, "It's just a matter of cause and effect."

4. "Emphasizing achievement and being accountable are just other ways of teaching to the test." Do you agree or disagree with this statement? Why?

5. Kathie Dobberteen says, "Demographics don't have to define student performance." If you agree with her statement, why do you think there are so many failing and low-performing schools?

6. Do you think that education is filled with too much activity and not enough achievement? Explain why or why not.

7. What are "Christmas tree" schools and how can principals keep their schools from becoming like them?

8. If you hear someone say, "The research says . . . ," how do you know if it really does?

Rapid Rewards Goals

You can choose your own, but here are two goals related to the Producer trait that will bring rapid rewards.

- Do the Force Field Analysis with your faculty regarding raising achievement in your school.
- Like Dale Skinner, choose one student outcome that seems to cause problems for students, prepare a lesson for your faculty, and then ask them to develop their own lessons that improve upon yours.

Exhibit D.1   Sample Force Field Analysis

"To become a school in which all students are powerful mathematicians, effective writers, responsible citizens, and confident readers" (Juanita School, 2002).

Facilitating Forces	Goal/Problem	Restraining Forces
→		←
Dedicated, caring, hardworking, and knowledgeable faculty		Too many students below grade level when they enroll at our school
Well-organized staff development program		Lack of parental support
Core group of high-achieving students and parents		School not high priority for students—extracurricular activities and work interfere
Good climate and culture in school		Low expectations regarding what we can realistically accomplish with low-achieving students
		Too much on our plates already
		Lack of time
		Scheduling problems

Form D.8   Force Field Analysis Worksheet

Facilitating Forces	Goal/Problem	Restraining Forces
————————————▶	◀————————————	

Reflective Writing Assignment

Reflect on your Rapid Rewards Goal experience.

Assignment for Next Meeting

Read Chapter 9.

Trait Number 9: The Character Builder

The highly effective principal is a Character Builder—a role model whose values, beliefs, and ideals are marked by trustworthiness, integrity, authenticity, respect, generosity, and humility.

Materials

Chart paper, markers

Energizer: Why Do I Trust You?

Ask the participants to think of an individual who is completely trustworthy. This person can be someone from their professional *or* personal lives. Ask participants to write the name of the individual on a page in their Ten Traits Journal and then write three characteristics that make them trustworthy. Poll each person for the traits they have written and collate them on a chart. Ask the participants to come up with specific behaviors and attitudes that would facilitate the development of trust in them by their teachers, parents, and students.

Process Activity: Character Builder Gallery Walk

Post a piece of chart paper for each of the qualities mentioned in the Character Builder trait: trustworthiness, integrity, authenticity, respect, generosity, and humility. Divide the group into triads and conduct a Gallery Walk. Ask each trio to write down one action or attitude by a principal that would demonstrate the quality under consideration.

Questions for Dialogue

1. Comment on Terry Beasley's position on honesty being the best policy when it comes to the evaluation process. Describe one of your evaluation experiences in the light of this comment.

2. Comment on Jim Ratledge's statement: "I have always believed that we should love children more than adults in our business. By that I mean that children's interests should take precedence over staff interests."

3. Does character matter? Why or why not?

4. How can schools become virtuous?

5. What does Terry Beasley's statement, "A principal has to have a good heart," mean to you?

6. Are the qualities of generosity and humbleness rewarded in education?

Rapid Rewards Goals

Here are two goals related to the Character Builder trait that will bring rapid rewards.

• Carry your clipboard around with you this week to make note of how many acts of kindness, words of encouragement, and positive statements you hear. While you're listening for the incidences of Character Building language, also be on the alert for gossip, sarcasm, hostility, criticism, and words that can tear down and damage those to whom they are directed as well as the character of those who speak them. Once you have collected this qualitative data, develop a short presentation to give to your faculty. Praise and affirm the positive. Ask them what they can do to eliminate the negative.

• Reread the Albert Schweitzer quotation at the end of the chapter and consider what acts of kindness you as a principal can perform in your school during the week. In order to qualify for inclusion in this goal, they must remain totally anonymous in your school.

Reflective Writing Activity

Describe an incident in your tenure as a principal that has tested your character.

Assignment for Next Meeting

Read Chapter 10.
Our process activity next week will tap the artistic creativity and ingenuity of participants. Please bring along any kind of materials that might prove useful in developing a large poster: construction paper, glitter, yarn, stickers, and markers of unusual colors.

Trait Number 10: The Contributor

The highly effective principal is a Contributor—a servant-leader, encourager, and enabler whose utmost priority is making a contribution to the success of others.

Materials

Markers, glue, construction paper, tissue paper, stickers, and so on

Piece of poster board for each small group

Energizer: The Best Boss I Ever Had

Ask participants to list as many attributes as they can that describe the best "boss" or "leader" they have ever worked for. Have participants get into groups of from three to five members and share these attributes and then pick the two that were most frequently mentioned. Ask a reporter from each group to share their two most frequently mentioned traits with the large group.

Process Activity: The Principal I Want to Be

Ask participants to form groups of from three to five individuals with at least one elementary, one middle school, and one high school principal in each group. The assigned task is to develop a poster to be titled, The Principal I Want to Be, creating a visual image that incorporates all ten traits.

Questions for Dialogue

1. Speculate regarding the reason for the low number of votes received by the Contributor trait.

2. Comment on how you have experienced the Elijah Effect in your principalship.

3. What is your reaction to the concept of servant-leadership? Do you find this chapter somewhat disconcerting? Encouraging? Impossible? Irrelevant? Annoying?

4. Marjorie Thompson related this comment made to her by a new student: "You don't act like no principal." She asked him what a principal was supposed to act like, and he responded, "They're supposed to sit in their office, shuffling their papers, not scrubbing no tables." If you become a servant-leader, will your followers understand and appreciate what you are doing, think you are out of character, or try to take advantage of you?

5. Roland Barth said, "A principal may comply with all 64 characteristics of an effective leader as seen by the state department of education, but if the teachers don't experience their principal as a leader [or a Contributor], then the principal isn't one." What should principals do if their teachers do not experience them as leaders?

6. Do principals have a moral obligation to meet the needs of teachers? Why or why not?

Rapid Rewards Goals

Here are two goals related to the Contributor trait that will bring rapid rewards.

• Choose four individuals on your staff—one student, one teacher, one parent, and one classified staff member—whom you will serve in some way during the coming week. You can either ask them how they would like to be served or you can offer to help them spontaneously as the need arises.

• Using Lola Malone's list of the needs her teachers have, choose one or two and intentionally act upon them during the upcoming week.

Reflective Writing Activity

Reflect on what happened to you and to those you served while implementing your Rapid Rewards Goal during this week.

Assignment for Next Meeting

Read the Conclusion.
Prepare Reflective Writing Activity regarding Rapid Rewards Goal.

Conclusion

Materials

Agree, Strongly Agree, Disagree, Strongly Disagree signs for corners of the room

Energizer: Do Principals Really Matter?

Imagine that your board of education is debating the elimination of all building principals. The principal's responsibilities will be given to an administrative clerk who will handle all paperwork and management responsibilities and an instructional supervisor who will handle curriculum and instruction. The combined salaries of the two positions will be less than your salary and benefits package. Jot down the three most compelling reasons you will give to the board of education when they ask to hear your on-the-spot opinion during the board meeting.

Process Activity: Spend a Buck

This process is a unique way for participants to determine the relative importance of the ten traits. They spend a limited amount of imaginary money to "buy" the traits that are of most value to them. Give each participant ten 3×5 cards. Ask them to write each trait on one of the cards. Instruct participants that they have a total of one dollar to spend on the traits according to each trait's relative importance to them. They must spend a minimum of twenty cents on each item chosen. Ask participants to first sort their cards into three piles: most-valued traits, least-valued traits, and the traits that are left over. Then instruct them to write the amount they wish to spend on a given trait on that trait's card. When everyone has spent their bucks on the traits they value most, collect the cards and sort them by traits, tabulating the total value of each trait. Then rank the traits by total value. Analyze what the rankings mean (McEwan, 1997, pp. 134–135).

Questions for Dialogue: Agree or Disagree

This dialogue will be both active and interactive. Post signs on chart paper in four corners of the room: Agree and Disagree on the corners of one wall, and Strongly Agree and Strongly Disagree on the corners of the other wall. Arrange two concentric circles of chairs in the middle of the room. Read the first statement in the list that follows and ask participants to choose their corners. Then ask three representatives of the Agree group and three representatives of the Disagree group to sit in the inner circle to present the reasons why they agreed or disagreed with the statement. Repeat the procedure with the second statement, asking participants to go to the corner representing their feelings about the statement. Choose six different people from the Agree and Disagree positions to talk about the second statement. Continue down the list of statements as time permits.

1. All of the ten traits are essential to some degree in order to be a highly effective principal.

2. Highly effective principals know themselves, and they are works in progress.

3. The ten traits interact with each other in synergistic and often inexplicable ways.

4. It is impossible to rank the ten traits or to identify one that is more critical than any other.

5. Becoming a highly effective principal is definitely more of a process than a product.

6. Highly effective principals are continually monitoring and adjusting their responses to the various schools, faculties, communities, and challenges they encounter.

7. Highly effective principals make a difference wherever they go.

8. Highly effective principals are masters of timing.

9. Highly effective principals are emotionally, physically, and spiritually healthy individuals.

10. All principals, including the thirty-seven highly effective ones featured in this book, possess totally unique combinations and permutations of the ten traits.

**CORWIN
PRESS**

The Corwin Press logo—a raven striding across an open book—represents the happy union of courage and learning. We are a professional-level publisher of books and journals for K-12 educators, and we are committed to creating and providing resources that embody these qualities. Corwin's motto is "Success for All Learners."